D0961310

BELLE

Belle

THE BIOGRAPHY OF BELLE CASE LA FOLLETTE

. . . .

by Lucy Freeman, Sherry La Follette
and George A. Zabriskie

. . . .

Beaufort Books   Publishers   New York

Library of Congress Cataloging-in-Publication Data

Freeman, Lucy.
    Belle: the biography of Belle Case La Follette.
    Includes index.
1. La Follette, Belle Case, 1859-1931.
2. La Follette, Robert M. (Robert Maron), 1855-1925.
3. Legislators' wives—United States—Biography.
4. Legislators—United States—Biography. 5. United States.
Congress—Biography. I. Zabriskie, George Albert, 1926-
II. La Follette, Sherry.
III. Title.
    E664.L155F74 1985 973.91'092'4 [B] 85-9124
             ISBN 0-8253-0314-1

Published in the United States by Beaufort Books Publishers, New York.
Designed by Helen Barrow
Printed in the U.S.A.
First Edition
10 9 8 7 6 5 4 3 2 1

For Fola and Mary La Follette
with abiding love and admiration.

And with appreciation and thanks to the friendly, helpful, and dedicated people at the Library of Congress, the State Historical Society of Wisconsin, and the New York Public Library. Without them, *Belle* could never have been realized.

CONTENTS

....

INTRODUCTION

....

From the child who never missed a day of school, except when she had the measles, to the first woman chosen to be a United States Senator, Belle Case La Follette was an American original.

From the moment she won the University of Wisconsin's Lewis Prize for her senior oration, "Learning to See," Belle went through life seeing the world a little differently from most people. She saw the injustice in not allowing women to vote. She saw the inequality in denying black women and men their lawful civil rights. She saw the terrible waste of war. She did something about these inequities. Belle Case La Follette spent her life fighting for justice, equality and peace. Her weapons were words.

She fought from the speaker's platform in school auditoriums, in churches, in Chautauqua tents and in the halls of Congress. She fought in her weekly, then monthly, columns in La Follette's Magazine, which later, under her direction, became The Progressive. She fought in letters to presidents, senators, congressmen and ordinary citizens. She communicated her concerns to all her friends and associates in her effort to create a more humane world. But perhaps the most important of all her life's outpouring of words were those she spoke to her husband, Senator Robert "Fighting Bob" La Follette. He described her as "My best and wisest counselor, altogether the brainiest member of the family," and her words determined his actions more than those of any other person.

From her birthplace in Baraboo, Wisconsin, to her homes in Madison, Wisconsin, and Washington, D.C., Belle Case La Follette blazed the way in most of the issues that still confound us. The world has become much more complicated in the fifty-four years since Belle's death, and while progress has been made in some areas, the great issues of justice, equality and peace are still with us. For this gen-

eration of concerned individuals, Belle's words are as cogent as the day she first uttered them.

But there was more to Belle than her public persona. She was also a devoted and concerned wife and mother. She considered marriage a partnership, a union of two people who would share life's experience, each supporting the other. For Bob and Belle, it would be an equal partnership. By mutual consent, the word "obey" was dropped from their wedding ceremony. It was an idealistic concept in 1881 but for this particular couple it worked remarkably well. They went through life together giving their best to each other, their children and the causes they espoused.

Early in their marriage Belle realized that Bob suffered from a variety of maladies that often defied diagnosis. The symptoms were nausea, dizziness, mysterious pains, physical weakness, and exhaustion. All her life Belle steadfastly believed in the interaction between a sound mind and a sound body. For her, the combination of simple, nutritious food and proper exercise was the key to mental and physical health. Belle practiced what she preached and lived a long, active, and generally healthy life. She attempted to treat Bob's various ailments with the prescription that worked so well for her. But the senator was a recalcitrant patient and more often than not was unable to abide by her program of diet and exercise.

Since Bob projected such energy and endurance when well, Belle tried to protect him from public view when he was ill. Her protective policy worked for a while but as Bob became more prominent the press became more insistent in probing the causes of his illnesses. In the end Belle switched from protection to press release to explain his various medical problems. That she could not help Bob achieve continuous good health was perhaps one of her great personal disappointments in their life together.

In an interview during Bob's 1924 presidential campaign, Belle stated: "I have been fortunate, marvelously lucky, in having during all these years a companion. True companionship is the greatest thing in the world. We have been through everything, my husband and I, bad times and good times, disappointments, illness, poverty, hard work, the struggle for principle, the climb to success, but when you have a companion to count on through thick and thin, it's all easy. We two have kept together because . . . well, because our minds and hearts matched." Bob and Belle matched, not like two peas in a pod because they were identical but like two pieces in a jigsaw puzzle that complemented each other.

Belle was also a dedicated mother and her four children—Fola, Bob Jr., Phil and Mary—openly adored her. She believed in their freedom as individuals right from the start and encouraged them to grow with as few restrictions as possible. From an early age her children's opinions were sought out and respected. The children were included in all family affairs. In this family, such activity meant political affairs as well as private activities. Because their early life was so often split between Madison, Wisconsin, and Washington, D. C., Belle often became teacher as well as mother. For her, the two roles were completely compatible and she relished both. When her children were seriously ill, as was Mary for a short period and Bobbie for many years, Belle was a constant nurse and companion.

Along with her caring support and encouragement for freedom of expression went great expectations. Belle assumed her children would excel in whatever they did. At times they disappointed her but in the last year of her life she could take deep satisfaction in her children's lives. Both Mary, a gifted painter, and Fola, a respected actress, were happily married and leading fruitful lives, young Bob was a member of the United States Senate, and Phil was governor of Wisconsin.

Not only was Belle's influence on Bob and her children profound and lasting, her influence on her whole generation was considerable. Belle was like a one-woman "think tank." She was an avid reader and researched every issue important to her. This inquisitive side of her mind was balanced by the logic she had learned in law school. Once Belle felt she possessed the necessary information, she pursued a reasoned course of action. Though a naturally private person, she did not labor alone. Jane Addams, Carrie Chapman Catt, Elizabeth Evans, Emily Bishop, and Elizabeth Brandeis were not only intimate friends but associates in an effort to make women an effective force in creating a more humane world.

For those who believe that change for the better must be achieved and that a logical train of thought is the best compass to follow, Belle pointed the way.

Here, often in her own words, is the story of Belle Case La Follette.

THE AUTHORS

PROLOGUE

....

Abraham Lincoln said it at Gettysburg in 1863: "This Nation shall have a new birth of freedom, and government of the people, by the people, for the people shall not perish from the Earth."

Fifty years later, in 1913, Belle Case La Follette repeated those familiar words in testimony before the Senate Committee on Woman Suffrage. Then she added a question. "Are not women people?"

The stunned all male committee was silent for a moment and then broke into applause. There was but one answer to Belle's question. The injustice of denying half of the people of this nation the right to participate in the affairs of government made a mockery of both freedom and democracy.

Her blue eyes sparkling, her hand raised, her forefinger pointing directly at the gentlemen who composed that Committee, Belle continued, "Government is not a man's problem nor a woman's problem alone. It is their mutual problem. And it is only when women are given their share of responsibility in the solution of public questions, that the affairs of government will be brought into the home for discussion. Not until then will government become a familiar subject, interwoven in the family life and understood as it must be if democracy in its best form is to endure."

In her testimony Belle also pointed out that women do most of the buying. "Ninety percent of the ten billion dollars spent in the United States for food, clothing and shelter is spent by women . . . If the tariff in any way affects the cost of what we wear and what we eat, if the trusts and [corporate] combinations have anything to do with the high cost of living, in that the price of great staples like beef and sugar and oil and woolens and silks are fixed by monopoly, then women should know about it, because the only way to remedy those wrongs is through national legislation . . . I can not think of a single important question that has been before the Congress of the United States in the last twenty-five years in which women have not been equally concerned with men."

Toward the end of her testimony Belle stated, "I am not one of those who expect any great radical change because of equal suffrage—that is, any great radical *immediate* change. It has always seemed to me very natural that women and men of the same family should have somewhat similar views on political questions . . . It is to the general uplift that we must look for the great benefit of equal suffrage. Granting equal opportunities to women in education—and that movement, remember, met with much the same bitter opposition that this movement meets with—granting equal opportunities in education did not suddenly change the status of society. But who questions the powerful influence upon society today of the liberal, educated woman? . . . Your Committee has been very patient and generous in listening to the extended discussion of this subject in all its phases; but I wonder if—after all has been said—you will not agree that it resolves itself into a simple question of common sense."

Once again applause swept through the Committee Room. And after others testified the Committee unanimously recommended passage of the Susan B. Anthony amendment to the Constitution. However, the Congress in general was not yet willing to accept women as *people*—capable of sharing with men in the responsibilities of government. It would not be until 1919 that the equal voting rights amendment would become the law of the land. In the interim the most destructive war in history had ravaged Europe, killing and maiming millions of people on both sides of the Atlantic. During this First World War, Belle became one of the founders of The Woman's Peace Party, which later became The Women's International League for Peace and Freedom, an organization still active today. After the War, Belle became a leader in the Woman's Committee for World Disarmament.

On Christmas Day in 1920—one year after she had won the right to vote—Belle led a disarmament rally on Pennsylvania Avenue in Washington. Freezing temperatures and a blustery wind did not stop this fighter for world peace from speaking her mind. "We women have the power to compel disarmament. We need not plead or beg. We have the ballot. On this issue of militarism we hold the balance of power. We propose to be practical. We propose to watch Congress.

And here on this day precious to the Christian World, at the very door of the Capitol of our beloved nation, we vow to use our votes to *defeat* those senators and representatives in Congress who stand for Militarism and War; and to *elect* senators and representatives who stand for Peace and Disarmament . . . *Real* disarmament of nations will relieve the people of the world from the grievous burden of military taxation, thus paving the way to transfer to education and public welfare the aid so long denied."

Through Belle's efforts, and thousands of women like her, pressure was put on senators and representatives to pass a bill calling for the first disarmament conference in history—The Naval Arms Limitation Conference of 1922. Although the influence of women had been largely responsible for calling the conference, no woman was chosen to participate. Belle was furious and took to her typewriter. "This conference was called in response to the demand of the great masses of people, especially women, for disarmament and the end of war. But the delegates selected to sit at the council table were all (male) representatives of the conservative class. Whatever progress occurred was made from their point of view. These delegates sought to lessen the chance of war and to mitigate its horrors, but they continued to think in terms of war. There was no strong, forward-looking spirit at that table, *demanding* that the will of the great masses of plain people be made effective . . . that there be NO MORE WAR!!!"

In 1925 Belle's husband, Senator La Follette ("Fighting Bob") died. In Wisconsin, from the Governor to the "plain" people in the street, Belle was the unanimous choice to serve out his term. Had she accepted, Belle would have been the first woman to sit in the United States Senate. But Belle preferred to let her older son, Bob Jr., represent Wisconsin. She then addressed her fellow women, "because your petitions present to me the most compelling reason why I should become a candidate. I realize that my election might pave the way for other women to be elected to the Senate and I am deeply mindful of the importance of women sharing the responsibilities of high office and of having direct voice in shaping a government of the people. But due to the special obligations circumstances placed upon me, I cannot, however, bring myself to believe that it is my *duty* to enter the political field. For many years I have gladly shared with Mr. La Follette the rewards and hardships of public life. My faith in the righteousness of his chosen work has been, like his, unshakable; but I know from long experience the exacting demands, the ceaseless strain of public service. At no time in my life would I ever have chosen a public career for myself. It would be against nature for me to undertake the responsibilities of political leadership." Instead, Belle wanted to complete the biography of Fighting Bob and to continue as Editor and Publisher of *The Progressive*.

To make the world a better place was the thrust of Belle Case La Follette's life. It was a life that began in a log cabin, on an inauspicious homestead, along the Wisconsin frontier.

BELLE

Young Belle of Baraboo

[1859–1875]

In the Juneau County wilderness of Wisconsin, a baby girl with auburn hair and eyes of cornflower blue was born on April 21, 1859. She was named, appropriately, Belle.

Her first home was a log cabin her parents had built in a place called Summit. Her father, Anson Case, and her mother, Mary Nesbit Case, worked hard to wrest a living from the inhospitable land. While Anson harvested what crops he could from the soil, Mary cared for the children, a flock of chickens and a cow. She sold her produce in town, always setting aside a portion of her butter and egg money for a rainy day. Six children were born to Mary and Anson. Two survived, Belle and her older brother Roy. The Cases, like thousands of others, had settled in what they believed to be the promised land.

In the early 1800's Wisconsin was a pristine territory of 55,000 square miles of untouched wilderness. It was possible to see a silver dollar laying on the bottom of Green Bay through sixty feet of water. The primordial forests that shielded the land were thick and tall. There were giant white and yellow pine, balsam, cedar, hemlock and spruce, rock maple, ash, basswood and hickory. Indians and a variety of game lived in the forests.

John Jacob Astor had formed the American Fur Company to trade cheap whiskey with the Indians for expensive pelts. By 1820 Astor had become America's first self-made millionaire. He was followed by men more interested in the trees than the animals. The new America was expanding westward with vigor and transportation —wagons, ships, boats and barges—were all built of wood. Houses, stores, factories, sidewalks and even whole cities were built of wood. Chicago was created, board by board, house by house, block by block, out of Wisconsin wood. There was a frenzy in the forests as lumbermen cut and sawed their way through timber, square mile after square mile.

Only the straightest logs, the easiest to handle, were moved to the mills. The tops, branches and slashings, about sixty percent of the cut, were left behind. Where once a forest grew, piles of dead debris dried in the sun and rotted in the rain. Sawmills sprung up along the Wisconsin River. By 1848 there were twenty-four and ten years later one hundred mills were producing 100 million board feet of lumber a year. It was boom time in the timberlands.

Animals for their furs and lush forests for their timber were exploited in the northern part of the Wisconsin Territory. To the south lay prairie land, rolling grass-covered hills that led to the Great Plains of the Midwest. The Mississippi River was the western boundary of the territory. Lead was discovered in the southwestern corner in 1819 and ten years later a mining boom exploded. Spurred on by widely distributed handbills that proclaimed *"Lead Mines on the Upper Mississippi River,"* settlers flocked into the southern part of Wisconsin. The handbills promised: "This tract of country is first rate farming land. Springs of the purest water are to be found in abundance. The interior is healthy. No local causes of fever exist. The climate is pleasant and desirable. Snow seldom exceeds twelve inches in depth during the winter. All fruits, vegetables and grain which grow in the East will succeed equally well here."

From a population of 200 permanent settlers in 1825, the area grew to 10,000 by 1828 and 31,000 by 1840. The men who came to mine the lead had no time for farming, or even building a house. Like Astor, they surged in only to make their fortunes. They lived in caves dug into the sides of the hills next to the mines. Since they existed like badgers, they were called badgers and Wisconsin, which became a state in 1848, was dubbed the Badger State. The miners worked at such a feverish pace that by 1850 the lead was depleted. But the image of Wisconsin as a state in which to make a fortune persisted.

Fifty-three persons gathered on March 20, 1854, in the little white schoolhouse at Ripon, Wisconsin, to establish a political party with the goal of stopping the spread of slavery. They called themselves Republicans. So great was their appeal in Wisconsin that two years later a Republican, Coles Bashford, was elected governor. Four years later Abraham Lincoln was elected the first Republican President of the United States.

The year 1854 was also the year Anson Case's parents, Archibald and Lucetta Moore Case, left their homestead in Avon, Ohio, and headed for Wisconsin. They settled in Baraboo, Sauk County, thirty miles northwest of Madison, the state capital. Anson, at twenty the oldest son, was not completely happy about the move to Baraboo. As soon as land was claimed and he had helped build a cabin for the rest of the family, he returned to Avon to marry the girl he left behind, Mary Nesbit. Wanting to homestead in Wisconsin but also wishing to be on their own, the young couple settled in Summit, about fifty miles from Baraboo. But when Belle was three, Anson gave up his hopeless stake in Summit to rejoin his parents in Baraboo, where money was to be made growing hops.

Traditionally, hops had been produced in New York and Pennsylvania. New York City and Philadelphia had been the major beer brewing areas since Colonial times. But in 1861 the hop louse devastated the Eastern crop. Thirsty Pennsylvanians and New Yorkers felt the pinch as the price of their favorite beverage went through the roof. Though it seemed peculiar, the area around Baraboo was uniquely suited to meet the hop crisis.

Baraboo had been founded by an enterprising and wealthy but eccentric Hungarian nobleman, Count Agostin Haraszthy. By the late 1830's he had secured for himself much of the land in and around Baraboo and in 1842 he built the first structure in town, a general store. The area around Baraboo reminded him of the fertile plains of his native Hungary and he was determined to turn Sauk County into a cornucopia of the finest European produce. He teamed up with a wealthy Englishman, "Lord" Bryant, and together they started the first ferry service across the Wisconsin River, then a steamboat service up and down the river. Soon after, they built a brickyard to produce the material for European-style buildings more durable than the wood shanties and log cabins commonplace on the prairie.

The Count was most interested in agriculture. He introduced sheep and hogs into the area on a large scale. He experimented with fruit trees and a variety of grains, including the first extensive cultivation of Indian corn. His passion was viniculture. He dreamed of establishing a major wine-producing industry in Sauk County and imported thousands of European grape cuttings, only to see them perish in the harsh Wisconsin winters. Broken-hearted, the count pulled up stakes in 1848 and moved on to California, where he became so successful he was credited with founding the California wine industry. He left behind in Baraboo, and Sauk County generally, a spirit of agricultural experimentation led by a large number of German settlers with an established taste for lager. The place was ripe to fill the hop gap.

In the spring of 1862 Sauk County farmers began growing hops in earnest. Within three years hops had become the major produce of the area. The price had risen from fifteen cents a pound in 1861 to sixty-five cents a pound in 1865. By 1867 Sauk County held the distinction of being the most intensively cultivated hop producing area in the world, earning its farmers that year over two million dollars.

The establishment of breweries was the next logical step and again the German settlers took the lead. With pure spring water and locally grown grain and hops, the breweries became an instant success and the settlers soon became intoxicated with their new affluence. Farmers dressed their daughters in satins and silks and purchased pianos for them to practice on. Farmers' sons went in for purebred horses and fancy phaetons. Hop-picking time was carnival time. The railroad added extra trains to bring in bright-faced girls and ambitious boys bent on filling their purses and pockets with dollars. In the evening under the harvest moon, there was feasting, fiddle playing and jigging to the latest fad, the hop dance.

The dizzy flow of money made everyone a little heady and extravagant. Unfortunately, the hop louse now discovered Sauk County. In 1868 it destroyed half the crop while in the East, which had been slowly recovering, there was a bumper crop. By 1870 the Wisconsin hop boom was over. The joyous carnival of riches had lasted only a few years but they were the formative years of Belle Case's early childhood.

Because Mary and Anson's time was totally consumed producing hops, Belle turned to her grandmother for the attention she quite naturally desired. Lucetta adored her bright and inquisitive granddaughter, to whom she devoted much time.

Lucetta Moore Case had been born in Vermont of English and Scottish parents. When she was ten, in the winter of 1808, her parents left Vermont for the less rocky land and more temperate climate of Ohio. They traveled by an ox-drawn wagon over barely discernible roads, settling finally in Avon.

Lucetta's mother, pregnant at the time, died in childbirth. The ten-year-old girl, the oldest of the children, took over the role of mother. Of necessity she became experienced in child rearing and the other housekeeping duties of an adult frontier woman. She had no chance for formal schooling but she taught herself to read the only book available, the Bible. She absorbed not only the spirit of the book but tended to speak in the eloquent King James English.

Lucetta also learned the art of herbal medicine and became the one to whom the family looked in times of illness. She was expert at making such foods as maple sugar and cheese. She kept bees and put up honey. She made her own vegetable dyes, taught herself to spin and weave and fashioned all the family's clothing, not the usual plain homespun but Scottish plaids and English checks to brighten the wardrobes.

Lucetta was fascinated by the natural world. She learned all the primary constellations and could tell time by the stars. Throughout her life neither her hands nor mind were idle except in sleep. One day at the farm Belle and her grandmother were cutting and sewing rags to make a rug. Belle complained, "Grandma, don't you hate to sew short rags that take such a long time to do and make such a small ball when you're done?"

Lucetta Moore Case looked over her glasses at the little girl and replied, "No, child. I don't hate to do anything that needs to be done."

Aware that her granddaughter was unusually bright and sensitive, Lucetta determined Belle must receive the education she had been denied. And so, with her mother and grandmother's pride and encouragement, Belle was sent to school. The schoolhouse was a mile from the Case farm but never, throughout the twelve years Belle walked to and from it every school day, was she late for a class. She loved learning and the only time she was absent occurred when she fell ill with the measles—even her grandmother's medical skill could not prevent that.

The end of the hop boom was followed by the Depression of 1873, triggered by the failure of the New York banking firm Jay Cooke and Company, and causing the collapse of other banks and industries. Panic spread from Wall Street to all parts of the nation. Railroad construction almost stopped, steel production dropped, farm prices fell. The only thing to rise was the size of the average family's debt. The American Dream of that era had faded.

In June 1875, when Belle was sixteen, she graduated from the district school in Baraboo. She decided to take the "classical course" at the University of Wisconsin in Madison. Anson and Mary knew they would have to work even harder to pay Belle's room and board but they were determined, especially Mary, their Belle would receive a college education.

First and Only Love

[1875–1881]

When Belle set off for the University of Wisconsin in Madison, thirty miles southeast of Baraboo, it was the farthest she had ever been from home.

She was assigned to live in Ladies Hall, the dormitory for female freshmen. Her roommate was a German girl from Sauk City who, Belle later wrote, "possessed one of the rarest spirits I had ever known. She taught me more than any of my teachers how to appreciate Heine, Schiller and Goethe."

Owing to gaps in Belle's rural high school curriculum, she had to make up several required courses at the university. One was first-year German, taught by Miss S. A. Carver. One day shortly after the college year started, Miss Carver found it necessary to reprimand a group of young men who were disrupting the class.

Belle noted at the edge of the group the earnest face of one young man whose name she learned was Robert La Follette. In spite of his sober look, she suspected him as "the prime cause of mischief," even before becoming better acquainted with him.

Bob and Belle were attracted to each other at once, discovering they shared a similar farming background, a love of learning and a delicious sense of humor.

Bob was born in Primrose, Wisconsin, a small town twenty-four miles northwest of Madison, on June 14, 1855. His father, Josiah, had built a double log cabin near a spring, not far from the road, on a piece of land consisting mostly of prairie.

Josiah La Follette and Mary Ferguson had been sweethearts in their teens in Indiana. Josiah had asked Mary to marry him before she was ready and she refused. Miffed, Josiah returned to his boyhood home in Mount Sterling, Kentucky. Perhaps believing she would never see Josiah again, Mary was persuaded by her family to marry another man, Alexander Buchanan, in 1840. But he died within the year, leaving her pregnant with her first child, a daughter, Ellen.

When Josiah learned of Buchanan's death, he threw down his ax in Kentucky and returned to Indiana, still intent on marrying Mary, though it took him five years to convince her. They lived on the Buchanan farm where their first two sons, William and Marion, were born. Marion did not survive childhood. Their third child, a daughter, Josephine, and youngest son, Robert, were born in Primrose where the family moved in 1850. Bob and Jo, as he called her, were inseparable in childhood and, according to Belle, remained "always at heart very close."

Josiah was a handsome man, six feet, two and three-quarter inches tall. He had a high forehead, expressive brown eyes, thick wavy hair and a heavy beard and eyebrows. Mary was only four feet, ten inches, but she held herself as straight as an arrow, giving the impression of being taller. She had a pretty but determined face, with fair skin, blond hair and intense blue eyes. Bob inherited Josiah's thick hair and heavy beard but he had Mary's eyes and, like her, was short, growing only to five feet, six inches.

When Bob was eight months old Josiah died from a complication of pneumonia and diabetes. He knew he was dying and told Mary he had no fear of death but "dreaded to be forgotten." Mary made a point of repeating Josiah's fear to Bob often and it made a lasting impression on him. Bob idealized the memory of his father and later confessed to Belle how often he thought of his father by day and dreamed of him at night.

After Josiah died, Mary wanted the body of their little son, Marion, which had been buried on a hillside in sight of the house, to be placed with that of his father. The boy's coffin was taken from the grave, brought to the house and opened. "The child's face was perfect, as if asleep," Belle recalled Bob's telling her. "While they were looking, it fell to ashes. Father and son were taken to the Postville Cemetery on Green's Prairie and placed together in one grave."

An unexpected and heavy blow was dealt Bob in 1862 when he was seven. His beloved mother, a widow for six years, married John Z. Saxton of Argyle, Wisconsin, a widower with adopted children. Twenty-six years older than Mary, Saxton was known locally as Uncle John and, as town chairman, postmaster and merchant, was a leading citizen of Argyle. Though a rival store had recently sprung up, Uncle John had a good country trade and was considered prosperous, even wealthy, for those times. At one time he even owned a hotel.

Saxton was an ardent Baptist, a deacon and leader in the church as well as the community. Bob hated his stepfather from the start. Resenting his attempts to convert him, Bob became expert at playing sick on Sundays to escape Saxton's sermon. While everyone else was at church Bob stayed at home with his pet pony, Gypsy, teaching her tricks such as going up and down the steep hall stairs.

Mary was ambitious for her children, eager for them to have the education she lacked. She had hoped John Saxton would provide as liberally for his stepchildren as he had for his adopted ones. But it annoyed Saxton greatly that Josiah and Mary's children not only rejected his religion but also refused to take his name. Bob was especially irreconcilable announcing, if strangers addressed him as Saxton, "My name is La Follette!"

After a prolonged illness that required constant attention from his young wife, John Saxton died leaving nothing to Mary and the children, not even a house. For the next two years, until he was nineteen, Bob supported his mother and sisters by growing and marketing produce from their old farm, selling it in Madison. It was a day's drive over dirt roads and steep hills with a team of horses and a load of grain, butter, eggs and poultry.

"There was no work on a farm Bob could not do well," Belle later wrote. "He plowed a straight furrow and plowed deep. He handled a scythe with an ease and rhythm delightful to watch. He knew how the crops should be planted, the stock cared for; how the haying, harvesting and all the things that are a part of the day's work on the farm should be done."

In the early 1870's Bob took note of the Granger movement which, through local granges, provided farmers with a channel for economic protest and a forum for political organization. He later called the movement the first powerful revolt in Wisconsin against the monopolies, the "arrogance" of railroads and the "waste and robbery of public lands."

Belle believed both the experience of the Granger movement and listening to "the great address" of Wisconsin Chief Justice Edward G. Ryan, who spoke at the university, "did more than even Bob himself realized to shape his political career." Bob never forgot, she said, the "prophetic words" of Justice Ryan: "There is looming up a new and dark power. . . . The enterprises of the country are aggregating vast corporate combinations of unexampled capital, boldly marching, not for economic conquests only, but for political power. . . . The question will arise, and arise in your day, 'Which shall rule—wealth or man; which shall lead—money or intellect; who shall fill public stations—educated and patriotic free men, or feudal serfs of corporate capital?"

Bob moved Mary and his sister Jo—and the family cow—in June of 1873 to Madison, where he had applied for admission to the university. Still keeping their log home, the three La Follettes rented a house near the university. Mary and Jo cooked meals for twenty paying college boys and Bob helped out by selling books and teaching at a country school in nearby Burke, riding Gypsy each day the five miles to and from school.

Jo told of a day in his freshman year when they walked to the cemetery to hear an impressive Memorial Day address by Colonel William F. Vilas, a well-known Madison lawyer. On the way home Bob suddenly stopped, grabbed Jo's two shoulders and looking earnestly into her eyes said, "Jo, I can do that! Some day they will be coming out to hear me!"

An important part of nineteenth century college social life revolved around fraternities, sororities and, for the intellectually inclined, the literary societies. There was keen rivalry among the literary societies to attract the most promising students to take part in special programs of weekly debates, orations, essays and declamations. On weekends the libraries were filled with young men and women preparing for these lively events. Regular society meetings were held Friday nights in rooms reserved in university buildings. Public meetings frequently took place in the assembly chamber of the capitol and these were open to townspeople as well as students. Such events drew enthusiastic audiences, if for no other reason than they were the only show in town.

Belle became a member of the Laurean Literary Society while Bob joined the Athenae Oratorical Society, the oldest one, organized in 1850. His experience in this society quickly developed his natural gift as a dynamic and compelling speaker. It was not long before other students sought his help in the preparation and delivery of their orations.

In the spring of his freshman year Bob started to fight against what he considered "injustice." The university had joined the Inter-

State Collegiate Association, made up of 10,000 students in fifty colleges in the six states of Ohio, Indiana, Illinois, Iowa, Missouri and Wisconsin. A mass meeting was called to elect representatives for the home oratorical contest. Winners would represent the university in competition with the other colleges in the final Inter-State contest.

The fraternities Bob refused to join as too elitest had made up a slate without consulting the rest of the student body. They then presented this slate at a meeting and it was accepted. Bob and others who did not belong to a fraternity felt this a particularly serious example of fraternity manipulation to dominate college politics by electing members to all the important posts. The literary societies, largely composed of nonfraternity students, feared they would be undermined in their oratorical territory by the "secret societies," as fraternities were also known.

At a meeting of all the literary societies Bob spoke out against what he called a flagrant abuse of power. After the meeting he organized a room-to-room canvas of the nonfraternity students and persuaded two hundred to sign a protest against the slate to be presented at another mass meeting of the student body. The protest included a demand for reconsideration of the names offered as speakers for the oratorical contest. The college authorities approved the protest and a second mass meeting was held. The slate offered by the fraternities was rejected. The "antis" triumphantly presented their list, which was subsequently accepted.

Belle took no part in the antifraternity rebellion, "little understood what it was all about," she later confessed. "But I remember the excitement and the milling about of the students on the campus. Most of the girls from Ladies Hall, where I lived, who attended the mass meeting, were 'pro-frat' and very much disgusted when the 'antis' won out."

One of Belle's classmates, an ardent champion of the secret societies, later wrote Belle of the second mass meeting, where "feeling ran high" and "we looked upon Bob as an outsider and a demagogical disturber of the peace." But she soon held a different view after Bob brought word that one of her close friends, a girl she loved and admired, was to be expelled from the university that afternoon because of a trifling infraction of rules connected with a fraternity dance the night before.

Through a faculty leak the news had reached Bob ahead of the official announcement. He went to Belle's friend at once, out of "a burning sense of the injustice of this extreme penalty," to ask her aid "in uniting the class in common protest." The letter ended: "What thrilled us was the glimpse we got of Bob's inner nature—the quick sympathy and understanding, the revolt against injustice, the utter absence of anything like resentment of our earlier opposition, with, instead, perfect confidence in our friendship and loyalty and a certainty that we were as ready as he to take a stand against injustice."

In the summer of 1876 Bob borrowed $400 to buy the *University Press*, the semimonthly college newspaper. It was financed by subscriptions, about 1,000, and advertisements, often paid for in merchandise. Bob ran the *Press* for the next three years of his college life. He worked day and night, writing the editorials, gathering college news, sometimes even setting type and soliciting ads. The *Press* netted $700 a year, and the experience of publishing created in Bob a longing to own his own press someday.

He tended to put most of his energy into these extracurricular activities that both interested him and helped somewhat to defray his college expenses. As a result his classwork suffered. And though he was generally well liked, he was considered a poor student by his teachers. Belle, on the other hand, was a natural student and excelled in every class she entered—except public speaking. Not as mercurial as Bob, she was not a particularly exciting orator. Early in their friendship they began to help each other, she with his studies, he with her platform appearance. This was the beginning of a lifelong partnership of mutual support.

What little leisure time Bob had they spent together. Belle admired Bob's dedication to everything he undertook, his natural gift for public speaking, his mischievous wit and sense of humor. Bob was as attracted to Belle's inner, as well as outer, beauty, her analytical mind, her compassion for the downtrodden, and her zest for life. People described Belle as possessing the most contagious laugh they ever heard.

During junior and senior years each student had to give "orations" that had a considerable effect on scholastic standings. When Belle delivered her first oration she failed to remember a single word, gave up and returned to her seat "overwhelmed with a sense of disgrace." Her instructor told her that to get credit for rhetorical work for her junior year she would have to write a new oration. With Bob's help she did just that and recited it perfectly.

Bob met a similar crisis in very different fashion. Belle later told of this day: "Short and slight, there was nothing striking in his appearance as, head slightly bent, he walked up the aisle with long strides until he stood upon the rostrum and faced the audience. Then his fine brow, keen eyes, mobile face and that something we call magnetism arrested and held the attention. But suddenly, in the middle of an impassioned sentence with fitting gestures, he forgot his lines.

"The prompter had lost the place and Bob quietly waited for him to find it, without the slightest change of countenance, holding his arm upraised, his body outstretched from toe to fingertips, until he heard the cue. Then, apparently unconscious of any break, not reacting to an audience convulsed with laughter, he continued his oration."

Bob told Belle afterward that he had felt "deeply humiliated" but she said she could not believe this because of the cool self-mastery with which he had recovered his ground and effectively closed his oration.

The "Junior Ex"—exhibition of final orations—was held once a year in the assembly chamber at the capitol. The program consisted of a presentation by one representative of each literary society. As a junior Bob represented the Athenae and Belle, the Laurean. She helped him with his research and he coached her in delivery and stage presence. The title of Bob's oration was "The Stage." *The Madison Democrat* reported Bob held his audience because of "his grace and it was evident that he believed what he said." He described drama onstage as a medium of arousing people to awareness of injustices, causing them to find a remedy.

In reporting the exhibition for his own paper the *University Press*, Bob omitted all reference to his oration but praised the others. Of Belle's part in the program he wrote: "The audience were on the *qui vive* as the president announced the next orator's subject—'Children's Playthings'—and Miss Case, of the Laurean Society, took the stage. She fully sustained her reputation as a writer of uncommon merit. Gracefully, and in a clear ringing voice heard easily in every part of the assembly chamber, she pronounced an oration that for force and originality of thought and finish of composition was probably not equaled during the evening."

Following her successful oration, Belle was told by her English professor that her talent for writing was worth cultivating, that he believed she might achieve a place as a contributor to current literature. She did not take the suggestion seriously at the time but later wrote she would consider it if she "were beginning life over again. . . . I realized that even the occasional writing and speaking had more value for me in after-life than anything else at the university. To learn to speak and write easily, as a matter of course, whatever we have to say, should be one of the first objects of educational training."

At the end of their junior year Bob asked Belle to marry him. He would later tell their four children, "Mama laughed when I proposed to her."

Belle explained to them, "If I did, it was Papa's fault, he had been so disposed to make me laugh when I was in his company, how could I be sure he was not joking?"

In recollecting their courtship she said, "And it was true, our relationship had been free from sentiment, so lighthearted and joyous that I preferred to keep it on that basis—at least until we finished college. But he had his own way, as he usually did; so before we parted for the summer vacation it was settled that we were to travel the road together."

In her senior year Belle was doing so well in all her courses, amassing more than enough credits to graduate, that she elected to take an extra course in natural science. The course was taught by a young instructor, Edward Birge, who later became president of the university. He offered the course, without credit, to anyone interested in the natural sciences.

Belle was the only woman to take it and one of the few to stay with it through the year. There were no special science laboratories in those days so the classes were held at the end of an unused passage with a kitchen table and several chairs. The hours Belle spent at that kitchen table discovering the natural world—the unseen life in a jar of pond water, the intricate beauty of a dragonfly's wing—aroused her intellectual curiosity and called out her powers of observation, a profound experience she soon put to good use.

The outstanding event of Bob's senior year was winning the midwest Inter-State Oratorical Contest in May of 1879. He chose Iago as his subject. Belle recalled the day he first read the oration to her, asked for her advice and comment: "We walked out along University Drive and sat down on a knoll under a big tree. He took the manuscript from his pocket and read reflectively, without emphasis, as though to himself. I had no knowledge by which to judge his conception of the character of Iago, but I knew how he had read and studied, how carefully every word had been chosen, every phrase considered. Before the home contest he had worked out the delivery as definitely as the thought and composition. This does not mean that his gestures were mechanical, for he studied to make them interpretative, just as he always tried to have the right word."

The home contest was held in the capitol on August 25 and Bob won first place. The state contest, which he felt he had to win for the university as well as himself, was held at Beloit, Wisconsin, a week later. A number of classmates were among the crowd of students who accompanied Belle and Bob on the train to Beloit. The engineer and conductor shared the excitement as they allowed the students to ride in the engineer's cab two at a time. For Belle it proved "a real adventure," except she was sorry not to cross the state line, still never having been beyond the state of Wisconsin.

She described the church where the contest was held as "long, narrow and not well lighted," and reported the character of Iago therefore "seemed more sinister, the effect of the oration more somber than at Madison. There could be no doubt about the result, for Bob won his audience from the start." After the judges announced Bob's victory, which meant he had been chosen to represent Wisconsin in the Inter-State contest, the male students from the university swung him up on their shoulders and marched from the church to the train, cheering and singing.

At Madison, Bob and Belle were met by a crowd of students with a band. Elation ran so high that students drew Bob's carriage up the hill to the university, where he was formally welcomed. That evening he was given a reception in the state house and Belle sat beaming with pride as his praises were sung by Colonel Vilas, the Postmaster and Republican political leader, whom Bob greatly admired, and by members of the faculty. But the climax of this day was "the happiness and pride of his spirited little mother," as Belle put it.

The final contest, the midwest Inter-State Competition, took place at Iowa City, Iowa, on May 7, 1879. Bob held the listeners spellbound and won easily. One of the judges commented, "His words fitted his thoughts and his thoughts filled his words. The truth concerning Iago was so in his mind that he was able to present to the hearer the truth and the image in such a way as to make them appear living realities."

Winning this honor undoubtedly helped Bob get his diploma,

for his general academic standing was low. When the matter of his graduation came up in a faculty meeting everyone conceded that in spite of his poor marks he had not loafed, that his time away from studies, including his work as editor of the *University Press*, had been worthily spent. University President John Bascom cast the deciding vote to allow Bob to graduate.

Despite his poor grades Bob always had a profound regard for scholarship and more faith in the conventional system of education than Belle did. "Even with my limited grasp of what constituted 'education,' " she wrote, "I was impressed by Bob's better knowledge of some subjects we were both studying, and his ability to apply what he knew. Most of my time was spent striving to get my lessons, and I had higher marks than he, in mechanics, for example, but his understanding of the principles and application of the screw and lever was practical; mine was confined to what the book said."

The commencement day program on June 18, 1879, consisted of essays and orations by members of the graduating class. Students' average marks over the four years determined whether they had a place on the program, which meant Belle's consistent A's made her one of sixteen in the class to take part in the exercises. The program started at nine in the morning but so many arrived early at the assembly chamber that hundreds had to stand outside within hearing distance. In those days a university graduation ceremony was a community event.

On that day an honorary prize was to be awarded to the participating student whose essay or oration was judged the best. Inspired by her work on Dr. Birge's kitchen table, Belle selected as her subject "Learning to See." One afternoon Dr. Birge had assembled a few corals, sea urchins and starfish, and handed them to his students to describe, saying, "Tell me what you see." It had been a new educational experience for Belle and "I was amazed how little I knew of the art of seeing," she wrote.

She prepared her oration with her usual care and then asked Bob to critique it. He did not suggest changes in content but "touched up the language and gave the oration rhythm and ring, as he knew how to do. Then he began drilling me in its delivery and kept me at it until he had done all he could for me. I think he expected me to win the prize. I had little confidence in winning."

But this time Belle spoke so winningly and her topic was so interesting the judges awarded her the coveted prize. "I was so greatly pleased when it was awarded me," she recalled. But she was especially gratified that her father, "who almost never left the work of the farm," and her mother, "who made so many sacrifices to keep me in school in spite of the hard times," had come to Madison to see her graduate.

"I remember seeing their faces while I was speaking," she wrote. "I was happy most of all for their sakes to hear the applause that followed the judge's decision."

To Love, Honor—
But Not Obey

[1881–1885]

Before graduation Belle and Bob had a long talk regarding the profession he might best pursue as his life's work. Besides the law, the stage had a strong appeal for him but he gave up this goal since he felt he was much too small at five feet six inches to play either a leading man or a villain.

He was so interested in literature and teaching that he also considered a university instructorship, which would lead to a professorship and a "congenial and attractive career." But after "talking it over seriously," Bob and Belle agreed that the most practical and ideal plan was to study law and, sometime in the future, buy their own farm.

Belle decided to teach after graduation so she could help earn the money Bob and she would need to marry. She was offered a job in the fall teaching high school in the town of Spring Green, thirty miles west of Madison on the Wisconsin River. Bob started his legal courses at the University's law school and also was accepted as a clerk in the law office of R. M. Bashford, a Madison attorney. Train connections to Spring Green were good and Bob visited Belle as often as he could.

During her first year as teacher, Belle was assistant principal of the Spring Green High School. The principle, Walter Delamatyr, an experienced teacher, was a Civil War veteran who "exercised an easy, natural control over the school," Belle noted. "There were apparently no rules. Great freedom and much give-and-take existed between teachers and scholars, but never a suggestion of disorder or disrespect. When I asked the secret of his philosophy, Mr. Delamatyr laughed and said, 'I put them on their honor and then watch 'em.' " Belle described the students as "there because they were eager for an education. They were paying tuition, more often than not with money they had earned themselves. Some were older than I; some were district schoolteachers. I had to work hard to keep in advance of them in the branches I taught."

The strain of "keeping in advance of them" took its toll on Bob as well as Belle on at least one occasion when she appeared uncharacteristically insensitive to his feelings. Bob kept a diary he called *Private Journal and Night Thoughts.* He wrote on November 7, 1879: "Had the evening mainly with Belle and was puzzled not a little to understand her. I hardly know why, but she, at times, did not seem like herself. Nor could I shake this off nor dispute it all the time she was with me till Monday evening."

He wrote of their enjoying a play and his taking the train back to Madison so he would not miss an important law lecture. He ended the entry: "But, oh, how reluctantly and what a miserable day I passed. My Dear Journal, I tell you everything, but I can't tell you that—I cannot form misery in words—*it is a feeling.*"

Bob may not have attempted to describe the misery he felt in his journal but he obviously revealed his depressed state to Belle, for on November 9 his journal read: "Had a lovely letter from Belle's mother which I think helped to save me from one which Belle sent in reply to a note written her Monday night. Oh how she has misunderstood and how much pain her words cost me. I know she did not mean to hurt me, but it seemed like the black days of the past and it brought me face to face with my old enemy. I had thought him well out of my way but he came, dark creature that he is, with a power that I had nearly forgotten."

But their good times together far outweighed the unhappy. Once when Bob visited Belle at Spring Green their spirits rose so high that Belle challenged Bob to a race "right in the village street." It was not recorded who won but Belle stated, "I was a good runner for a girl. When I was nine years old, there was only one boy in school who could run faster than I could."

She taught school for two years while waiting to marry, the second year in her hometown, Baraboo. Her pupils there were all in the seventh grade, ages ranging from twelve to fourteen. One pupil, a tall, heavy, dark-eyed boy named John Ringling, was "good-natured, full of fun but had little taste for lessons or books." When it came to "composition," Belle was wise enough to ask the class to write of things they knew. When John Ringling "read a long account— interrupted with giggles from the school—of the sideshows he and other boys had been giving every night," instead of praising his first attempt at self-expression, Belle told him to take his lessons more seriously. She later wrote, "Fortunately, the scolding had no effect. Soon after, he and his older brothers started a small circus in which they themselves took the leading parts as musicians, tumblers, clowns, ringmaster and animal trainer. Such was the beginning of 'Ringling Brothers' Circus.' "

Bob was admitted to the bar on February 5, 1880, after studying law for only five months at the university. This single term at the law school was possible because the faculty, who admired and liked Bob, made an extraordinary exception in allowing him to enter without paying the usual fees. They knew he was supporting his mother and sister and also wanted to marry Belle when he could afford it. The faculty were also aware that during his college years Bob had attended court when important cases were being tried and listened to arguments by leading lawyers. This proved excellent training for his bar examination and his subsequent law practice.

That summer Bob decided to become a candidate for district attorney on the Republican ticket. He wanted the political position because the salary was $800 a year, with an allowance of $500 for expenses, and this seemed a golden opportunity to get married. He was, as he put it, "as poverty-stricken a young lawyer as ever hung his shingle in the wind." Also, criminal trial work appealed to him.

As he campaigned for the nomination as district attorney, he suddenly realized he was taking on the Republican "bosses" who completely controlled all elections. It was a daring act for him to announce he was a candidate for district attorney of Dane County without the consent of the local Republican boss, Colonel E. W. Keyes, postmaster of Madison. Keyes had publicly praised Bob's victorious delivery of "Iago" but running for public office was a different matter.

Keyes summoned Bob to his office where he told him he was wasting his time and money. The next district attorney had already been picked—and his name was not La Follette! Bob later wrote in his autobiography: "Boss Keyes did not know it but opposition of that sort was the best service he could have rendered me. It stirred all the fight I had in me." Bob described Keyes as "a good representative of old-time politics: the politics of force and secret management. He was absolute dictator in his own territory; he could make candidates, and he could unmake political office-holders."

Bob went to work campaigning "as though his life depended on winning the office," Belle wrote. His method was a simple one—he adhered to it through the years. He determined to go directly to the people. With his gray mare, Gypsy, and a buggy loaned by a friend, he canvassed Dane County. It was harvest time and he knew how few moments the farmers had to talk or listen to speeches. So he visited them evenings in their homes. His opponents called him the "night rider." He covered the ground thoroughly and kept a list of the men he met, particularly the ones who expressed interest in his ideas. The retiring district attorney had been inefficient, employing a large staff, which increased taxes, and Bob promised he would do all the work himself. The chief complaint he heard was "Ain't you over-young?"

There were five Republican candidates and it was the voters in the section around Primrose, Bob's birthplace and boyhood home, who decided the outcome. Eli Pederson, a prosperous farmer and local political leader who had known Bob's father, was the spokesman at a critical moment between ballots at the Dane County caucus and his moving speech describing Bob as "our boy" resulted in Bob's nomination.

Though the district was normally Republican, Bob had a difficult fight ahead because Boss Keyes spoke out for the Democratic candidate rather than support the young Republican rebel who had defied him. Again, Bob personally canvassed the county and organized his friends to work for him.

He won the election for district attorney by ninety-three votes. He was determined to carry out his pledge to the Dane County voters to do the work himself. Nights and Sundays found him at his office "digging, digging." When a crime was committed he tried to be the first to interview all the witnesses and examine the scene. He believed, "It is the facts that settle cases; the law is always the same." A leading lawyer described Bob's style as a prosecutor: "La Follette mastered every conceivable detail of a case. . . . He tried his cases like a trip hammer. There was no groping about; fact followed fact in quick succession, creating to the jury the picture which the young district attorney had framed in his mind."

Bob was especially good at cross-examination. Belle said he could tell by the posture and expression of a witness whether he was lying. His successful trial of criminal cases soon brought him a larger civil practice than he could handle. He established the firm of La Follette and Siebecker in the fall of 1881 with Robert Siebecker, a college friend who had boarded with Bob's mother and met and married his sister Jo. Setting up the firm was a brave venture for two young lawyers without financial backing. Belle heard Robert Siebecker voice doubts and fears but Bob expressed only confidence they would be more independent and successful by themselves rather than taking in as partners older, more experienced lawyers.

Bob was right. They soon had more civil cases on the circuit court calendar than any other firm in Madison. With money coming in, Belle and Bob could now marry. He asked Belle to set the time. She made what was then an unusual request.

In the standard marriage service of the day the woman promised to "obey" her husband whereas the man promised to "cherish" his wife. Belle asked that the word "obey" be omitted from her part of the marriage vow. Her independent spirit rebelled against what she considered an anachronistic demand on the part of the male marital partner.

Bob agreed. He wanted equality for the citizens of his country and he also wanted it for the woman he loved.

They were married on the evening of December 31, 1881, at Belle's home in Baraboo by a Unitarian minister. Her grandfather had recently died but, she wrote, "Our wedding would have been simple under any circumstances—just Bob's folks and mine."

Bob spent the day of the wedding in court trying an important case. A lawyer friend noticed a memorandum on the table in front of Bob that read, "Five p.m. Go to Baraboo." The friend asked to what this referred. Bob explained, "I am going to Baraboo tonight to be married. I mustn't forget that." He left work in time to catch the train and returned to Madison following the ceremony. There was no time or money for a honeymoon. They bought a large house on West Wilson Street where they lived with Bob's mother and his sister and brother-in-law, Robert Siebecker.

To help buy this large home, Bob had sold his beloved farm in Primrose. It "cost him a struggle to part with the farm, but he consoled himself with the thought that he would buy it back some day," Belle wrote. The new home was a dignified old mansion with high ceilings, French windows, marble mantels and spacious grounds. Though two families and Bob's mother occupied the house, it was so large that some of the rooms were closed off. Later it was made into separate homes.

One of the newly married couple's first purchases was books.

Bob owned a small collection of poetry, novels, histories and speeches, as well as several editions of Shakespeare. He had given Belle sets of Goethe's and Schiller's works. They now bought editions of Walter Scott, Washington Irving, George Eliot and James Fenimore Cooper, among others, which, with an *Encyclopaedia Britannica,* filled a bookcase they ordered specially for their library.

Bob felt the need of more thorough preparation in elementary law. The first year of marriage he and Belle spent many evenings reading Blackstone, Kent's *Commentaries* and other lawbooks. When difficult questions arose in his cases, they worked together in his office searching for precedents. Belle later revealed this highly stimulated her interest in law; she "found it a keenly enjoyable intellectual training, quite different from any other studying I had ever done."

With Bob's encouragement she continued to express her independence of mind, including her style of dress. She refused to be hemmed in, literally, by what she considered the ridiculous costume of the 1880's and discarded the bustle and corset to wear loose-fitting, comfortable clothes.

Bob and Belle's first baby, Fola, was born in 1882 and the experience made Belle "profoundly happy. During the first year of her infancy her care absorbed my thought and time. I experienced wonderful contentment and restfulness of spirit." Though Belle believed the "supreme experience in life is motherhood," she also "had never been troubled over problems of a career," and in 1883, at Bob's suggestion, she enrolled in law school. "It did not require much urging to convince me I could do so without neglecting my child and other home duties," she wrote. She had the honor in 1885 of being the first woman to graduate from the University of Wisconsin Law School.

At the end of two years as district attorney, Bob was so successful that not only were the politicians and voters satisfied with his administration, even Boss Keyes did not oppose his renomination. Wisconsin had been a Republican state since that party's founding in the little white schoolhouse in Ripon. But the Republican machine had become corrupt and unable to cope with growing social and economic distress. Consequently, in 1882 Dane County went Democratic, except for Bob, who ran two hundred votes ahead of the rest of the Republican ticket and won by 118 votes. Bob did not disappoint the voters for in his second term he continued to enhance his reputation as a fighter for justice.

During his two terms as district attorney Bob became aware of the depths of the political corruption that existed in Wisconsin. The bosses were all-powerful in the election or appointment of sheriffs, police, usually the district attorney and often judges. Bob began to feel pressure in all sorts of cases as witnesses faded out of reach of the sheriff's office.

In one particularly provoking adultery case involving a friend of Boss Keyes, Bob found himself "facing parties who brought powerful influence to bear," and suffered his first failure to convict in his initial attempt to prosecute. Exhausted and disheartened, he fell ill and took to bed for a few days. Hoping to take advantage of Bob's collapse, Boss Keyes used his influence to try to have the case dismissed. Bob heard of this and "although too weak to walk, I had myself rolled into a blanket and driven to the courthouse. I entered my appearance and asserted my official authority against having the case dismissed. There was a good deal of a fight. . . . I was threatened with being sent to jail for contempt. But finally I secured a postponement and afterward convicted my man."

In fact Bob broke the record for convictions in Dane County as he "worked the sheriff half to death. . . . If there was evidence any-where to be obtained in my cases I got it, regardless of work or expense." In one case he sent a sheriff to England to gather evidence.

During these four years he had little to do with politics. Then one day Sam Harper, another of Bob and Belle's classmates at the university, visited them. Sam had taught school for a while, then studied law. He stayed at the La Follette home for several weeks and they "talked as such friends will." One night Sam asked, "Bob, why don't you go to Congress? You can go to Congress just as well as not. You have the opportunity of a public career and you have the stuff in you."

Harper continued, "There are five counties in this district [the Third Congressional District]. The two big counties, Dane and Grant, outnumber all the others in voting population. Now I live in Grant and you live in Dane. I'll carry Grant for you and you carry Dane for yourself. They will control the convention—and you will go to Congress."

Bob thought hard about this and after considerable discussions with Belle, decided he might try to run for Congress. He delivered the Memorial Day address on May 30, 1884, before a number of Civil War veterans in Madison. Belle later wrote she thought Bob's speech materially helped his nomination and election to Congress. After he started to talk "it seemed no one moved until he had finished." She then confessed, "No one was more spellbound than I. The cadence of his voice, the rhythm of his words carried me along, quite unconscious of who was speaking . . . he was at one with his audience, in perfect accord with the spirit of the day."

Belle later admitted her "instinctive love of home and dread of change" led her "in a mild way" to take the negative side of the argument when Bob announced his decision to run for Congress: "Madison offered every advantage of a permanent home for ourselves and the children we wanted. Why sacrifice such a prospect for the uncertainty of a public career with its inevitable change in our mode of living?" But, as usual, Bob had his way.

An indispensable factor in Bob's election to Congress was his backing by General George E. Bryant. Bryant was a lawyer and judge, as well as a general. He had become impressed with Bob's courage, honesty and ability as district attorney. Bryant was a close friend of General Ulysses Grant and had a large following among the old soldiers in the Third Congressional District, many of whom served in his Wisconsin regiment. Bryant was also a farmer who understood the farmer's point of view.

As in the race for district attorney, Bob faced the machine of Boss Keyes and, as before, he went out on the road to speak to the people of Dane County. But now he was widely known and had many supporters. Harper, as he had promised, spent thirty days making a similar horse-and-buggy campaign in his home county of Grant. General Bryant worked the other districts.

The convention was held at Dodgeville in November of 1884. Though the corrupt machine opposed him, Bob was nominated on the first ballot. The Keyes crowd then tried to beat him at the polls by throwing their support to the Democrats but Bob won by four hundred votes, carrying both Dane and Grant counties, as Harper had accurately predicted. After the votes were counted, old Boss Keyes was reported to have said as he looked over the crowd, "It's the young fellows that did it." General Bryant must have felt flattered.

Bob's term as district attorney ended January 1, 1885, and though his first term of office in Congress and his salary began March 4, he was not due to take his seat until the following December. He intended to make good use of the time by continuing his law practice.

But first he had a trip to make. He had never been further East than Chicago. In January he traveled to Washington to remain there until President Grover Cleveland was inaugurated March 4. Bob attended the sessions of the House of Representatives as faithfully as though he were already a member. He studied the rules, followed every debate, read the *Congressional Record* each day. When there was an all-night session he remained until the dawn. He wanted to study the terrain of the new territory he would be exploring far more fully in his new career.

Belle recalled "how vividly he related his impressions when he came home." More than ever she realized what a change the move East would be, "what a break in the current of our quiet home life."

At this time it was the practice of railroad companies to give passes to public officials and their families in return for favors. Bob thought this unjust and when he received two passes as a new congressman, he and Belle conferred with General Bryant and Harper as to whether he should accept them.

Bob argued that he did not want to be under any obligation to railroad companies which, if he had his way, would be subject to restrictive legislation. It was agreed that he might become involved in a controversy if he returned the passes since the question was not then a public issue. So the passes were delivered in a sealed envelope to Harper for safekeeping and Bob paid for his and Belle's tickets to Washington.

Belle commented, "Doubtless Bob's attitude was a reflection of the Granger movement and the deep impression Chief Justice Ryan's warning had made. 'Which shall rule, wealth or man?' "

La Follette
and La Follette

[1885–1891]

When Bob and Belle left for Washington their plans were "tentative"—Belle's word. Congressmen who could afford it built their own homes or stayed in hotels, as there were few apartments. A boardinghouse was the only choice for the congressman totally dependent on his salary.

Before the move to Washington Belle could foresee that boardinghouse life might not be the best home for a young child. Because of this dilemma Belle made the painful decision to leave Fola, now two and a half, with Bob's mother, Mary, until "we could adjust ourselves to the new environment and find the right place to live."

They wanted to be near the Capitol and initially found a room in a private house in southeast Washington. Like many homes at that time, it had only gas heaters for warmth. When a cold wave struck the city it was virtually impossible to keep warm. Belle's decision to leave Fola at home proved prudent as "in all our hard Wisconsin winters, we had never suffered so much from the cold indoors." Eventually they located a back parlor with a grate fire and "use of the front parlor."

Belle commented of the new life: "There were always some interesting people wherever we lived, although the social life was too much influenced by women without any special occupation, whose thoughts were centered on society, dress, cards, and gossip."

Those were not Belle's interests. Her concerns were social reform, literature and the law. She was happier than ever Bob had urged her to get a law degree. It taught her a more disciplined way of thinking.

Belle sat with other congressional wives in the family gallery of the House of Representatives as the December 1885 session opened.

At twenty-nine, Bob was the youngest member. Belle watched with "quickening pulse" as the members of the House of the Forty-ninth Congress assembled on the floor: "The calling of the House to order, the prayer of the chaplain, the taking of the oath, the allotment of seats, were all matters of absorbing interest to me."

She particularly was struck by Congressman Thomas Bracket Reed of Maine, who stood six feet four inches and was reported to weigh almost three hundred pounds. Belle thought him "cordial, democratic and magnetic," with a "kindly humor and the attitude of a friendly philosopher who enjoyed his fellow men." His report in favor of women's suffrage was under discussion and Belle listened intently.

She met Senator (and future President) William McKinley of Illinois, whom she described as "a fine speaker, earnest, often eloquent. He inspired the admiration of spectators and the affectionate regard of his associates. He had an innate dignity and at the same time a warm, sympathetic nature." Mrs. McKinley was an invalid and her face "had a worn look, but it was evident she had been a beautiful girl." Belle revealed that Mr. McKinley was devoted to his wife. At a party Mrs. McKinley told a friend that when her husband was away from the house he sent a message to her every day. The friend asked what he could possibly find to say. Mrs. McKinley replied, "He can say he loves me."

No sooner did Bob appear in Washington than he felt the influence of the senior senator from Wisconsin, Philetus Sawyer, leader of the Republican party in that state. Because Bob had been elected to Congress without the assistance of the Republican machine, indeed in defiance of it, he was not known to the Senator personally.

Sawyer was a self-made millionaire lumberman, possessing great physical strength and a shrewd, active mind. He had tramped the forest, cruised timber, slept in the snow, built sawmills. He had little education and it was jokingly said he signed his name "P. Sawyer" because he could not spell Philetus. He was cunning in both political ways and political means. He believed in getting all he could for himself and his associates whenever and wherever possible and regarded money as the chief influence in politics. Bob wrote in his autobiography, "Whenever it was necessary, I believe that he bought men as he bought sawlogs."

Sawyer called on Bob one morning and invited him to meet the President. Bob described Sawyer as a "short, thickset, squatty figure of a man with a big head set on square shoulders and a short

neck—very matter of fact—looking at me from time to time with a
shrewd squint in his eye. He had no humor but much of what has
been called 'horse sense.' His talk was jerky and illiterate; he had
never made a speech in his life."

They called on President Cleveland and then his cabinet officers.
Sawyer's introduction of Bob was the same at each place they stopped.
He did not seem quite sure of Bob's last name, even when prompted,
continuing to introduce him as "Follette."

As they drove away from their last call Sawyer asked if Bob had
in mind any particular committee in the House on which he wished
to serve. Bob said he wanted to be on some committee that would
allow him to make use of his legal knowledge. He knew he could not
hope to be assigned to the great Committee on Judiciary so he told
Sawyer he would like to be on the Committee on Public Lands and
grapple with the legal and ethical questions raised by land grants.
Sawyer looked at him "benignly" and said, "Just leave that to me;
don't say another word to anybody. I know Carlisle, served with him
in the House. Just let me take care of that for you." Speaker of the
House John G. Carlisle of Kentucky was the one who appointed
congressmen to committees.

Gratefully, Bob awaited his appointment. But when Carlisle announced the committees, Bob was astonished to find he had been
assigned to the Committee on Indian Affairs. He later realized he had
been too frank with Sawyer in expressing his interest in land grant
forfeitures.

Disappointed, but eager to get to work, Bob at once invested
money in second-hand books about Indians. He also asked that all
treaties and documents relating to Indians be sent to him. It all added
up to quite a library. After studying the books and papers he told
Belle he now felt "a good deal of sympathy with the Indians."

Bob soon learned why Sawyer had him appointed to this committee—the first "illuminating glimpse I had of the inside methods
of political chicanery." Assuming that Bob was under Sawyer's influence, the chairman of the committee appointed Bob as a subcommittee of one to consider a bill to be introduced in the House. It was
a bill Sawyer had introduced in the Senate, which had passed it.

The bill concerned selling pine timber from the Menominee Indian Reservation and offered, in Bob's words, "unlimited opportunities for stealing the timber from the Indians." Bob informed the
congressman who introduced the bill in the House that he would

report on it adversely. As a result, the bill died in committee. Sawyer never mentioned the matter to Bob but Bob understood Sawyer well enough to realize his defiance would not be forgotten.

Belle spent most of her time in the family gallery, listening with deep interest to all discussion. Often she made notes she thought would be helpful to Bob. A press clipping describing Bob and Belle at the time was headed "La Follette and La Follette." Because Belle had a law degree it was assumed she was Bob's legal as well as matrimonial partner. In a very real sense she was his partner in all aspects of their lives together. This partnership began at the university when she helped him with his academic subjects and he helped her with her public speaking. It was manifest in her desire to eliminate the word "obey" from their marriage vows. It was evident when he was district attorney and she coached him on legal precedents. In Washington she continued in her role as coach, sitting in the gallery on the side lines, observing his performance, as well as that of his adversaries, reporting her observations and counseling him. Belle performed a unique role as a congressman's wife because they were a team. In effect there really were two La Follettes representing the Wisconsin third congressional district in Washington.

The Washington social season opened with the New Year's reception at the White House, the most elaborate official function in Washington social life. President Cleveland was still unmarried and his sister, Rose Elizabeth Cleveland, was the hostess. Belle described her as "unassuming but gentle, and especially kind to the public. . . . She was perhaps the last 'first lady' to keep open house" at the White House.

As a new congressman's wife Belle had the official privilege of calling on the first lady and the wives or social representatives of all members of the diplomatic corps, the Supreme Court justices, the cabinet members and those senators and representatives who had served longer than Bob.

This privilege was in the nature of an official obligation and Belle proceeded to do this social "stunt" religiously. She met the same women, also visiting, day after day and within a few weeks was surprised to find how many women she knew, how well acquainted she felt and "how easy it all was." She wrote: "Fortunately, I did not take it too seriously. I soon realized that most of these acquaintances were 'for the time being.' In Washington 'good morning' and 'good-bye' were said with equal ease, whether for the day, the season, or forever."

Throughout these first years in Washington, Belle and Bob were well aware the old-line politicians back home were laying plans to defeat Bob at the next election. They knew they must start working right away if he were to be more than a one-term congressman. They had no illusions the machine would support a rebel like Bob.

Belle now became Bob's chief political organizer. She and Bob selected key people in the five counties in his district who had supported his candidacy and set up regular mailings to them of his and other congressmen's important speeches. Bob had to pay for the printing which was a financial burden. In those days a congressman, unless he was the chairman of a committee, had neither office nor clerk. So Belle personally mailed out all the public documents including, whenever possible, a free packet of new varieties of seeds which were available from the United States Patent Office. She knew this personal touch would create good will among the farmers back home. In going over the list so often, Belle became familiar with the names and addresses of Bob's supporters. As a result, when she accompanied him on his campaigns through his congressional district, she was able to keep him informed who was who.

Belle also answered routine departmental correspondence, thereby freeing Bob to use his mornings to take care of those matters requiring his personal attention. Congress did not meet until noon. Belle's afternoons were often spent piloting constituents who visited Washington through the Capitol, the National Art Gallery, the Smithsonian Institution or wherever they wished to go, including Pennsylvania Avenue, the principal shopping center.

Congress adjourned in August of 1886 and Belle wrote, "It was wonderful to be home again. After the long strain of the first session, a respite from politics would have been welcome, but never were we allowed to forget that the campaign for renomination and election was at hand." Enough caucuses and county conventions had been heard from to indicate Bob would be nominated by a large majority, though the same forces that originally fought his nomination were still opposing him. Belle admitted, "The persistent efforts to oust him troubled me much more than Bob, who accepted the hostility of the Keyes machine as a part of the game."

At that time there were no direct primaries. This meant that party politicians, not the voters, selected the candidates for Congress, as well as local judges, county sheriffs and district attorneys. This was the "caucus and convention" system. At the state conventions that preceded the national ones in presidential election years, the bosses openly bought the votes of delegates of both parties, as they did during local elections.

Despite the opposition of the bosses Bob was renominated to run for a second term at the Republican congressional convention held September 15, 1886. He then had to make the race against his Democratic opponent. Belle was now so in touch with the voters, had acquired such a practical understanding of politics, that when Bob and she were conferring on his campaign for the election General Bryant advised, "Bob, you better take Belle along." And so, unlike his first congressional race, but like most that were to follow, Bob and Belle set out on this campaign together.

Bob seized every possible occasion to reach the voters. He spoke at picnics, fairs and local celebrations as well as political meetings held at night in halls or churchyards. Whatever the hour he finished, the crowd besieged him to shake hands and have a personal word. Everyone called him Bob and when he and Belle would say good-bye, "it was like parting with old friends," she said. Sometimes people could not bear to let him go and would follow him and Belle back to their hotel. If it had been up to Bob they would have kept him up all night; Belle said she had "to be the ogre and insist on his getting his sleep."

On a number of occasions when Belle thought Bob had been talking too long, she would signal him to stop, to which he would sometimes respond, "There's my wife shaking her head and looking daggers at me. She thinks I'm talking too long." The crowd would laugh and urge him on. One farmer later recalled, "Why he talked so long every darn cow in this part of the county was bellerin' to be milked but the crowd just kept hollerin' for Bob to go on."

Once a man sitting next to Belle in a hotel late at night asked, "Are you his wife? I thought when I saw you shaking your head you didn't like what he was saying and was sure you must be a *Democrat!*"

Bob won the election in November 1886 by a majority of 3,510. He ran 537 votes ahead of his ticket in his congressional district. Interestingly, many Democrats had voted for him.

Belle was determined "never to go to Washington again" without their little Fola, now three. They decided also to take Bob's mother for the short session that convened on December 6 and were pleased to note Mary's fascination with the congressional debates as she sat next to Belle in the gallery.

During this session Bob spoke in favor of what became the Transportation Act of 1887, which created an Interstate Commerce Commission for the regulation of the railroads. His early impressions of the Wisconsin struggle for railroad regulation and his interest in passing such legislation on the federal level kept him constantly alert to what he considered a vital issue. For nearly four years he fought for regulation of railroads. His fundamental principles were outlined in the closing sentence of a speech he made in the House on January 20, 1887, in which he asked that railroads "provide efficient service . . . be fair and impartial . . . [make] just and reasonable charges . . . and discriminations and favoritisms, such as free passes to public officials and their families must be forbidden."

During the Fiftieth and Fifty-first Congresses Belle, sitting in the gallery, saw Bob become a national figure in the Republican party. During both sessions of the Fifty-first Congress the La Follette family were comfortably ensconced at 52 B Street, N. E., where the Senate Office Building now stands, facing Capitol Park. "This view of the park is always associated in my mind with Fola," Belle recalled, "as I could see her from my desk at the window, roller skating. I had tried sending her to kindergarten, but it did not seem to agree with her, so I began teaching her myself. After lessons were over, the park was her playground."

As Belle noted, the more familiar Bob became with the inside workings of Congress, the more clearly he saw the encroachment of private interests upon public rights. In his first term he had discovered and thwarted an attempt to steal the timber of the Menominee Indians in Wisconsin. His service on the Committee on Indian Affairs brought another revelation during his second term, one with more far-reaching consequences.

While listening to the reading of a bill in committee to open for settlement 11,000,000 acres of the Sioux Indian Reservation in the Dakota Territory, Bob was surprised at a provision to ratify an agreement made with the Indians by the Chicago, Milwaukee and St. Paul and North Western Railroads for a right of way through the reservation. Each railroad, in addition to the right of way, was granted 160 acres every ten miles for "station privileges." Bob told the committee it looked like a "town-site job" and asked to have the pertinent paragraphs "laid over" to the next session of Congress. A committee member whispered warningly, "Bob, you don't want to interfere with that provision. *Those are your home corporations!*"

Shortly after the committee adjourned, Senator Sawyer sent word to Bob he would like to see him in the cloakroom. After casual conversation, Sawyer remarked that when the Sioux Indian bill came up again in committee he wished Bob would look after the provisions "for our folks up in Wisconsin." Bob said the bill had already come up and he was opposed to the "town-site" scheme. He explained he believed the railroads should have the land needed for the right of way, yards, depots and shops but thought it unjust to the Indians and the public to give the railroads land for speculative purposes. He added he was proposing an amendment along these lines. Sawyer "showed no ill temper" but said he would see Bob again about the matter.

As soon as a train could bring him from Milwaukee, Henry C. Payne, a lawyer and lobbyist for the St. Paul Railroad and other large corporations, appeared in Washington. He and Sawyer met with Bob night after night for a week as they tried to persuade him to stop his fight against the bill. Bob would not compromise and put through his amendment. It gave the railroads the lands necessary for transportation but prohibited the use or sale of any land for town-site or speculative purposes. It also provided that the railroads forfeit their lands to the government unless the roads were built and in operation within three years.

Bob was to clash again with Senator Sawyer over a pending ship-subsidy bill. Bob denounced this as a "flagrant effort of private interests to dig into the public treasury." It was generally supported by Republicans and opposed by Democrats. One afternoon Bob left the cloakroom and headed up the center aisle of the chamber to see Sawyer coming at him, white with rage. Sawyer exploded, "Young man, young man, what are you doing? You are a bolter. The Republican platform promises this legislation. You are a bolter, sir; you are a bolter."

Equally furious, Bob warned, "You get out of here or I will call the Speaker's attention to you."

Though Bob often crossed swords with Senator Sawyer, his relations with members of the House and with the Wisconsin delegation were "cordial and friendly," Belle wrote. When the Department of Agriculture was created, President Benjamin Harrison appointed as its first secretary general Jerry Rusk of Wisconsin, who had served as governor for seven years. Belle found Mrs. Rusk "quiet and dignified . . . ever gracious and kind," and her daughter Mary, who had been a friend of Belle and Bob's at the university, "wise politically and helpful to her father."

At a New Year's reception in the Rusk home Belle first met Theodore Roosevelt, then Commissioner of the United States Civil Service. Roosevelt was "talking with his usual vigor and emphatic gestures" to Massachusetts Senator Henry Cabot Lodge. Belle reported: "It chanced that when I offered [Commissioner Roosevelt] a cup of coffee, his hand struck the cup, and the black coffee spilled over the front of the white dress I wore. He was terribly distressed; he feared I was burned and my dress ruined. I assured him the coffee was not hot and the dress of no consequence."

He sent flowers and a "charming note" to her the next day and many times when they met afterward he referred to the episode "and made a good story of it. I remember that he once said, 'I blush when I wake up in the dark and think about spilling that coffee over Mrs. La Follette's dress.' "

Bob was unanimously nominated to run for a third term at the Wisconsin Republican Congressional convention in August as he continued working in Congress. This left less than a month for his state-wide speaking campaign. Allen R. Bushnell, a lawyer appointed United States District Attorney by President Cleveland, was his Democratic opponent.

When Bob went home to deliver a few speeches at various locales in his district, he believed his election so secure that he responded to the urgent requests of the Republican State Central Committee to speak in other parts of the state on behalf of their Republican candidates. Speaker of the House Thomas B. Reed came to Madison on October 29 to help the Republicans and Bob escorted him to the capitol, where he introduced him to the largest audience ever gathered there.

Midway in Reed's address he stopped to comment on Bob's work in Congress. He described Bob as "one of the ablest members of the Ways and Means Committee" and predicted that "if the Republicans of this district do their duty" Bob had "a great career before him, and you and your state may well be proud of him." The audience cheered wildly for its native son and "all the surface manifestations indicated a tremendous Republican victory," according to Belle.

After dinner on election day eve, awaiting returns in their home, Belle wrote: "Bob sat thrumming his guitar, whistling an accompaniment. I remember that I remarked that I did not believe his opponent Bushnell was whistling."

She told of Bob going "uptown later to get the returns," and she thought it only a question of how large a majority he would receive.

She ended the account: "I couldn't believe him when he came home about eleven o'clock and called upstairs in a matter-of-fact way, 'Well, Belle, Bushnell is elected to Congress from the Third District, and I am elected to practice law.' "

CHAPTER
5
....

Motherhood in Madison

[1891–1901]

The Democratic landslide in Wisconsin was attributed to a new law that required parents to send children between seven and fourteen to a private or public school for not less than twelve weeks each year. The law defined "school" as one that taught reading, writing, arithmetic and United States history in the English language.

The large Lutheran and Roman Catholic populations in Wisconsin considered the new law a blow aimed at their parochial school systems which sometimes taught in languages other than English and expressed their anger by refusing to go to the polls. According to Belle, the "stay-at-home vote in Dane County alone would have elected Bob." Hard times also probably influenced a general Democratic sweep.

When Bob first told Belle he had been defeated, she thought he was joking. When she realized he was serious, her first thought was "Republicans were ungrateful." She was indignant that his four years of "devoted service" had not been rewarded. She expected her husband to be a good sport and meet a setback gracefully, as was his custom. Yet even she was "amazed at the way he accepted defeat. There was no break in his habitual good cheer, not a word of complaint, nor one moment wasted in regret. I learned then that he valued life too much to let the ordinary chances of politics spoil it for him."

Bob went directly home after Congress adjourned but Belle remained in Washington with Fola, who had caught the measles. On their return to Madison, Belle wrote, "Our house felt desolate." The hall was filled with bags of documents that demanded attention and she had a "funereal feeling about the task."

They were also poor and in debt. When they had changed residences each year from Madison to Washington, she had not minded that the house in Madison was "meagerly furnished, the rugs worn and many things in need of repairs, but it was different now we had come to stay."

She spoke of Bob's income as "uncertain" but shortly he returned to his profession, confident he could soon build up a good practice again. Fola was happy to be back in Madison and relieved to be assured, in answer to her "anxious inquiry, that lawyers did not have to be elected to practice law."

During Belle and Bob's absence in Washington, Robert Sie-becker, Bob's brother-in-law and former law partner, had been appointed Dane County circuit judge. Sam Harper had replaced Siebecker in the law firm and another young lawyer, Gilbert Roe, from New York, also joined the firm in Bob's absence.

Not long after Bob's return the firm did so well that "it was overwhelmed with work at the circuit," according to Bob, and Belle was pressed into preparing briefs. One case on which she worked broke new legal ground and her brief won the case when it reached the Supreme Court. About a year after the decision, as Bob told it, Supreme Court Justice W. P. Lyon "in the presence of a group of lawyers, complimented me on the brief . . . saying, 'it is one of the best briefs submitted to the court in years, and in writing the opinion I quoted liberally from it because it was so admirably reasoned and so clearly stated.' "

Bob replied, "Mr. Chief Justice, you make me very proud. That brief was written by Mrs. La Follette, an unknown but very able member of our bar—altogether the brainiest member of my family." Though Belle never actually practiced law, she continued to prepare briefs and do other work for the firm whenever her talents were needed.

One of the major forms of political graft at that time in Wisconsin was the depositing by the State and its agencies of public funds in favored banks. After the office of governor, the most sought-after office in the state was that of treasurer. A treasurer could deposit public monies in any banks he chose, with terms satisfactory to the bankers and profitable to himself. Interest on this money was regarded as a political reward for the treasurer.

When the Democrats won the state house they discovered Republican state treasurers had been involved in this type of graft for a number of years on a grand scale. One of the first acts of the Democratic state administration was to institute suit against all who had occupied the office of state treasurer over the preceding twenty years. Since Senator Sawyer had been the principal bondsman for quite a number of these treasurers, his personal liability amounted to several hundred thousand dollars.

Shortly before the cases came up for argument before Bob's brother-in-law, Judge Siebecker, Bob received a letter from Sawyer. It requested him to be in Milwaukee at the September state fair to consult with Sawyer on "matters of importance."

"Please answer by telegraph," Sawyer directed. "All you need to say, if you can meet me that day, is merely telegraph me, 'Yes.' If not, simply mention the day you can meet me."

The letter was typed on a single sheet of paper. Curiously, the top part of the sheet had been torn off, nearly to the date line, leaving only the printed words, "Dictated, Oshkosh." This did not impress Bob at the time but eventually led him to discover the letter had been written on the office stationery of one of the five treasurers being sued, Henry B. Harshaw, a close friend of Sawyer's.

After conferring with Belle and Sam Harper, Bob decided he should meet with Sawyer. He sent a telegram with the single word, "Yes."

He took a train to Milwaukee on September 17 and met Sawyer at the Plankinton House. The state fair was under way and the hotel was crowded. Sawyer told Bob he had been unable to reserve a room and asked him to go with him to a large parlor on the second floor. They sat in a section of the room "remote from the entrance," according to Bob.

"I want to talk with you about Siebecker and the treasury matter," Sawyer told Bob confidentially. "These cases are awfully important to us and we cannot afford to lose them. They cost me a lot of anxiety. I don't want to have to pay."

Then, with a wallet in one hand and a roll of bills in the other, he said, "I don't want to hire you as an attorney in the cases, La Follette, and don't want you to go into court. But here is fifty dollars. I will give you five hundred more—or a thousand—when Siebecker decides the case right."

Bob was thunderstruck at Sawyer's assumption he would even consider taking a bribe. He later wrote it was all he could do to keep his hands off Sawyer's throat: "I had always had a pride in my family—in my good name. It had been the one thing that my mother had worked into my character. It was the thing that she emphasized when she talked with me about my father."

Leaping to his feet in rage Bob replied, "Senator Sawyer, you can't know what you are saying to me. If you struck me in the face you could not insult me as you insult me now."

"Wait—hold on!" Sawyer said.

"No! You don't want to employ me as an attorney. You want to hire me to talk to the judge about your case off the bench."

"I did not think you would want to go into the case as an attorney. How much will you take as a retainer?" Sawyer asked, realizing he had once again misjudged Bob's character.

"You haven't enough money to employ me as an attorney after what you said to me," shouted Bob as he ran blindly from the room.

"Let me pay you for coming down here!" cried Sawyer.

"Not a dollar, sir," Bob called back as he flew down the stairs and out of the hotel.

He returned to Madison and the moment he opened the front door Belle noticed "there was something in his face that made me ask, 'What happened?' He did not answer but remained silent until we sat down to supper. Then he said, 'Belle, something *has* happened. Our life will never be the same."

"And it never was after that," Belle wrote, recalling the incident.

Bob decided to confide in a few close friends of Sawyer's bribery attempt. He wanted their opinion of his conviction that it was his "plain duty" to report what had happened to the circuit court. They pointed out that Sawyer, with his great power, could destroy Bob. Recalling these days Belle wrote, "I well remember the anxiety of those conferences and how glad I was when it was suggested that the matter be submitted to Judge [Romanzo] Bunn, the federal judge of the western district of Wisconsin, who was held in highest esteem by everyone who knew him."

Knowing Bob, Belle was certain his mind was made up and nothing would stop him from placing the matter before his brother-in-law, "but it was great support to have Judge Bunn, after listening to the statement of the Sawyer interview, respond, 'You must tell Judge Siebecker. You cannot permit him to sit in the case without telling him all about it. I doubt very much whether he will feel that he can try the cases. That is for him to decide—you must tell him.' "

Siebecker decided immediately that being privy to Sawyer's attempt to bribe the court made it impossible for him to sit as judge. He called in the attorneys on both sides, telling them only that he was obliged to withdraw from the cases and would select any judge on whom they agreed. He did not give any information or take any action that might prejudice the trial of the cases.

Judge Siebecker's announcement caused surprise and consternation and was followed by sensational stories in the leading newspapers in Wisconsin and other states. The headline in the *Chicago Times* on October 23, 1891, read: *"Bribery Their Game—Persons Interested in the Wisconsin State Treasury Suits Attempt Desperate Means—Startling Disclosures Expected."*

The morning after the publication of this particular story, Sawyer's friend, former State Treasurer Harshaw, came to Bob's office to ask, "Bob, will you meet Sawyer at the Grand Pacific Hotel in Chicago tonight?"

"No," Bob said. "I will never meet Sawyer or have any communication with him as long as I live."

Sawyer was in Milwaukee awaiting Harshaw's return, prepared to go to Chicago. Harshaw reported to Sawyer that Bob refused to meet him. Sawyer then gave an interview to the *Milwaukee Sentinel*. In it he protested his innocence though no official charge had been made connecting him with Judge Seibecker's refusal to try the treasury cases. Sawyer implied an "improper interpretation" had been placed on the conversation by Bob. Sawyer asserted it had never entered his mind "to influence the action of the court" and that it was impossible for him to think his "conversation with Mr. La Follette" was the basis of the judge's refusal to try the cases.

The publication of Sawyer's interview, wholly misrepresenting the facts, made it necessary, Bob felt, to make public the truth. On October 28, after consulting with Belle, he published a signed statement giving a detailed account of what took place at the Plankinton House. It was published in the *Milwaukee Sentinel* the next day.

Belle noted that probably nine-tenths of Wisconsin did not doubt the truth of Bob's story but party loyalty and fear of the powerful Republican organization were so strong that "had Bob accepted Sawyer's bribe, been prosecuted and convicted of it, he could hardly have been more completely ostracized." Even those who had been close to Bob believed that regardless of Sawyer's behavior, Bob should have kept silent "for the good of the party." The La Follettes' intimate friends, who admired Bob's honesty, feared he would "never rise above the political ruin this conflict with Sawyer would bring," Belle added.

The suits were finally tried and resulted in judgments in favor of the state amounting to $608,918. Of this amount Sawyer was liable for nearly $300,000. Yet even after the trial the mostly Republican press continued to condemn Bob's act and prominent politicians denounced him. Besides Belle and a small group of his courageous friends, no one raised a voice in his defense. Bob wrote in his autobiography, "No one can ever know what I suffered. As I recall the fearful depression of those months, I wonder where I found strength to endure them."

Belle knew the extent to which Bob was in agony. She recalled, "Though he was determined that the outside world should not know what he suffered, in his home, and with his intimate friends, he made no attempt to appear the same. I feared he might not recover his buoyant spirit, wit and humor again."

Anonymous threatening letters came in droves, some of them warning if Bob dared reenter politics he would do well to "arrange in advance for a lot in the cemetery." The threats were so serious Belle said, "My only anxiety was for him. I knew he was followed, and sensed the sullen hatred and real danger which menaced him."

But out of this ordeal Belle and Bob gained a clearer picture of the magnitude of the corruption in the Republican party and of the power wielded by a small group of politicians and lobbyists. And, as Belle wrote, she and Bob were "determined the power of this corrupt influence should be broken in Wisconsin." But before they could be effective in crushing the machine, they knew they would have to prove Bob had not been annihilated by Sawyer, still the most powerful boss in the state.

The Republican National Convention, which met in Minneapolis on June 7, 1892, provided Bob with the public recognition and respect he sorely needed. Attending the convention was a former congressman, now governor, William McKinley. It was generally believed he would be Wisconsin's choice for the Republican presidential candidate in 1896. Ignoring the animosity and coldness of the other Republican leaders, Bob sought out McKinley, who greeted him openly with a warm handshake and an "understanding look." Bob persuaded McKinley to be the National Day speaker on July 29 at the Monona Lake Assembly, a well attended local event.

McKinley arrived the day before he was scheduled to make his address and spent the night with Bob and Belle. The next day Bob introduced him before a large crowd. Belle wrote: "Only those who had lived through the period following the break with Sawyer could realize the real aid and comfort McKinley's visit was to Bob. To meet his friend again on the old basis of good fellowship and understanding and to be so cordially greeted by the audience and elsewhere, lightened the load he had been carrying and inspired him with new confidence."

Six months later on January 24, 1893, Theodore Roosevelt, still Commissioner of the United States Civil Service, arrived in Madison to address the Wisconsin State Historical Society. On his first evening there Belle and Bob gave him a reception at their home. Belle reported: "It was in the nature of open house and was largely attended. Politicians, reformers, scholars, big-game hunters, and people generally were much interested in meeting him. And [Roosevelt] was 'delighted' to meet them. In introducing the callers, Bob gave the cue as to who they were, and Roosevelt came back with just the right response. The occasion was a success, as were all the social events of his visit." When he returned to Washington Roosevelt wrote Belle and Bob to say he had enjoyed every moment of his stay and the reception at their home "most of all."

At this time Belle became interested in the Emily Bishop League, a physical culture organization. Her interest may have been due in part to Bob's depression and her desire to help him through it. Miss Bishop's philosophy was that "the body is only the agent of the mind." She prescribed a regular set of exercises to be carried out while reciting phrases such as "Slower, deeper breathing means calmer, healthier thought" or "Strengthen the diaphragm and you strengthen the will." Exercises were accompanied by a diet of fresh vegetables, citrus fruit, eggs, lean meat, and skim milk. Sugar and fat were completely avoided.

Emily Bishop first visited Madison at Belle's suggestion and spoke on health and dress at Ladies Hall where Belle had lived in her university days. So many women were interested in Emily's ideas that an informal school was organized in Madison, of which Belle became president. Emily was "a born teacher," Belle said, adding, "There are few friends to whose influence I owe so much."

Bob's mother died on April 21, 1894, and Bob, as Belle wrote, "was wholly unprepared for her passing. Although seventy-six, all winter she had attended a physical culture class, greatly enjoying the exercises, which she practiced with delightful absence of self-consciousness. Bob worshipped his mother; they had been inseparable. It seemed as though he had never thought she might die."

Belle might easily have resented Bob's closeness to his mother yet she wrote: "Bob's mother was very dear to me and I missed her greatly. My own feelings helped me realize Bob's sense of loneliness and irreparable loss. He kept hard at work, as always, and time healed, as it must if we are to go on living . . . but Bob's memory of his mother was always singularly fervent."

Bob chose this time to move his father's body, which had been buried in Primrose, next to his mother's grave in Madison. Standing beside his father's grave after exhuming the body himself, Bob wept as he held his father's skull in his hands and exclaimed, "Oh, my idolized father, lost to me before your image was stamped upon my childhood brain! What would I not give to have known the sound of your voice . . . to have received your approval when merited."

For Belle and Bob, work was always the antidote to grief. They decided to begin their fight to reform Wisconsin politics by finding a strong Republican candidate for governor in the 1894 election campaign. One who would command respect and guarantee that "the new movement against corruption was launched in staunchest faith," as Belle wrote. Had Bob believed himself the strongest candidate, he would have run. But he and Belle felt it was too soon after the Sawyer affair. They feared the contest would inevitably focus on the quarrel instead of what they believed the real issue—overthrowing the political machine. After appraising the various possibilities, they convinced Congressman Nils P. Haugen to lead the revolt as candidate for governor.

Haugen had been a member of the state legislature and a state officer and also had served nine years in Congress "with an independent spirit and distinction," according to Belle. He would also appeal to Wisconsin's large Scandinavian population. Bob set up headquarters in his law office. As with his own campaigns, he characteristically worked night and day, dictating letters to voters, holding meetings, organizing workers all over the state.

Belle turned their home over to campaign work. Her heart was set on Haugen's becoming governor: "It seemed to me the people of Wisconsin must seize this wonderful opportunity to nominate a candidate of such superior character and ability tested by years of public service." Yet she knew unless Bob could be sure of carrying Dane County by the time he went to the state convention, the Haugen campaign would collapse.

No other political contest in which she and Bob had been involved seemed "quite so desperate" as the fight for delegates. Their work paid off. The Dane County convention endorsed Haugen for governor and Bob was chosen to lead the delegation to the state convention in Milwaukee.

The day before the convention opened, a Milwaukee reporter wrote, "Bob La Follette struck the Pfister [Hotel] like a young cyclone today and if he has only done half what rumor credits him with, he must be about as pleasant company for the bosses as a wildcat would be at a picnic. He is working tooth and nail for Haugen, and has alarmed the bosses so that every henchman in the employ of both Spooner and Sawyer has jumped into the fight intent on downing La Follette first, and looking for candidates afterwards. Promises, money and whiskey are all in the scale against the doughty little champion from Dane, and although he will probably be beaten, he has the sympathy of a large number of delegates who dare not declare themselves in his favor. The reason why the Sawyer men fight La Follette is obvious. He refused a bribe and is therefore considered a dangerous lunatic by the sawdust contingent."

The convention became a verbal battleground. "We are giving them a pretty fight," Bob wired Belle. But the three candidates representing the machine united, thereby succeeding in their effort to defeat Haugen and nominate their candidate, William Upham. Belle wrote she was "mystified by the triumphant way our returning delegates discussed the convention results." It was Bob who made her realize their victory: they had succeeded in nominating some of their candidates for other state offices, an act that could serve to launch a movement whose power would grow.

The campaign of 1894 was a sweeping victory for the Republicans as the compulsory school-attendance issue was all but forgotten. With Upham elected governor, the Sawyer machine was again in power. The new state government's first act was to relieve the former treasurers of the "hardship" of paying their full indebtedness to the state.

A second child was born to Belle and Bob on February 6, 1895. "Bob had longed for a son," Belle wrote, "and I rejoiced that his wish was fulfilled. We decided without hesitation that his name would be Robert Marion, Jr."

In the winter of 1896, after Bob had exhausted himself during a long and difficult term of court, he fell seriously ill. The family physician, Dr. Philip Fox, who had taken care of Bob since university days and, Belle claimed, had more influence over him than anyone else, prescribed a rest cure in Florida and took time from his own work to accompany Bob. Belle stayed at home with the new baby and Fola.

The day before the two men left, William Osborn, a cousin of McKinley, called on Bob at home to ask if he would support McKinley against the Sawyer-backed candidate, Congressman Thomas Reed. Bob told Osborn he was confident the voters of Wisconsin were for McKinley and while he had to go south to regain his health, promised that his friends would take his place in the campaign until his return.

While Bob was in Florida with Dr. Fox he kept a journal in which he described his symptoms and complained of "feeling bad." On their way home they spent a week at French Lick Springs, Indiana, where part of Dr. Fox's "cure" for Bob was to insist he drink two gallons of Pluto mineral water at the springs every day. Belle meanwhile was counseling in her daily letters: "Why not cut loose altogether from medicine as a habit. . . . I have the feeling that as long as you resort to these artificial aids—even if not injurious—you will never really and truly realize the strength and recuperative power that is in *yourself.*"

Back in Wisconsin Belle and Bob's friends were not only working for McKinley; they also elected Bob as a delegate to the Republican National Convention, to be held that fall in St. Louis. "Boss" Keyes had been a candidate against Bob but Bob carried all the counties except one.

In balloting for the vice-presidential nomination at the convention, Henry Clay Evans of Chattanooga was running second. Evans was a former Wisconsin man who had fought in the Civil War with a Wisconsin regiment, and most of the Wisconsin delegation supported him. At the last moment, the Tennessee delegation unexpectedly asked Bob, who had served in Congress with Evans, to second his nomination. "Seconding the nomination of Mr. Evans was the greatest oratorical success of all the nominating speeches," read one newspaper report the next day. "And it was delivered on the briefest notice to a tired-out audience."

Sam Harper, who had gone to the convention with Bob, returned home elated over his participation in the proceedings. He told Belle that Bob's speech had made him an entirely "different man in the eyes of the nation." Belle laughingly replied, "I am glad he looks the same to me."

But Belle caught the mood of Sam's earnestness as he helped her understand a presidential convention was a national political stage with delegates and spectators on hand from every state. "All the leading newspapers had representatives there and Bob made a great hit," Sam told her in front of Bob, adding this could only serve to strengthen Bob's leadership in Wisconsin.

As Sam talked, Bob was silent and thoughtful. Finally he said, "Sawyer is not going to last many years. I ought to be a candidate for governor in Sawyer's lifetime and try out before the people of Wisconsin the issue that has been raised by the trouble between us. I don't want it said that I waited until he was dead before I dared to hazard the contest."

At first the Sawyer henchmen ridiculed Bob's candidacy. But when they realized he was making headway, they marshaled all their forces to defeat him. Even so, at the Milwaukee convention on August 5, 1896, Bob was nominated on the first formal ballot, along with five other candidates, including a "machine" nominee.

Shortly after midnight, Bob later reported to Belle, Charles Pfister, another Sawyer cohort, came to Bob's headquarters and asked to speak to him alone. He said, "La Follette, we've got enough of your delegates away from you to defeat you in the convention tomorrow. Now, we don't want any trouble or any scandal. We don't want to hurt the party. And if you will behave yourself, we will take care of you when the time comes."

Bob told Pfister he could take care of himself and would "smash their rotten machine." He confessed later to Belle he was not sure but that they had him beaten but he did not propose "to run up the white flag. I didn't have one."

When the balloting ended the next day Bob was defeated, as Pfister had predicted. But defeat only stoked his burning faith. He intended to run for governor in the next election, two years away.

A second son entered the family on May 8, 1897. He was named Philip Fox after the faithful family physician. Sensitive to the effects of Bob's intense devotion to his first son on his second son, Belle often told Phil that with her first sight of him she thought, "This is *my* boy."

During the summer and fall of 1897 Bob again took to the road in what Belle referred to as "the country-fair crusade." The theme of his campaign was "the menace of the political machine." He described the evils of the caucuses and state conventions used by both parties. He illustrated how readily they led to manipulation by bosses, short-circuiting the will of the majority.

He outlined a system of direct nominations for all county and state offices by both parties on the same day. This was the first presentation in America of the direct primary nominating system—the system in use today. Bob's speeches stirred the people and started at last to break down party lines. He also attacked Governor Scofield for shipping all his personal belongings, including a cow, to Madison on free railroad passes. "Scofield's cow" became both a joke and a symbol of corruption.

Belle attended and evaluated as many of Bob's talks as she could. When he spoke at the state fair in Milwaukee on September 24 she sensed the audience excitement over his crusade. She and Bob felt his speeches had never produced better results than those given at the country-fair crusade. Audiences listened "without that prejudiced partisanship which characterizes political campaigns," she wrote. "The bosses didn't know to cope with it. It was a growing power that baffled the political machine."

Intent as Bob was on carrying his crusade to the people, he sorely missed his family when away. "I talk to you and the children every night when I go to bed," he wrote Belle from Union Depot in Saint Paul.

His work for reform legislation was now widely known outside Wisconsin. On his return home following a speech on primary elections at the University of Michigan at Ann Arbor, he found his close friend and adviser and law partner, Sam Harper, critically ill with pneumonia. Belle had seldom left Sam's side throughout his illness and now Bob joined the vigil. Sam died March 19, 1898. Ever since he and Bob had been freshmen at the university they had been "inseparable in mind and heart," Belle recalled. "The sympathy between them was closer than any ties of kinship." Since returning to Madison Bob had lost both his mother and his closest friend.

Bob had been overworking himself for months. Sam's death was a hard blow and it cost Bob considerable effort to reenter the political conflict and become a candidate for governor. But no one else was willing to take on the machine. He formally announced his candidacy on July 15.

The extent to which Bob's political strength had grown was clear in that the platform was "practically dictated" by him and the other Republican Progressives. It demanded corporate taxes based on real property, a direct primary, the abolishment of lobbies and an end to railroad passes. Bob would have been nominated on the first ballot had money not again been used to buy off his delegates. It cost the machine $8,300 to defeat Bob and assure Scofield's renomination.

After the convention ended, Bob remarked as he bid farewell to a supporter, Judge Albert Long, at the Madison station, "Well, Albert, we lost the day. But we made a fight that was worth the making. There is another day coming and I shall expect to see you again."

Though Bob's political strength was increasing, his physical strength was depleted by his exhausting campaign. While trying a lawsuit he collapsed and spent, in Belle's words, "the greater part of the next six months in bed and convalescence." Once again Dr. Fox prescribed a rest cure in a warmer climate and offered to accompany him. This time Bob would not leave without Belle. She made arrangements for Bobbie and Phil to stay with her mother, in Baraboo, and Fola with Jo, while she accompanied Bob to California sunshine. Belle was now pregnant with her fourth child.

They took the train to San Diego, then a city of less than 20,000. Belle wrote to their friend Alf Rogers, "The first few days we were here Mr. La Follette seemed to rest and recuperate very rapidly. I think he has turned his mind to old channels [which has] interfered with his improving. He is not sick but in something of the condition he was while campaigning—diarrhea, headache, and not sleeping very well." After a few weeks Bob's health seemed restored, and "as always after recovery from serious illness, he promised to be more careful in the future," she wrote.

A second daughter was born on August 16, 1899. She was named Mary after her two grandmothers, one of whom she would never know. In the first twelve years of their marriage, Belle had given birth to only one child. She now had three in the four years between 1895 and 1899.

While Bob was away on one of his speaking trips, he wrote Belle, "I am proud of the kiddies, Mama. They are a rare combination of qualities. They could not be otherwise with such a great woman for mother. It is the mother that makes the children what they are."

In the four children's early years Belle was the dominant parental influence. And despite the political turmoil that whirled around them, for the children those years seemed mostly happy. Bob idolized them, as they did him. At times he would put his arm around Belle and say, "Mama, aren't our children wonderful?" Belle wrote she might have smiled at his enthusiasm but she shared it: "My heart was full and nothing was wanting to make our life complete."

Bob took Bobbie, then four and a half, a blue-eyed boy with blond curls, to meet President McKinley's train when he came to speak in Madison in October 1899. Bob presented his card to the proper official with greetings to the President but was not invited to board the train. It was not clear whether this was an oversight or whether McKinley had decided Bob was too controversial to associate with. In any case, Bob reported to Belle after Bobbie and he returned home that Bobbie had not asked for an explanation of why they had not spoken to the President. Deeply sensitive even as a small boy to his father's feelings, "he understood without asking," Bob said.

Vera Parke, who lived a block away from the La Follettes, wrote her childhood chum Mary, many years later, of that era: "Your mother was the loveliest lady outside of my own family whom I ever knew. . . . One of my vivid memories is of one time when you, Robert and Philip had received a new tricycle. Of course I was promptly invited to try the new possession on your lovely big porch. That was my first experience with your mother's kindness to a little girl. Of course, having no brothers, I had no experience with such toys. I mounted and surprisingly enough there was a corner right there to turn. I tried but promptly tipped over. Your dear mother appeared as if she had been waiting for me. I was gathered up in loving arms and soon the hurt was all gone, but not for a long time did my embarrassment disappear."

Though the Progressives had lost in three successive campaigns for governor there had been a perceptible change in the political climate. Belle attributed this not only to the country-fair crusade but to the discussion of the issues in newspapers. "Wisconsin was so permeated with La Follette sentiment that Bob was certain, if a candidate, to be elected in spite of the old machine," she said.

The 1900 Republican state convention was held August 8 at the Exposition Building in Milwaukee. That morning General Earl M. Rogers, a spokesman for the apparently united Republican party, along with three other candidates for governor who had previously withdrawn, visited Bob and Belle. "Mr. La Follette," they announced, "we call for the purpose of striking our colors and surrendering to you. From this time forward we are all of us for Bob La Follette."

When the convention started there was no contest over delegates. The nominee and the platform were a foregone conclusion. Belle wrote of the "abundant enthusiasm" characterizing the congratulations that closed the day. She also noted that Bobbie, who had attentively followed the formal proceedings, edged his way through the throng to make sure his father was "not being hurt by the demonstrations." Farther back on the platform, Fola, Jo and Belle shared in the congratulations. Jo spoke of the happiness it would have given their "little pioneer mother" to have been with them.

The morning after the convention, Zona Gale, then a reporter on the *Milwaukee Journal*, later a well-known novelist, asked Belle whether she believed women were ready to have a voice in matters of state. Belle replied laughingly, "Yes, I think the women are. But I think . . . the state is not. That is the trouble."

Gale then asked whether Belle's position in Madison would change if Bob was elected governor. "Everything would be the same as it is now," Belle replied. Then she added firmly, "Excepting that the wife of the governor has an added social duty. I know the house would always be open—and though there would be only the plainest hospitality, it would be for everyone."

When Theodore Roosevelt, now candidate for vice president, opened the 1900 presidential campaign in September at La Crosse, Wisconsin, people from the surrounding farms streamed in by horse and buggy for hours. Regular trains added extra coaches and special trains were packed with visitors. Belle recalled, "Bob rode with Roosevelt in the first carriage of the procession, which wound through the gayly decorated city to the accompaniment of bands and enthusiastic cheers given for 'Teddy' and 'Bob.'" At the evening meeting Roosevelt received an ovation and there were calls for Bob as well but he did not speak, feeling this was not the place to do so.

As the campaign advanced, requests for Bob to be a speaker poured in from all over the state. Bob and Belle again conferred with General Bryant, chairman of the state central committee, about arranging for an engine and special car for a whistle-stop tour during the last weeks of the campaign. With easier traveling conditions Bob was certain he could make eight or ten speeches a day. But he told General Bryant to make sure the railroad companies were paid their regular rates "so as not to incur any obligations."

Belle and Bob left Milwaukee in October on a special train consisting of a pullman, a combination baggage car and a coach; on board were a cook and a porter. From then until election day, November 6, Bob spoke ten to fifteen times each day, except Sunday. Before the era of automobiles, this set a new record in Wisconsin campaigning. "It was dramatic and excited great interest," Belle wrote. "Farmers quit working, driving long distances to hear Bob. Factories, mines and schools were closed for the occasion. Arches were built, music provided, flowers strewn. A Young Ladies' La Follette Club was a striking campaign feature before women had the vote."

Together Belle and Bob covered 6,433 miles, traveling through sixty-one counties. Bob made 208 speeches, talking to nearly 200,000 people. But even these "easier traveling conditions" took their toll. A letter from General Bryant to Gil Roe, Bob's old law partner, dated November 1, noted: "Belle has been traveling with Bob most of the days. I ain't seen him for two or three weeks, but I guess he has lost fifteen or twenty pounds of flesh, from what folks tell me. But he has hung on to his voice pretty well, and made a host of friends throughout the state."

The work Bob and Belle had done paid off. Bob was elected governor on November 6, 1900, by the unprecedented plurality of 102,745 votes. One of Phil's earliest memories (he was three and a half at the time) was of Belle's mother coming into his room where he was looking at a picture book and sucking his thumb.

"Phil," said Mary Nesbit Case, "Your father has just been elected governor of Wisconsin, and we can't have the governor's son sucking his thumb."

Bob's campaign had been directed toward the farmers and the workers—what he and Belle called the plain people. Belle wrote of the victory: "Mindful of the great responsibility and hard work ahead, but believing the way cleared for the enactment of the bitterly contested platform principles, I was filled with a deep sense of satisfaction and contentment."

She summed up, "Perhaps at no time in all our years of political experience did a long hard fight seem so surely won, and the road ahead so smooth and certain."

"When We Were Governor"

[1901–1906]

After the hectic campaign Bob was exhausted once again. Dr. Fox sent him and Belle to French Lick Springs, Indiana, where Dr. Fox had taken him four years before when he became ill. Belle described Bob now as "looking young for his age [forty-five] though his life had been one of hard work, responsibility and strain, with more than his share of illness."

This enforced vacation brought about an improvement in Bob and, Belle later recalled, "The November weather was lovely; each day we enjoyed never-to-be-forgotten horseback rides along the beech-wooded hills of southern Indiana."

They both returned to Madison refreshed and Belle eagerly made plans to move to the governor's mansion, or "executive residence," as she preferred to call it. The mansion was fully furnished and the state provided heat, light and janitor service, as well as a man to take care of the stable. "We needed only to rent our house furnished, take our books and personal belongings, our horses and cow to the other side of town, and be settled in our new abode," Belle said.

Spacious grounds sloped down to Lake Mendota. The well-proportioned house was of native stone and had wide porches, long, deep windows, high ceilings and a center hall that separated a large drawing room from an equally generous library. The house held the historic charm for Belle of having been the home of a locally famous violinist, Ole Bull. In 1870 he had married the young daughter of a Wisconsin millionaire lumberman who lived in the mansion. Belle still remembered the joy she felt as a freshman at the university when she first heard Bull play at a concert.

As Phil recalled in his autobiography, "The Executive Residence was on what was known locally as Big Bug Hill. Our former home was on the opposite side of town, called the Bloody Fourth. These names aptly described their social status. The Executive Residence was in a neighborhood overwhelmingly Conservative Republican and bitterly opposed to my father. Our neighbors looked on him and his politics as a personal challenge to them and the particular niches they occupied in the economic and political system in which they had thrived for so many decades. Although it was the custom for their ladies to call on the governor's wife, few called on my mother."

Belle made no changes in the mansion other than instituting "more hygienic housekeeping." She discovered beautiful hardwood floors under a moth-eaten carpet in the drawing room and immediately removed the carpet. She then proceeded to take up the old carpets in other rooms, knowing they would be not only more hygienic but easier to keep clean. She elected to keep the massive bed and dresser brought from Norway by Bull, but the children never forgave her, she said, for removing from the library an Oriental "cozy corner" lit with a red lantern, adorned with colored tapestries supported by long bright spears, "suggesting a fortune-telling gypsy tent."

A summer house on the grounds, built for Bull, was converted to a study for Bob. An old barn that stored a large open carriage was dubbed "the ark" by the children. The family horse, Maid, and a horse named Max, loaned by a friend, became the carriage team. The barn also housed Nancy, the gaited Kentucky saddler that Belle and Bob rode, and Rowdy, the children's Welsh pony.

"The grounds echoed with Indian war cries and other games," Phil recalled. "There were no nursery schools but Mother hired a fine German teacher who came a few times a week. Mother also tried to have us learn to play the piano but it did not work. So we were sent to dancing school which all the boys my age detested."

It was the custom in Wisconsin for the governor to send his annual message to the legislature to be read by the clerk. Bob broke this tradition and delivered his message in person three days after his inauguration on January 7, 1901. "The occasion was impressive," Belle reported. "The senate and assembly met in joint session. The state offices and members of the supreme court were present and the galleries and floor were crowded. [Bob] had prepared his message with great care and was profoundly in earnest; yet he spoke with a natural ease as though talking to each individual in the audience personally."

She said that while Bob "always fascinated me, as though I were listening to him for the first time, yet I was ever critical, making a mental note of how he might improve his speeches. Sometimes I was so eager to point out where he might do better that I forgot to express my appreciation of how well he had done. He always listened patiently, knowing my wifely anxiety that he should attain a perfect standard every time. When he finished his address to the legislature, there was not one flaw to my way of thinking."

Bob was confident the legislature would enact the laws the people of the state indicated they wanted passed. So it was a "great shock" to him, two days after the inauguration, to read in the newspapers that the Stalwart Republicans, as the conservative element of the party now called itself, still controlled the senate and proposed to fight the Progressive measures. Typically, Bob still believed the majority of the senate would support his legislation. Not so Belle. As she noted, "Bob and I never quite agreed as to how much the back-home influence could be depended upon. When I would suggest that he overestimated the interest of the rank and file, he would always say, 'If they understood' they would make themselves heard. Time, for the most part, justified his confidence; but, oh, more often than not, it took years of abiding faith and patient waiting."

The big corporate interests and political bosses joined forces to defeat the Progressive legislation. It was a "heavy blow," Belle said, when, soon after Bob's inauguration, the powerful Milwaukee multimillionaire boss Charles Pfister bought the most influential newspaper in Wisconsin, the *Milwaukee Sentinel*. The paper proceeded to carry to every part of the state a campaign attacking Bob both personally and for his program, specifically railroad taxation and the primary election bill. As he had done in Congress, Bob continued to rely on Belle to keep track of the political climate and advise him. She determined to get to know the legislators and their wives, to try to sense which way each was leaning and how vulnerable they were to Stalwart influence.

Not surprisingly, politics was daily fare to the La Follette children. Belle admitted, "At home, among ourselves, we thought and spoke of little except politics. We soon began to realize the fight to hold our ground was every hour becoming harder. Bob worked night and day making every legitimate effort to bring public sentiment to bear on legislators who showed signs of weakening. At the end of each day I awaited his return from the capitol with mingled hope and dread. Would he have good news or bad to report about this senator and that assemblyman whom we had counted on absolutely; for one by one they were being picked off until our majority was getting dangerously low."

Belle both admired and envied Bob's ability to ignore attempts to vilify him in the press. He made it an "inviolable" rule, she recalled, not to notice personal attacks on himself: "Not because he did not feel like striking back, nor that he did not know how. He was not meek and had a gift for a quick answer and apt retort. But he believed that personal controversy was a trick to divert public attention from the real issues."

The legislature was battling over Bob's two main bills: one to increase railroad taxes by one million dollars, the other to institute primary elections. The Stalwart leaders used every trick of parliamentary procedure to stall and delay action. As a result, the primary election bill became so watered down, its wording changed to apply only to county elections, that when it was passed Bob vetoed it. After the longest session then on record in Wisconsin the Legislature adjourned on May 15, 1901, without passing any of Bob's proposed legislation.

Though Bob could tolerate personal attacks, the defeat of his legislation threw him into a deep depression. "He suffered intense pain and caused grave anxiety," Belle recalled. She had coped with his collapses and their mystifying mix of symptoms before. But his previous attacks occurred when he was in private practice. He could ease up for a while or take a rest cure. But now he was the highly visible and controversial governor of the state.

Bob wrote of this physical episode in his autobiography: "I broke down completely and for practically a year afterward I was ill. . . . This was made the occasion for unremitting attacks. . . . The newspapers published stories that I was losing my mind, that I had softening of the brain—anything to discredit me with the people of the state."

Belle cared for Bob as best she could, prescribing a simple diet for his indigestion and what she liked to call "mental gymnastics" to restore both emotional and physical health. Despite her efforts Bob remained in bed for months, leaving whatever official business was required to Belle. "Never during our twenty years of married life do I ever remember feeling so helpless," she admitted.

It was during this dark period that Phil was sent to live with Belle's parents in Baraboo. Phil revealed that even in the best of times

"Dad was often irritated with me—and in spite of himself, he could not help showing it. My restless energy seemed to be galloping off, unbridled, in all directions at once." Fortunately, Phil adored his grandmother who, as he put it, doted upon him, for he was to remain with his grandparents for nearly a year as his father recovered.

Early in October 1901 Bob went to Dr. Fox's farm, Foxhall, near Madison for further recuperation. According to Belle, "No one had quite the power over Bob that Dr. Fox did. He knew when and how to tell him the time had come to get out from under the strain so that Bob would heed the warning." Whether it was the "power" of Dr. Fox or the quiet, wholesome outdoor life at Foxhall, Bob's health improved rapidly and he was soon outdoors and riding horseback every day.

Meanwhile, back at the Stalwart's headquarters, the machine was actively organizing a campaign to defeat Bob's nomination for a second term. Belle and Bob knew that to win they would have to reach the voters with specific evidence as to the nature and cause of the bitter warfare against him. During Bob's convalescence Belle pondered his philosophy—that if the people "understood" they would support Progressive reforms. How could Bob make the people understand? The challenge was to educate farmers and merchants who had very little real information about the inner workings of politics—and Belle was a teacher. What was needed was a text, an accurate nonpartisan account of how each legislator had voted.

Bob and Belle debated the merits of this idea and then consulted with Bob's old law partners, Gil Roe and Alf Rogers. After a few of these pow-wows, as Bob called them, they decided to publish as a campaign document, the first *Voter's Hand-Book*. In 144 closely printed pages, the *Hand-Book* presented Bob's program and recorded, for the first time, the votes of all the individual legislators on various issues. It gave the people a chance to know exactly who was to blame for the failure or success of proposed legislation. Copies were distributed to every precinct in the state.

The opening of Bob's campaign for a second term began with a speech on March 19, 1902, at the roundup of the Farmer's Institute at Oconomowoc. He stressed the point that in taxation "the burdens borne by real property were nearly twice as great as those of certain corporations" and that farmers were the "largest property owners." He urged these tax burdens on farms be lessened, saying "equal and just taxation must come."

Bob's self-confidence returned with his health. At Belle's insistence he entrusted the details of the preconvention campaign to others and the La Follette family actually indulged in a small vacation. Belle described it: "We took a plain little cottage at Colladay's Farm, Lake Kegonsa, several miles from the railroad station, yet near enough for Bob to ride horseback or drive to the office when necessary. The Siebeckers rented an adjoining cottage and we renewed the happy relationship of living next door to each other."

Belle took this occasion to once again put into practice her philosophy of the interdependence of mind and body, her conviction that regular exercises performed with a positive mental attitude constituted the best route to mental and physical fitness. She recalled, "Soon all of us were devoting a number of hours each day to physical training. Bobbie, Phil and even little Mary, together with the Siebecker children, became ardent gymnasts rivaling each other in games and stunts. Bob, throwing off all care, joined in their sports with the single-minded zest that characterized his pursuit of any object which had once awakened his interest."

Bob, Belle and his other advisors broke with tradition when they decided to move the site of the 1902 Republican state convention from boss-ridden Milwaukee to the more friendly town of Madison, then holding a population of 25,000. Wisconsin had a total population of about 3,000,000. The Stalwarts screamed in protest at the change but the Progressives were now in control of the Republican state central committee that organized the convention.

Bob was renominated as the Republican gubernatorial candidate on the second day of the convention, winning 790 to 266 against the Stalwart candidate. When Bob spoke at the capitol he received a rousing ovation but warned the fight had not been won, the same forces arrayed against Progressive legislation would still be present. It was vital, he said, to elect only those men who would publicly pledge support of the promised legislation.

Bob concluded by suggesting, "Let all else of this contest be forgotten. . . . I do not treasure one personal injury or lodge in memory one personal insult. With individuals I have no quarrel and will have none. The span of life is too short for that."

Belle reported that when he finished he took a moment to turn to her and the children in the midst of tumultuous applause and "as we clasped hands, I suddenly realized how differently I felt than at the close of the 1900 convention. He had won a more significant and striking victory in his second nomination. His leadership and the principles for which he had long contended were more firmly established. My joy and satisfaction were no less sincere and profound now than then; but I better understood the nature of the struggle. Never again could I take for granted that the fight was won and the war was over."

Belle put all her educational and managerial skills to work during this reelection campaign. She was fortunate in the spacing of her children. Fola, twelve years older than Bobbie and now at the university, fell naturally into the role of a sometimes bossy big sister and mother's helper. Belle said that all her life she felt guilty over the burden she believed she had placed on Fola at such an early age. If, indeed, it was a burden, it did not affect Fola's performance at school. She, like Belle, was a stellar student, graduating from high school with honors.

Despite the demands of public life Belle tried to provide her children with social pleasures as well as exposing them to social and political concerns. Another letter from Vera Parke recalled one such event: "It was the custom at the Unitarian Church to sponsor a church picnic across Lake Monona each summer. We boarded a steamer at Askew's landing at the dock on South Henry Street. It was a short but thrilling trip across to the Chautauqua grounds, near the present Esther Beach. At last, but much too soon for us, the return whistle sounded. Amid the scurrying around, there was one child missing. That was Philip La Follette. We called and called but no little boy. After quite a few minutes Fola stood on the side of the hill and called, 'Philip Fox La Follette, you come here at once!' Very shortly a sheepish but determined little boy appeared and announced, 'I am not ready to go.' Your mother gently, but sternly, guided him to the boat where he had to sit between her and his sister. That was quite a day!"

The Democratic state convention met in Milwaukee on September 3 and nominated David S. Rose, mayor of that city, as the Democratic gubernatorial candidate. As a delegate to the Democratic National Convention two years before, he told the Wisconsin delegation that "standing up and dying for principle" was "all rot." During his administration as mayor of Milwaukee valuable railway franchises had been secured by the Pfister interests. A number of leading Wisconsin Democrats, disillusioned with Rose, now came out openly for Bob.

Bob made fifty-five speeches throughout the state before Election

Day. Wisconsin, on November 4, 1902, reelected him by a plurality of 47,599. The *Voter's Hand-Book* had accomplished its aim. However, half the senate was not up for reelection and it remained a Stalwart bastion. The 1903 legislative session was a time of hard work but Bob kept his health. In April, President Theodore Roosevelt stopped off in Madison. Bob met him at the station and rode in the carriage with the President to the capitol, where he introduced him to a large crowd.

Belle and Bob felt deep satisfaction during Bob's second term at the election of Charles Van Hise, their former classmate, as president of the university on April 21, 1903. Bob and Belle supported adult education and extension services, often conferring with President Van Hise. When possible, Bob appointed experts from the university to important state boards. The university and governor had as close a relationship as could be found in any state between such groups. In fact, government's willingness to look at the university community for assistance became known as the "Wisconsin idea." It has proved a fruitful concept at both the state and national levels.

Closer to home, Bob continued to seek guidance from Belle. Though she never actually practiced law, Bob felt "this training brought her into closer sympathy and companionship with me in my professional work, and in my political career she has been my wisest and best counsellor. That this is no partial judgment, the Progressive leaders of Wisconsin who welcomed her to our conferences would bear witness. Her grasp of the great problems, sociological and economic, is unsurpassed by any of the strong men who have been associated with me in my work."

Through Belle's influence Bob came to believe that women should play a larger role in governing the state. He wrote in his autobiography that during his campaigns in Wisconsin he had been struck by the fact women were "as keenly interested as men in the questions of railroad taxation, reasonable transportation charges, direct primaries and the Progressive movement. As a result my political meetings were generally as largely attended by women as by men, and these questions were brought directly into the home for study and consideration. It has always been inherent with me to recognize this co-equal interest of women."

He added, "My widowed mother was a woman of wise judgment; my sisters were my best friends and my wife has been my constant companion."

In his messages to the legislature Bob recommended the appointment of a woman as factory inspector, and also that women serve on the board of University and Normal School Regents and the important Board of Control, in charge of all the charitable, penal and reformatory state institutions. Bob attributed one of the factors in the improvement of conditions in Wisconsin to the selection of able women for positions in the state service and readily admitted Belle exercised a great influence in securing the legislation and in making the appointments. In later years Bob was fond of referring to their six years in the Executive Residence as the time "when we were governor."

His salary as governor was only $5,000, and expenses like the *Voter's Hand-Book* he had to pay out of his own pocket. Bob and Belle were in constant debt, so it seemed "inevitable," Belle said, that he should go on the Chautauqua platform. It offered substantial fees plus "a wonderful medium for reaching the people and extending his political usefulness."

The Chautauqua platform took its name from a western New York lake and town where it originated. In the 1890's and until the 1930's, the Chautauqua was a distinctive feature of a small town life. For six or seven days, usually in July or August, a large tent with platform and folding chairs was set up for an audience between 1,500 and 2,000. There were morning, afternoon and evening appearances by lecturers on education, government, travelogues, art, singing, domestic science, literature. Six weeks on a Chautauqua circuit quickly weeded out the amateur from the professional speaker.

Bob's appearance on the Chautauqua began in 1902 with several speeches in neighboring states. The following summer he made an extended tour of the Middle West and also traveled to New York and Maryland. He gave two talks, one on representative government and the other on *Hamlet*. The latter was used for Sunday programs or when he spoke twice in the same town.

In the days before motion pictures and television the traveling lecturer was a popular and important form of local entertainment. Bob was a natural on the platform—people loved to hear him speak almost as much as he loved to talk. He wrote Belle after a meeting in Iowa, "I feel very sure that my work is going to do good the country over. Of course I can get in but here and there, and the country seems large. Yet it has already spread out from Wisconsin wonderfully and I am adding a number of radiating centers with this summer's work."

But the travel took a lot out of him. He would come off the

platform dripping with perspiration, change clothes at the hotel or, if pressed for time as he often was, on the train that took him to his next engagement. Trains were often late, connections poor. He carried two heavy grips, one weighted with documents to substantiate, if need be, each statement he made. In spite of such hardships he found strength and inspiration in the response his message evoked from the "real folks." One night he wrote: "Belle, the women are interested in these public questions; it is wonderful how well they understand, and how responsive they are in all my audiences."

His speech at Chautauqua, New York, on July 8 was Bob's first invasion of the East. Newspaper editors wondered in print what "La Follette's object" might be, some suggesting he was after the vice-presidency. Reports of his speeches, often garbled, were published in Wisconsin where the newspapers controlled by the Stalwarts raised the alarm that the governor "was betraying" his state, "injuring" its reputation and "hurting business." Belle reported even when he spoke in Madison his speeches were "grossly misrepresented in the press and he was bitterly assailed."

Bob's exhausting schedule played havoc with his digestion and since he was often unable to get the simple foods Belle prescribed, he turned to the medicines of Dr. Fox. Though devoted to Dr. Fox—after all, they had named their second son in his honor—Belle sometimes questioned his therapy. After Bob wrote, in August, he was feeling no better, she advised him to "cut loose from all medicines. I cannot think it is really an important factor in your digestion."

Belle was as concerned over Bob's mental health as with his physical well-being. "I am like Bobbie," she told him. "I want you to be perfect in all things. I want you a model in physical health as well as moral character."

In addition to Bob's fragile health, another concern was the family finances. So worried was Belle that she wrote Bob suggesting they let go their "nurse girl" and cut down on the number of horses they both loved and owned. Bob's response was to describe in a letter that arrived three days later how he had to pay his entire speaker's fee of $150 to get the railroad company to carry him to his next destination, as he had missed a connection. With his usual optimism he told her, "Dear girl, don't worry about the bills. We are going to make a good cleaning up this summer."

How heavy a price Belle and the children paid for their father's absence much of the time was evident in a letter Belle wrote Bob on

August 11. Addressing him as "Dear Papa," she confessed, "Robert is especially anxious each night to know if I think he has been good. I understand that he is looking forward to your coming home. With love, as always, Belle."

Being the governor's wife and chief advisor had not changed Belle's philosophy much. As always, she sought perfection from herself and from her family. She believed the path to this goal was through the application of will power to excel—"mental gymnastics" as she called it. At the same time she continued to maintain an informal approach to the La Follette family's way of life.

"Our way of living had always been simple," she once wrote. "We usually had one maid but if, as sometimes happened, none was to be had, I could do my own work and was glad that health and strength permitted. Our social contacts were chiefly with our university, neighborhood and political friends. Bob liked to bring someone home with him when he came to his meals, and I always planned for an extra plate. We were both inherently hospitable, and there were many gatherings of friends at our home; but we took very little part in the formal social functions of Madison."

One afternoon as Belle held a reception for the wives of state legislators, she noticed as the women entered the drawing room they all seemed to suppress chuckles. During a slight lull in the parade of arriving guests she seized the opportunity to look toward the front door. There she saw Bobbie seated in a chair, his feet up on the porch railing. In his hand was a piece of string attached to the screen door. As guests approached, remaining seated he pulled open the door. Laughing out loud, Belle returned to her duties as hostess.

Since Bob often brought his political friends and associates home to dinner, there were occasional social gatherings from which the children, of necessity, were excluded. One day Bobbie and Phil discovered a register under a rug in their bedroom that had not been used for years. It was set right over the dining room and provided a perfect opportunity for the two boys to spy on events they were not allowed to attend. Their chance came during a formal white-tie-and-tails affair for some important university guests. Phil recalled: "Everything was going splendidly at the dinner. We rolled up the rug and carefully opened the register and looked down into the dining room. To our horror a large black spot appeared right in the middle of the white tablecloth. The accumulated dust and dirt of a decade had been dumped on the table. Bobbie and I thought we were surely in for it now. We were wrong. Mother and Father treated it as a joke and we went scot-free for that one."

Although the ladies who dwelled with the La Follette family on Big Bug Hill may not have deigned to call upon Belle, their curiosity often forced them to, as Phil put it, "pump" the children for inside information about formal social affairs. "I remember particularly when I was asked how Mother arranged the seating of the guests at formal dinners. Of course I knew the answer: 'She seats first a dull one and then a bright one, and so on around the table.' That one went around town in a hurry. And thereafter, guests at our table would good-naturedly wonder who was who."

Though the La Follette children may not have understood the fine points in the battle waged over their father's program, they knew well that La Follette supporters were called Progressives and the old guard Republicans were known as Stalwarts. This was made especially clear one fall evening when Bobbie came home and announced, "I am wearing a black eye that Philip Sanborn gave me in a football game at school. I am a fair player and would not slug back. Philip is a Stalwart, you know."

Belle's approach to education was amply rewarded in June, 1904. Like her mother and father, she and Bob became proud parents as they not only witnessed Fola's graduation from the University of Wisconsin but saw her elected Phi Beta Kappa. She, too, had set a record of excellence for the younger children to follow.

Belle did not remember an actual discussion between her and Bob regarding his running for a third term as governor in 1904. They simply took it for granted he would continue to lead the fight for the primary-election law and a state commission to control railroad rates. Without this power the taxation law would prove an empty victory. The railroads would simply raise their rates.

While Bob was out running for reelection, Belle attracted some attention running in her own way. Under the headline "*Mrs. La Follette Can Run,*" a Detroit newspaper reported: "The wife of the governor of Wisconsin is said to be an enthusiastic dress reformer and builds much also on physical exercise of all sorts. She is said to get up early and take a two-mile run before breakfast."

During the winter of 1904 two candidates for the Republican gubernatorial nomination emerged, Judge Emil Baensch and Samuel A. Cook. Both had at one time been personally friendly to Bob and were to some extent identified with him in the public mind. The

Stalwart strategy was to secure support for these two at the caucuses as "nonfactional" candidates. Then, at the proper moment, the Stalwarts expected to pool their strength, capture the convention and in one blow strike out Bob, the "agitator" and "troublemaker." The railroads, the Stalwart newspapers and the Congressional old guard under Spooner and Pfister were united in their pursuit of this strategy.

Bob had the support of a number of smaller newspapers, as well as the backing of a fighting organization and strong leaders throughout the state. But with most of the large newspapers against him, his only way to reach the voters was by word of mouth and the *Voter's Hand-Book*. It seemed an almost superhuman task to overcome the power, money and prestige of his enemies.

In his campaign speeches he effectively used a preliminary report on an investigation he had asked the 1903 legislature to authorize. The report showed that during the two preceding years four railroads had paid Wisconsin shippers over $1,298,000 in rebates and had failed to report gross earnings amounting to over $400,000, totaling more than $1,698,000 on which they had failed to pay taxes. The investigation also revealed that large Wisconsin manufacturers and shippers who had opposed legislation to tax or regulate railroads received annual rebates amounting to between $40,000 and $60,000.

Bob dramatized these facts as he spoke from the platform so that every man, woman and child who heard them could understand how the rebate system gave the railroads tyrannical power, demoralized business owners and robbed the state. As it became evident Bob's county-fair speeches were arousing the people, the railroads grew reckless in their determination to defeat him. They told employees their jobs depended on defeating La Follette. One conductor on the North Western courageously resigned, saying he was giving up his job rather than "break faith" with Bob.

Belle wrote that throughout these years of strife, she was aware that Bob ran a constant risk of being the victim of violent acts. He received many threatening letters. One time the state capitol was set afire and Belle and Bob were warned the executive mansion would be next. There was often a strange ringing of doorbells and pounding on doors, "which, though the house was carefully watched, remained a mystery," she wrote. "I tried to accept the hazards of political struggle in the same spirit Bob did: recognizing there was danger in all undertakings; that fear and worry were futile and wasted energy which should be conserved for the work in hand."

Belle also had to accept what would be the greatest loss in her life to date. She wrote Bob, on the platform trail, at four a.m. on January 28, 1904: "I am at Baraboo. Mother ill." Concerned as she was about her mother, she nevertheless added, "I feel anxious about you dear, if only for your work's sake. It would be a great God-send—as they would look at it—for the Stalwarts, if you should get sick. I don't just see how you can stop but if you were sick you would *have* to stop. You could at least make a less number of engagements and give yourself a little chance to breathe. *This* much is within your control. With abiding love, Belle."

Her mother died shortly thereafter and Belle often remarked that there was not a day of her life she did not miss her.

Prior to the caucuses of the Republican state convention to be held in Madison on May 18, Bob brought something new into his campaign. He now began systematically to read to his audiences the legislative roll call. In senate and assembly districts where representatives had violated their platform pledges, he presented these facts at public meetings and cited each legislator's vote on important issues. He made the *Voter's Hand-Book* come alive.

It was a new idea to judge a legislator by his vote instead of his appealing manner or his good standing in the community. Even so, some of Bob's friends urged him to omit the roll call. His answer: "This is not the time for bouquets or soft words. We are getting none."

Belle said she sat on the platform with him many times and "felt the audience 'freeze' as he began to read the ayes and nays disclosing the record of senators and assemblymen to their constituents." Once again, Bob did not deal in personalities but only informed the public how a legislator had voted on crucial issues.

It was a daring and original undertaking. But Bob knew the election of a legislature that would carry out the will of the people when it met in 1905 by passing the proposed reforms was even more essential than his own election. He turned the simple reading of the roll call into a weapon that has had a far-reaching effect on the political history of this country. It was not until 1933 that the precedent set by the *Voter's Hand-Book* was finally accepted and the *New York Times* began publishing the votes of New York congressmen.

When Bob arrived home from his exhaustive speaking campaign on the Saturday morning before the convention, he greeted the family, then said anxiously, "I must get right at work on a speech of acceptance." Whereupon he collapsed in an easy chair in the library and fell asleep. Belle closed the door, made sure he was not disturbed, and he slept all day. He would often catch up on sleep this way.

At the convention Bob's name was placed in nomination, seconding speeches were made by leading Progressives and the entire state ticket was unanimously renominated. When Bob appeared on the platform, one reporter said, Bob charged the four words, "I accept the nomination," with "hypnotic power which made the gathering feel the load suddenly lifted from its shoulders and transferred to his own."

At this time Lincoln Steffens, the renowned writer and investigative journalist, arrived in Madison to interview Bob. Belle said when she first learned of this, "I was moved to tears." She explained: "Although I had become inured to the continuous false and ruthless attacks of the Stalwart press, still, each time after reading one of Steffens's articles in *McClure's* telling what he had seen in Chicago, St. Louis, Missouri, Illinois and elsewhere, I would say to myself, 'Oh, why doesn't he come to Wisconsin?' It had become a subconscious prayer with me."

She added, "Of course, I didn't expect him to tell the story as I saw and felt it. But it would be wonderful to have the history of the Wisconsin struggle written up from the standpoint of so expert and impartial an observer. I was confident he had the ability and insight to get at the truth in spite of the maze of lies he would encounter."

Bob telephoned one day from his office at the capitol to say Steffens was in his office and he would bring him home for supper. "I was very happy," she later wrote. "I simply took it for granted he was our friend and gave him a fervent welcome."

But she felt "greatly disappointed that he was so unresponsive." She noted, "It did not occur to me he was still investigating the facts and had not yet reached his conclusions. My assumption that he was on our side of the case—in fact, a wholehearted sympathizer—doubtless impressed him as premature and tactless. He was polite but reserved."

Following an exhaustive inquiry into Bob's life and his fight against corruption in government, Steffens interviewed many representative Stalwarts. Later, accompanied by Mrs. Steffens, he traveled all over the state interviewing politicians on a list of Stalwarts suggested by Senator John Spooner's brother Philip.

The Steffens article was to appear in the October issue of

McClure's magazine and Belle wrote, "I awaited the verdict with an anxious heart." Undoubtedly she realized this would possibly be the most important article ever written about Bob, certainly the most important to date.

Bob began filling Chautauqua engagements in neighboring states, needing the money to carry on the political fight. In his absence Belle took charge of publicizing his record. As was her custom, she went over every document. Appreciating her writing and editorial skills, Bob often said, "If this gets by Belle, we're all right." It was estimated more than a million pamphlets "got by Belle" and went to Progressive headquarters for 100,000 supporters. All of it was paid for by Bob and Belle personally.

Bob went into crucial legislative districts and "campaigned them as they had never been campaigned before." He spoke forty-eight days in a row, averaging more than eight hours a day on the platform. He used two cars in case one broke down (the auto was not yet in common use). He took Bobbie, then nine, and Phil, seven, on one trip, both excited to be on their first campaign journey with their father—and in a car.

Belle was surprised when, in August, Steffens sent her a copy of the proofs of the article he planned to publish in *McClure's*, for Bob and her to go over. She wrote Steffens on August 14, 1904:

> My dear Mr. Steffens:
>
> I can never make you understand what your article means to me. It is something I have longed for, yet hardly dared hope for, and really never expected. To have you turn your searchlight on Wisconsin's politics is better than anything our guardian angel could do for us—on earth at least.
>
> I do not regard it as an ordinary magazine article—and I do appreciate its great importance from that standpoint also—but you are an authority on your subject. You have wonderful insight—wonderful gift of synthesis. You have ideals to which you are true—and a fine literary style. I believe that you will be greater than you are and that your books will take permanent place in history—and what you say will have great weight in the final estimate of the men you study. So I prize your estimate as a legacy to our children. But why explain further. God bless you and Mrs. Steffens for "taking sides." It may be, I see only one side, but I have seen that side from the *inside*. I know the stuff Mr. La Follette is made of, and what the struggle has been. I saw him—who

could have been the idol of his party—choose his course, realizing better than anyone else what it meant—in that Sawyer affair. I saw him after he made that choice, accept the consequences without complaint or bitterness, although it left him almost friendless personally—and quite friendless politically. He stuck to his law practice for three or four years and every one regarded him as "dead" to a public career. I saw him rise from this position of political friendlessness without money or any influence to help, except his own personality, and overcoming all obstacles, in spite of defeat after defeat, keep fighting for certain ideas. When all this abuse was being heaped upon him and all this fight being made against him under cover, he never turned from his course to make a personal attack on anyone, but simply stuck to his ideas and made his fight for them. You know what it is, that makes me *glad* to have this Wisconsin situation shown up in its true light by *you* for the *first time.*

Lebt wohl. Auf Wiedersehen.

Belle C. La Follette

Steffens's article in *McClure's* appeared on the newsstands the last week in September. Belle called it "a veritable bomb in the camp of the Stalwarts." A large edition sold out the first week. The *Wisconsin State Journal* claimed in an editorial that La Follette had "hypnotized" Steffens.

Bob had said in a Chautauqua speech, "I am not going to be swerved from my purpose . . . If I should be defeated on the eighth of next November, you will find me out early on the morning of the ninth on a new campaign."

He did not have to cope with another defeat. On November 8, 1904, he was elected by a 50,000 plurality. The vote for a direct-primary law was carried by about the same plurality as Wisconsin became the first state in the nation to have such a law. At last both houses of the Wisconsin legislature were largely Progressive.

This event was also recorded in Vera Parke's memories of childhood in a letter to Mary: "Our door was alerted by a ring. It must have been the morning following election for there stood Philip in top hat (well down over his ears and swinging a cane.) He greeted my mother with 'Good Morning, Mrs. Parke, I am Philip Fox La Follette, the son of the newly elected governor of the state of Wisconsin.' Of course there was no TV or radio in those days, only a newsboy crying 'Extra, Extra' on the streets."

Bob was inaugurated governor for the third time on January 2, 1905. In the fight to prevent his nomination and reelection, the Stalwarts had given little attention to the fact the 1905 legislature would elect a United States Senator. Throughout the state and in the legislature, Bob was believed the only man who could be elected senator without a prolonged, bitter conflict that might arouse animosities that would defeat legislation pledged in the state platform.

A joint session of the legislature on January 25 elected Bob to the United States Senate. He received 100 of the 123 votes. Belle later wrote, "I would not say he was unwilling to be chosen. . . . but he took no part in bringing it about." Some of his close friends and advisers, interested in his political future, urged him not to accept.

But he decided to accept the election conditionally. He said in his address before the legislature, "If there should appear any conflict in the obligation I entered into when I took the oath of office as governor, and that of United States senator-elect, then I shall ask you to place it in other hands of your own choosing."

No conflict appeared and he was free to become Wisconsin's junior Senator. When the state legislative session adjourned on June 21, 1905, it had achieved an extraordinary record of reforms for which Bob, Belle and the Progressives had so long worked: the primary-election law; taxation of railroads and other public utilities on the basis of actual physical valuation; the railway-commission law, which included regulation and control of telephone and telegraph companies; a civil-service law; an antilobbying law; a state bank law, and conservation and water-power franchise laws.

Belle said of Bob at this time: "The work in Wisconsin was the rock on which he built. The sentiment he expressed in regard to the legislation achieved in his state never changed: 'If it can be shown that Wisconsin is a happier and better state to live in, that its institutions are more democratic, that the opportunities of all its people are more equal, that social justice more nearly prevails, that human life is safer and sweeter—then I shall rest content in the feeling that the Progressive movement has been successful.' "

She felt she "could hardly endure the thought that after months of constant strain he must start off on the wearing summer's work without a moment's breathing spell; but he looked forward, as always, to enjoyment of his lecture engagements in the spirit of the crusader." In her first letter to him on his trip she warned his health was the important thing: "What you *have* done is great and *satisfying*. Why should you wear yourself out in further extreme effort?"

His answer: "Belle dear, don't worry about me. . . . am taking just as much care of myself as possible. I should really enjoy every hour of this if you were only with me. I think you ought to go part of the time. You see when I get a few of these long-range dates off all the work will be in a little radius and traveling expenses would be light for two."

She did join him at times during the summer when his schedule "made it convenient and not too expensive." She kept "urging him to conserve his strength and make his speeches shorter. He would promise to do so 'next time.' "

The family, she said, "had a good laugh, as he intended we should," when they read his letter from Omaha describing how he ran up stairs that were "longer than Jacob's ladder to catch a train that was an hour later." Belle worried about the strain on his heart caused by these recurring incidents of travel. He would write her almost every night a few lines about the audience or the reaction of his supporters in South Dakota, where, he was assured the state would vote for him "for President in the next convention." Bob added his characteristically humorous comment to her, she said, with the words, "So you see my [Presidential] boom is turned loose."

Before Bob started the 1905 summer Chautauqua tour, he and Belle decided they would sell the West Wilson Street home whether or not he was elected to the Senate. It still carried a mortgage but had increased in value. With its sale and the money that could be spared from his summer earnings, they planned to buy a farm. They felt it would make an attractive home for the children and be a good investment. Five years at the executive mansion had weaned the children from the old house where they had all been born, and they were reaching an age when farm life would mean much to them, as it once had to both Belle and Bob.

One "fine spring morning" when Belle and Bob were horseback riding around the Mendota Lake drive, they came to the lane leading to Maple Bluff Farm, three and a half miles from the capitol. Bob said, "Let's ride up and ask Sam Marshall what he will sell this place for." Marshall, son of a prominent banker, was a gentleman farmer, a former student at the Agricultural College of the university.

After the La Follettes and the Marshalls had talked pleasantries for a while, Bob asked Mr. Marshall, "What will you take for this place?" Without a moment's hesitation Marshall replied, "Five hundred dollars an acre." Sixty acres sloped to the south with 1,200 feet of shoreline on Lake Mendota. The farm adjoined a golf course. There was also a beautiful view of the city from the old brick house. But to Belle the price seemed far too high. She rode away laughing at the idea of buying the place. But she noted Bob was thoughtful on the way home.

Throughout the summer Belle hunted for farm "bargains" near Madison. When Bob came home from Chautauqua meetings for short visits she would place the possibilities before him. Each time he made the same answer: "I don't think anything you have yet found compares with the Marshall place." When Belle's father visited, Bob wrote her to be sure and have her father look over the Marshall place because *"he sees everything just as it is."* Maple Bluff Farm had deep rich soil which Bob knew would appeal to her father as the first prerequisite of a farm.

One morning in the fall as Bob and she were horseback riding they again turned in at the Maple Bluff Farm drive. Again they met Sam Marshall and again Bob asked, "What will you take for this place?" As before, Marshall replied, "Five hundred dollars an acre."

Bob dismounted, walked through the old house, talked about the age of the ancient grape vine shading the porch and covering the entire front of the house, discussed the value of the lake frontage and other details. It was "more in the nature of a social visit," Belle said, but their minds were made up. In less than an hour they reached an agreement to buy Maple Bluff Farm for $30,000. The high price was to others "a matter of surprise and comment," she wrote, "but when the transaction was completed I wondered how I ever had the least hesitation. The children were tremendously pleased. We were not to have possession for some months but we were all joyful in the thought that Maple Bluff Farm was to be our future home." Phil recalled he came home from school one afternoon to see his mother on the phone and "she hung up with a wonderful smile and said, 'Daddy has just signed the papers and we have bought Maple Bluff Farm.' " The mortgage, however, was to be a troublesome financial burden for the rest of their lives.

Lincoln Steffens had by now become a friend of the family. As Bob made the transition from governor to senator, Steffens visited Belle and Bob at their new farm and wrote about it: " 'Do you ride?' she asked me one day at their farm near Madison, and half an hour later there were two horses saddled at the door. She pointed to one, mounted in a flash the other, and, without looking back, she rode—she raced away as fast and as far as her horse could run. Then, springing to the ground, leaving me to tie the horses, she sat down by the lake side, and with a faraway look and a wide wave of her hand, she said: " 'That's what I would like to do, only faster and farther, much faster, much farther.'

"The next moment she began sounding me out most practically for my principles, my purposes; revealing hers; and since I had a working theory that to judge the staying power of a public man, one must know his wife, I let her plumb me. So, talking we remounted and rode at a walk all the way home, she judging me no doubt. I was getting the absolute certainty that Governor La Follette, United States senator-elect, would go through Washington as he was coming through the West, on a straight line. His wife would represent—she would personify at home what he represented in the senate: the people of their state.

"But aside from this, I got that day on that ride the romance of the woman who personified the people her hero represented. I sensed the love story of the flying hero with the watchful, adoring heroine; the public prosecutor's story, the congressman's, the governor's, the United States senator's, with a wife and a state behind him that understood. They were critical when Fighting Bob La Follette overdid; when he was too fast or too fierce or too obstinate, they told him so. The woman's intuition was surer than the man's; and that man sensed that. I have seen him bow to her judgment after resisting the very same criticism from others. She spoke, you see, not only for their state, but for their principles and their instinct.

"A great woman, this Belle La Follette, great as great men are great. She, too, was a statesman, politician, she could act, but she was content to beget action and actors."

During Bob's three terms as governor, Wisconsin more than any other state served as a laboratory for political and social reform for the nation. Wisconsin became a leader in labor legislation. Child labor was reduced and children kept in schools. Excessive hours for women workers were abolished. A new industrial commission was placed in charge of all the labor laws, with full power to enforce the laws and protect the life, health, safety and welfare of employees.

Bob officially resigned as governor on New Year's Day, 1906, and Lieutenant Governor James O. Davidson was formally inaugurated to fill out the unexpired term. Belle said, "Leave-taking of the executive residence cost me few heart pangs. It was a comfortable abode; but to this day a subconscious sense of official obligation is associated in my mind with the fine old place."

She and Bob were on their way to Washington for a second time. She was reluctant to leave the children behind but, as Bob was uncertain where they would live, it seemed wise to temporarily arrange for Bobbie, now eleven, Phil, nine, and Mary, seven, to go to Hillside Home School for a term. The school was run by the two maiden aunts of Frank Lloyd Wright. This would give Belle time to find a suitable home for the next six years in Washington.

Fola, who was in rehearsals in New York for a play, suffered the beginning of what were to be many exploitations by the press. Summoned by the company manager for what she thought was an understudy rehearsal, instead she found the theatre filled with newspapermen and cartoonists waiting for an interview. Fola tried to steer the questions to the play in which she was appearing, but she was continually pressed for intimacies concerning her increasingly famous father. Despite her refusing to cooperate, the papers carried illustrated interviews, quoting Fola as forecasting what Bob would "do to them when he arrived in the Senate." The day the stories were published Bob telegraphed: "How could you give out such an interview?" He and Belle understood what happened when she wired back: "How could you ever think I did?!"

The Senator's Wife

[1906–1909]

Looking down on Bob from the Senate family gallery as he took the oath of office on January 4, 1906, Belle "awaited the convening of the senate in a reflective mood," in her words. As she watched the Senators assemble and the crowd gather in the galleries she recalled that almost twenty years had passed since she first sat in the gallery of the House of Representatives waiting for the opening ceremony of the Forty-ninth Congress, of which Bob had been the youngest member.

This was the Fifty-ninth Congress. She said of the twenty years in between they were "twenty hard, trying years, yet in retrospect twenty years of useful effort and concrete achievement. I far better understood now the nature and significance of the struggle than I had earlier. I contemplated the future much more seriously; but I had faith in the outcome."

In those twenty years Bob and Belle had set the course of thought and action that would guide them for the rest of their lives and influence the lives of their children. Both Bob and Belle were fond of using the words "fight," "battle" and "struggle" to describe their activities. The words were appropriate. What they were attempting to do was nothing less than reform American politics and, with that, American society. It was a fight against a powerful élite, a battle for the rights of ordinary people and a struggle to see their Progressive ideals written into law. This was their cause. They sought to see it realized with missionary zeal.

Bob's old nemesis, Senator Spooner, escorted him down the aisle as he took the oath of office administered by the vice-president. That night Belle and Bob went to the White House to attend a reception for the diplomatic corps. Bob wrote in his autobiography that when they approached President Roosevelt, "He swore he was *dee*-lighted, overjoyed—that it was 'one of the greatest pleasures of his life to greet again his old friends, who had entertained him as a guest when at Madison,' and turning to his wife, and calling her by her first name, presented Mrs. La Follette with much unction."

While Mrs. Roosevelt "greeted each guest with pleasing grace," Belle thought, "as I read her psychology then and thereafter, her attitude was that of a spectator rather than a participant." Though she "gave generously of her time and strength to official entertainment," she "escaped public attention almost as though she had remained in private life."

Belle made the "calls" incumbent on a new senator's wife and noted changes since 1890: "While there seemed more wealth, there was less display, and good taste more generally prevailed; homes were more artistic; dress more becoming; manners quieter; voices lower. On the other hand, there were fewer social functions in the nature of open house; on cabinet and senatorial days you did not see the picturesque throngs of the earlier period. Social life had less color, less individuality; was more conventional, less democratic in spirit and purpose."

When she and Bob had left Washington in 1891, apartment houses were almost unknown but now "they seemed to have taken possession of the city." Her friend from college days, Lucy Daniels Thompson, who lived at the Ontario, discovered that one of the large apartments there could be rented furnished for $100 a month. Belle and Bob moved in at once. Lucy also "found a good maid for us, and we were soon comfortably settled," Belle wrote. She commented, "I was amazed at the convenience and quiet of the new mode of living as compared with the boardinghouses of our congressional days." Referring to the occasional howling of the wolves and roaring of the lions at the zoo, which their apartment overlooked, she said the noises and the sight of the wild animals added "to our sense of isolation."

As a new senator, Bob was given an insignificant committee to chair—the Committee to Investigate the Conditions of the Potomac River Front. The room for meetings and to store research documents was in the subcellar of the Capitol, reached by several flights of dimly lit stairs and long winding passages. Bob had great visions of cleaning up the whole Potomac River until he discovered the committee had never had a bill referred to it nor ever held a meeting.

In his autobiography he pointed out the vital importance of committee appointments in the Senate, saying, "They are the gateways of legislation. A powerful committee in secret session has almost autocratic power in deciding what laws shall or shall not be passed; and it is in the committees that the financial interests of the country have found their securest entrenchment."

He listed of first importance "the great Finance Committee, which has charge of all bills affecting the tariff, currency and banking." Then Interstate Commerce Commission, with its control of bills relating to railroads, trusts and combinations, and the Committees on Rules, on Appropriations, on Foreign Relations and the Judiciary.

Because of the inadequacy of his subcellar room in the Capitol, Bob rented another apartment at the Ontario in which to work. He covered every available space with reference material. He spent long hours preparing for a debate on the Hepburn bill, which dealt with the important question of amending the Interstate Commerce Act of 1887, legislation he had worked hard as a congressman to pass. This act created the Interstate Commerce Commission with power to ensure just and reasonable railway rates to the public and for ten years the commission assumed the right to fix rates. But in 1897 a United States Supreme Court decision took away this power, leaving the commission powerless except to make recommendations.

The Commission had repeatedly urged legislation to restore its power to control rates. Congress just as often had turned a deaf ear to these appeals. Now, however, it could no longer ignore the organized protests of the shippers against rebates and unequal rates. President Roosevelt helped call attention to the discriminations, creating sentiment for a "square deal." Bob's fight in Wisconsin against the unfair practices of railroads and his speeches in various states had awakened popular protest against the abuse by the railroads of their power.

Bob waited months for some senator to take action on this issue. He did not want to see the bill pass in its imperfect form but felt that as a new senator there was little he could do. He believed the President could use his influence to push the passage of important legislation. Bob, who had known Roosevelt for fifteen years, also knew the President had been warned "La Follette is dangerous and extreme" in his views. Bob did not want to offer unsolicited suggestions.

Belle described how, one evening after Steffens and a few other friends had dined with them, Bob was drawn into a discussion of the railroad problems and spoke at length of the defects of the Hepburn bill. Whereupon Steffens said, "I have been seeing the President, and

I am going to suggest to him that you have gone all over this question in Wisconsin, that you have been at it for years up there, and it will do no harm for him to have a talk with you about it."

He was as good as his word. President Roosevelt invited Bob to the White House for a conference on the rate bill at ten o'clock one Sunday night and they talked for two hours. At the President's suggestion Bob outlined amendments he thought necessary to secure reasonable rates for the public. Roosevelt objected, "But you can't get any such as that through this Congress," adding, "I want to get something through." Bob suggested if, while the bill was still pending, the President would send a special message to Congress pointing out what needed to be done, this would appeal to public sentiment that had been building up for nine years. Then, even if the current Congress failed to act, the next one would back the President more strongly.

Bob found Roosevelt "a very good listener," Belle said, and thought he had made an impression on the President. He told her that as he left the White House at midnight, he met Steffens going in to see the President. About two o'clock that morning the telephone rang in the La Follette apartment. It was Steffens reporting, "I have just left the President and he said you did a bully job."

But Roosevelt never sent a message to Congress recommending any of the changes Bob suggested. Since no other senator fought for the bill, Bob decided to expose its essential weakness himself and offer the necessary amendments to make it an effective statute. This was the subject that had most deeply concerned him as a member of the House and it had been a foremost issue in his Wisconsin fight. He knew that his suggestions would not be adopted without Administration support but he believed a move could be made in the right direction.

After weeks of careful preparation he arrived at the Senate chamber on April 19, 1906, with 148 printed pages in hand. It had been nineteen years and two months since he had spoken in the House advocating passage of the Interstate Commerce Act of 1887.

Belle, eagerly waiting to hear him, found the galleries crowded to capacity; people were even standing in line in the doorways. The country had been shocked by news of the San Francisco earthquake. The morning session had lasted way beyond the lunch hour. When the afternoon session was called to order, Bob rose to speak.

He started, "Mr. President, the people of this generation have witnessed a revolution which has changed the industrial and commercial life of this nation.

"The farmer knows that there are no open, free competitive markets for anything he may produce upon his farm. He knows that he must accept the prices arbitrarily fixed by the beef trust and the grain elevator combination. He knows that both of these organizations have been given control of the markets by the railroads.

"The independent manufacturer knows that he no longer has an open field and a fair competitive chance to market his product against the trust with its railroad interests. The consumer knows that the prices are made for him by those who control the avenues of trade and the highways of commerce. The public has suffered much. It demands relief."

As soon as Bob had started this speech a number of senators began to talk loudly among themselves, then stood up and left the Senate in a body. Bob ignored the exodus until he had completed the words quoted above. Then he stopped to address the presiding officer, Senator Chester Isaiah Long of Kansas, in a cool, deliberate manner which, Belle reported, "arrested the attention of everyone in the chamber."

Bob said: "Mr. President, I cannot be wholly indifferent to the fact that senators by their absence at this time indicate their want of interest in what I may have to say upon this subject. The public is interested. Unless this important question is rightly settled, seats now temporarily vacant may be permanently vacated by those who have the right to occupy them at this time." The implication was clear. He intended to read the roll of Senate voting to the populace at large during his next lectures.

Belle, listening carefully, said, "My heart stood still for an instant; then the conviction flashed upon me that his prophecy would come true as it had in Wisconsin. I believed the circumstances justified his calling the attention of the country to the Senate's lack of interest on this momentous question, and I was glad it had become a part of the record."

A spontaneous burst of applause sounded from the galleries, quickly hushed by Senator Long. That evening, Belle reported, "when our little group of friends came together to talk over the day's happenings," some urged Bob to leave the prediction out of his speech as published in the *Congressional Record*. Others argued that the effect on those who read it would be quite different from that on the audience in the galleries who, having heard the words delivered in Bob's eloquent voice, were moved to applaud. But Bob decided to let the record stand.

By late afternoon of the day after Bob's speech, Belle reported, the senators who returned to the floor started to recognize the significance of what Bob had said, including a large number of Democrats. "I felt sure the criticism of the fundamental defects of the bill was making an impression that could not be ignored," she wrote.

A verbal sparring match developed between Bob and Republican Senator Jonathan Prentiss Dolliver of Iowa over the physical valuation of railroad property as the fundamental basis for government regulation of railroad rates. Dolliver was a member of the committee in charge of the bill and at first opposed Bob's argument, though they had been good friends in the House and Dolliver had greeted Bob cordially when he came to the Senate. By the time they finished the argument Dolliver had been won over and thereafter agreed with Bob whenever the issue was raised.

In a letter to Fola, Belle informed her Dolliver had told President Roosevelt that Bob's speech was doing more to pass the bill than any yet made. Belle also wrote Dolliver's change of mind "was great backing and established at just the right moment the strength of the position Papa was taking." She said of Bob: "Papa was as free and at home as though he had been in the Senate twenty years. . . . He was completely master of himself and the situation. . . . We all feel very happy. I am deeply satisfied and you know I am hard to satisfy. My judicial and logical faculty compels me to see both sides. But there is no *other side* to this event, so far as its being a triumph—an unalloyed triumph for Papa. . . . Whatever comes, he has established himself right in the beginning, as the peer of any man on the floor of the Senate, and *new kind* of leader."

Belle returned to Madison on June 20, a few days before Congress adjourned, to get the new house ready for the children. Bob stayed in Washington and spent only one day at the farm before embarking on a long course of lectures that continued until December, interrupted only by several weeks of speaking in the Wisconsin gubernatorial campaign. This time the Progressives were divided on the nomination of a candidate for governor.

In his lectures in Iowa, Bob continued with his tactic of reading the roll call to show how senators had voted on national legislation. He wrote Belle on July 4, 1906, "I tried reading the roll call on some of my amendments which were 'tabled,' to see how it would go. It *goes* and some senators will find a back fire to look after. I suppose they will think I am the meanest fellow ever to 'go and tell.' "

In one state after another Bob's unprecedented procedure of ignoring party lines and reporting senators' votes to their constituents aroused bitter criticism. It was described as an "attack" upon senators, denounced as a violation of traditional "senatorial courtesy."

The candidate Bob supported as governor of Wisconsin in the first trial of the primary law was defeated. Bob was "deeply disappointed," Belle said, "but philosophical; he said we must accept the verdict." Steffens told her the outcome of this first primary furnished a far better argument for the direct-primary law than if Bob's candidate had won.

Belle spent the better part of the next year with her children as the family settled into Maple Bluff Farm. She and Bob envisioned it as "a real farm," she said. They planned to harvest the eleven acres of cherries and plums and raise and sell the offspring of the eight Shetland ponies Bob had bought.

Belle looked upon this period as a chance to put into practice many of her ideas concerning health, nutrition, education and management. Everyone was assigned duties and had specific responsibilities. Belle saw the combination of responsibility and a great deal of freedom as a solid learning experience for life. Bobbie, Phil and Mary jointly cared for the ponies. They provided the ponies with food and water, brushed them daily, kept their tack in order and cleaned out the stalls. Belle was a stickler for cleanliness, especially in barns and kitchens. Typhoid fever was still a serious killer, the house fly was the carrier and everyone was conscripted in a continuing war against flies, supplied with swatters, sprays and traps.

In return for their good care of the ponies the children were allowed the joy of riding them, training them and driving them hitched to a cart. Often during the summer and fall the children would load the cart with boxes of fresh vegetables or fruit and drive the few miles to town and sell their produce to passersby. The senator's children and their Shetland ponies soon became a familiar sight on the streets of Madison.

Belle loved the ponies. "No member of the family was more excited or happy than I when the little ponies came trotting up the drive from the main highway," she said. She learned the joys of a pony farm were, however, "seldom unmixed with trouble." One day

Rowdy, the Welsh pony, ran away while the boys were in a store attending to family errands and Mary was "holding the lines." But Mary's trying experience turned out to have some value when her father praised her courage and horsemanship. She was eight years old at the time.

There was plenty of open space on the farm for outdoor exercises. Belle supervised regular classes with the children. The farm also gave her the opportunity to jog a mile or two every morning in the privacy of their own land. All this activity created large appetites. Belle baked her own whole-grain, high-gluten breads and cakes and prepared low-fat, nutritious meals with produce from the garden.

Because she enjoyed teaching, Belle took the time to stimulate her children to develop inquisitive minds, to seek information and start learning about the world. During this period Bobbie attended the local public school while Belle educated Phil and Mary. Mary recalls that her mother "taught us to observe the environment, to do our best in all our endeavors, to treat others fairly and to share all good events in a joyous spirit." Mary also remembers Belle, like her grandmother before her, seldom had an idle moment, that "she was always at work doing something, whether related to her writing, to political issues or to the care of family, home and farm."

One of Belle's favorite objects was a small, framed inscription from an ancient Sanskrit text. It was called *The Salutation of the Dawn* and it always traveled with her, had its place on the wall in whatever house she and Bob were living. The poem summed up Belle's philosophy of life.

> Look to this day!
> for it is life, the very life of life.
> In its brief course lie all the verities
> and realities of your existence. . . .
> the glory of action,
> the bliss of growth,
> the splendor of beauty,
> For yesterday is but a dream
> and tomorrow is only a vision
> but today well lived, makes
> every yesterday a dream of happiness
> and every tomorrow a vision of hope,

look well, therefore, to the Day.
Such is the Salutation of the Dawn.

While Bob lectured on the Pacific coast, Belle wrote him, "The boys do pretty well about caring for the ponies. They get us up in good season to get the chores done and Robert off to school but he does not complain." She felt her faith in the inestimable value of the farm experience for her children was fully justified one winter day. Phil and Mary had hitched Topsy to their hand sled after bringing logs from the woodshed to the kitchen wood box. Belle heard Mary say in great earnestness to her brother, "Really, I don't see any use of having lessons. There is so much work to do on the farm we'll never have any time to read and write."

But they had time for other things, as Mary recalls. She tells how "when Phil and I played together, which we did a lot as the younger two, we would dress up in fancy clothes. Phil would be the king or Napoleon. I would be a princess. Bobbie wouldn't deign to play these games. He, being the Crown Prince, tended to lord it over Phil and me. He particularly liked to tease Phil. I would always come to Phil's defense."

Mary also remembers one day she and her mother went riding. Belle was on her Kentucky saddler, Nancy, and Mary rode Rowdy. They were trotting down the road when suddenly a piece of tar paper blew in front of Rowdy. The pony reared and Mary found herself on the ground. Belle dismounted and after making sure Mary was not hurt, held Rowdy's bridle and asked Mary to get back on. "I was frightened," Mary recalls. "I didn't want to get back on Rowdy. But Mother insisted. Reluctantly, I mounted Rowdy and with Mother leading the pony by the reins, we made our way home. Mother did not want me to be so frightened I would give up riding." Belle's strategy worked. Mary continued to ride and drive and care for the ponies.

Phil also fondly remembered the ponies. He wrote in his auto-biography: "Bob liked the ponies but Mary and I were devoted to them. I trained them to drive—single, tandem and four abreast. On one occasion when the Ringling brothers circus came to Madison, I took along one of the hired men, gave him one of Dad's old silk hats to wear, and we went to the starting point of the parade. Somehow I wangled a position just ahead of the calliope. As we circled the Capitol Park we apparently attracted considerable attention. For days afterward, we were the talk of the town."

The children decided to put on a circus of their own. "We rented a tent, put up seats and held a real pony show, charging admission," Phil recalled. "It was a good show and made a great hit. I think after expenses we had something like twenty-five dollars." He neglected to mention he broke his arm falling off a trapeze, which probably eliminated any profits. But the accident did not dampen Phil's enthusiasm for ponies, particularly his favorite, Jessie. He also wrote that "the big event of the year for me was the county fair. One year it was decided to have a pony race. That was my meat. I was in the lead as we came down the home stretch, when suddenly something frightened Jessie and she stopped abruptly. I jumped off, grabbed her bridle and led her over the finish line. The rules were not strict and I was declared the winner."

Bob had stationery printed for the boys headed "La Follette Brothers' Shetland Pony Farm." Phil said, "We were in business. But all the family became so attached to each pony that it was hard to sell even the colts. I am afraid it was not very profitable." The entire farm operation was always a financial burden.

When Belle wrote Bob about cutting back, he responded, "Dear Girl, don't worry about the finances. We will get even after a while for *sure*, and then do just what we please. There has not been a dollar spent which was not necessary. . . . Heaven bless you, dear heart, and keep you and my precious ones safe. Only another week and I shall see you."

Bob continued addressing audiences and reading the Senate roll call in Iowa, Nebraska, Kansas, Missouri, Indiana, Illinois and Colorado, among other states. His message never varied: "The object of our legislation was not to smash corporations but to drive them out of politics and then treat them exactly as other people are treated. Equality under the law was our guiding star," he wrote.

It seemed to Belle they had hardly begun to live at the farm when it was time for Bob to return to Washington for the next session of Congress. She thought it "wise and practical" to stay at home with the children, as this short session of the Fifty-ninth Congress, which began the first Monday in December, would end March 4, 1907. Bob could spend Christmas with them, so he and the family would be separated only two and a half months. She agreed to make permanent living arrangements in Washington for the next year so the family would be together.

It had been rumored that when Congress convened the Senators would punish Bob for his reading of the roll call throughout the country but no action was taken. On December 9, 1906, he wrote Bobbie: "My you must have real winter there, ice and snow everywhere. . . . As for ice in the Senate—well they have not applied any directly to me yet—and when they do things will warm up so it won't 'stay froze'—I fancy."

He wrote to Mary on December 11 as he worked on a bill limiting the continuous service for trainmen to sixteen hours. At that time trainmen were required to work up to twenty-four or even thirty-six hours without rest. He told Mary, "I have got one bill that I just have to watch so I won't lose my place. Did you ever play pussy wants a corner? You know if you have a corner and get away from it some one (who is playing pussy) dives in and gets your corner. Well I have got a game like that with a bill. So I just have to keep right in my corner every day and watch that bill." He won what the *Washington Times* described as "La Follette's sweeping victory" when, late in the afternoon of January 10, 1907, he Senate passed his hours of service bill by a roll-call vote of 70 to 1.

Belle wrote him that, judging from the *Congressional Record*, the newspaper accounts and the impression made on "the folks at home," it appeared "definitely understood" he had won an important victory. She said, "We all enjoyed and appreciated Moffett's write-up of the hours of service bill in *Collier's*. We read it aloud last night. It was fine. The *Times* write-up came at the same time—and I read the *Free Press* editorials to the children too."

President Roosevelt sent for Bob and they met on January 16. That night Bob wrote Belle he had called at the White House and the President had told him, "You have done another great piece of work in passing the hours of service bill and I am very grateful for it—because I was committed to it and it is right."

In a birthday letter to Bobbie, who would be eleven on February 6, Bob wrote: "It is hard to let a birthday go by for any of my little ones. It simply emphasizes the broken life we are leading and makes me repeat over and over again that we shall all be under one roof and around one table very soon I hope. You are coming now to the time when each year means a year of important growth in character as well as body. Look well to it that you grow in gentleness and tenderness as well as in strength . . . The boy Bobbie is a mighty important part of the man. As you are strong and kind as a boy so will you be strong and noble and tender as a man. Every day and hour of life is precious.

Every act lays the foundation for another. I love you, dear lad—and count on you for many things in the future."

The year passed swiftly and on December 13, 1906, Belle wrote Bob, "The children seem to be maturing very fast. Little Phil is growing quite reflective. It is beautiful to see how they all love their home. It is not a bad thing for them to spend a quiet winter here and get the perspective of your work and Washington life."

On February 21, she wrote, "It seems to me sometimes as though my life—inner life—was a long prayer that your strength may not give out under the strain to which you have been so long subjected and that the time is not far off when we can feel free to enjoy the time that *is*, not always wait for it to come."

Bob had sent her a clipping of a story appearing in the *New York Times* on February 11. It reported that, with the Senate session near an end, "La Follette is on top. The senators still snub him in the cloakrooms but not on the floor. He is bitterly hated, but also feared. . . . It is the Senate, and not La Follette, that is being rapidly brought to terms. . . . The main trouble with the Senate was that it chose to assume that he was a lightweight, a ranting demagogue. The industrious Spooner had spread that reputation for him before he arrived. La Follette does not rant, he is not a crank, he is extremely level-headed, and such an encyclopedia of information on every subject he takes up that any man who goes up against him in debate and has not devoted a couple of years to the subject is going to retire from the contest much the worse for wear."

Bob lost one enemy when Senator Spooner wrote a letter to Governor James O. Davidson of Wisconsin announcing his resignation as of April 30. Bob wrote Belle on March 4 from Chevy Chase, Maryland, where he was ill in bed, "No one yet knows what is behind it. . . . I think the Wisconsin situation taken all together was the underlying cause. . . . There are doubtless many things which made up the final judgment. . . . He shrank from the review of his record which he knew was coming. The deadly roll call deterred him."

A few nights later a telegram was delivered to Belle at the farm. It informed her Bob's illness had been diagnosed as severe influenza. The children were all asleep. Without disturbing them Belle packed a few necessities, left a note and on a bitter cold night walked the three and a half miles to town. She caught an early morning train and was in Washington the next day.

Her sudden departure created quite a shock at the farm. Phil,

then nine, wrote his father: "Dear Daddy, I am feeling fine. I hope
you are well. Mother has gone to see you. The ponies are fine. I think
Princess is with foal. I am just dying to go to Washington, not to
leave the ponies, not to leave the place, not to leave where I love to
stay, but because I will see you. . . . I want you more at home than
you are. How it did surprise Robert to find out that Mama had gone.
He pretty near fainted when he heard that she had gone. Your boy,
Phil."

Bob wanted Representative Isaac Stephenson to serve out
Spooner's unexpired term as senator and the Wisconsin legislature
followed Bob's wish. A meeting of Progressives in Milwaukee on May
31 was credited with starting the campaign for La Follette delegates
to the 1908 Republican National Convention. During the winter a
leading Kansas editor, also a member of Congress, had predicted if
Bob should become a candidate for President, he could carry the
Kansas delegation. A conservative Oregon senator had surprised his
colleagues by saying Bob could count on the Oregon delegation.

During the summer and fall of 1907 Bob's lectures took him to
distant states, from the Pacific coast east to Pennsylvania and south
to Missouri. He told the large audiences what had happened in recent
sessions of Congress. He explained why and how bills were killed in
committee. He described the fight against special interests that defeated legislation in the public interest and read the roll call on the
senators of each state he visited.

He wrote Belle from San Diego on April 28: "It made me very
homesick to be here without you. It made life seem so short. It made
it seem so wrong to be gone all the time. What is left will go so soon.
But this is not the way to write and not the way to feel, I suppose."

He lectured in July in states near Wisconsin and Belle accompanied him for a week. She worried about him for his audiences were
large, arriving from long distances and at the close of his speeches he
would shake hands with many people. He would come down from
the platform dripping with perspiration and at times tell her he had
felt dizzy, almost lost the thread of his speech. She felt he was taking
a serious risk talking so long on hot days in crowded tents and tried
to persuade him to shorten his speeches to a maximum of two hours.

She bought him an alarm watch and extracted a promise, which
he half seriously gave, that he would not speak longer than two hours.
The audience was quite startled when the alarm went off in the middle
of a sentence. Bob stopped talking, gathered up his papers and ex-

plained his wife had given him this watch to prevent his talking too long and he dared not say another word. The crowd laughed and cheered, insisted he go on. He yielded on condition they not tell Belle.

Once, when he was shaking hands with a long line of people, a woman said in a high-pitched voice everyone nearby could hear, "Mr. La Follette, I wish you would tell your wife for me that I think she wasted her money when she invested in that alarm watch." Bob, imitating her perfectly, would amuse other audiences with this story.

Phil wrote in his autobiography that with the school year of 1907-1908 began "the uneven and erratic primary and high school life that we three youngsters would have for the next seven years." They would start a school term in Madison, stay until Christmas, then pick up and move to Washington and try to fit into schools there until the close of the school year. Phil explained, "Mother and Father had to choose between that method of schooling or being separated from their children."

In the fall of 1907 Belle rented a furnished house at 2229 California Street in Washington. Besides Bob, herself and the three younger children, the residents included Nellie Dunn, Bob's secretary; Emma Gattiker, a friend of Belle's whom she had persuaded to be the children's companion and teacher, and Della Vallen and Laura Sachtjen, daughters of neighborhood farmers in Madison, who relieved Belle of household chores during the summer on the farm.

Belle wanted the children to attend the New Year's reception at the White House. The La Follettes ordered two carriages to drive them to the reception but only one appeared. They all piled into it. Phil, then ten, recalled, "Bobbie and I tried unsuccessfully to draw the curtains to hide our unseemly crowdedness from public eye. When we reached our destination, person after person stepped out until a policeman walked around to the other side to make sure that a line had not been formed by persons using the carriage as a passageway to the White House. As we passed down the receiving line all this was forgotten. The President greeted us with an enormous smile, gleaming teeth and 'Oh, the dear children!' in a voice that could have been heard for hundreds of feet."

Belle reported, "We were reminded, in moving about among the distinguished company, that Bob was a center of interest as a 'presidential possibility.' His record in the Senate, his achievement in Wisconsin, together with his lecture tours and roll calls in so many states, were creating a public sentiment that could not be ignored in

Washington political circles." The newspapers were mentioning him as presidential material for the next election.

From New Year's until the Republican convention in June, the La Follette family was frequently photographed and articles about them appeared in newspapers and magazines. The children's experience during the years Bob was governor accustomed them to this, Belle said, and "the inner life of the family was not overshadowed by anxiety or strain for the first year we were together in Washington." Bobbie and Phil never lost an opportunity to attend the Senate sessions: "Their interest in legislation sponsored by their father was almost as absorbing as his own. They had access to the Senate floor and were on intimate terms with their father's friends, most of whom they affectionately addressed as Uncle."

Bob's outstanding fight in the Senate during this session was against the Aldrich Emergency Currency Bill. It proposed issuing $50,000,000 worth of additional notes to national banking associations. The issues were to be based on state bonds, municipal bonds and, as reported by Senator Aldrich, also railroad bonds.

The first part of Bob's speech was devoted to the centralization of banking and industry. After presenting "evidence that less than one hundred men own and control railroads, traction, shipping, cable, telegraph, telephone, express, mining, coal, oil, gas, electric light, copper, cotton, sugar, tobacco, agricultural implements and the food products, as well as banking and insurance," Bob asked: "Does anyone question the overcapitalization of these consolidated corporations which cover the business of the country? Does anyone doubt the community of interest that binds these men together? Does anyone question their vital interest in maintaining their overcapitalization and protecting their stocks and bonds?"

It was seven weeks before the emergency currency legislation was again taken up. Bob felt sure, with the help of three or four Democratic senators, he could prolong debate until the worst features of the bill would bring such protest from independent bankers and businessmen that Congress would be forced either to defeat or radically amend the bill. With the help of Democratic senators, he entered on what would become a three-day, record-breaking filibuster starting at 12:20 p.m., May 29. Several attempts were made, as the temperature soared to over ninety degrees, to deprive him of the floor. Senator Nelson W. Aldrich proposed to keep the Senate in continuous session until the conference report was adopted.

From time to time during that afternoon and evening Bob sent messages to Fola in the gallery that he was "feeling tiptop." Until late in the evening his strength held out better than he thought it would. But at 11:30 p.m. an observant reporter noted Bob seemed under "great strain." Some time between ten and eleven he had taken a large swallow from a glass of milk mixed with an egg brought to him on the floor. As he swallowed, he noticed a "vile, bitter taste" and handed the remaining three-fourths of the drink back to the clerk, saying, "Take it away, it's drugged." Soon after, he was stricken with severe and painful dysentery, unlike any illness he had ever experienced. A subsequent chemical analysis of the liquid showed it contained enough ptomaine to have killed him had he swallowed the whole drink. By forcing several roll calls between 11:30 p.m. and 1:30 a.m. Bob managed to leave the floor for a few minutes, then return to his desk to resume speaking before each roll call was finished.

He spoke through the night until 7 a.m. when he concluded the nineteen-hour record-breaking speech: "Mr. President, I am rather reluctant to surrender the floor for the time being, but as others desire to speak and are in waiting, I yield the floor for the present."

But the odds were against him and the bill was finally passed. Though his filibuster had failed in its immediate purpose, he felt his effort was not in vain. The debate had exposed the character of the currency bill and had called national attention to the methods by which privileged interests put through legislation (including perhaps murder of the opposition). The applause in the galleries reflected a popular revolt that would affect the old guard in days to come.

An article by Steffens, based on interviews with Bob, President Roosevelt and Taft was published in *Everybody's Magazine* in late May. It was titled *Roosevelt—Taft—La Follette on What The Matter Is In America and What To Do About It*. While the currency-bill filibuster was still on, Steffens had written Bob that many of the letters he had received concerning the coming presidential election "express gratification that I 'appreciate' you and your 'lonely fight' in the Senate. You are deeper rooted in the heart of this nation than you think. Health is all I wish you, you have all else that *we* require of you."

Following the end of the legislative session the family returned to Madison. Ten days after Bob arrived at the farm, the 1908 Republican National Convention met at Chicago. With President Roosevelt and the administration machinery backing Taft for President,

Belle knew there was little chance of Bob's getting any delegates outside Wisconsin. The real object of his candidacy would be to bring a Progressive platform before the country by presenting it to the convention in the form of a minority report.

Bob's name was placed in nomination for President and his supporters staged a spontaneous demonstration lasting twenty-five minutes. But Taft was nominated and Bob backed Taft as the next President.

The *New York Times* on November 8, 1908, wrote of changes in the Senate, saying, "They no longer scoff at La Follette in the big white building on Capitol Hill; they are mortally afraid of him, and as respectful of him as of a rattlesnake."

CHAPTER
8
....

Editor and Columnist

[1909–1911]

One day late in the summer of 1908 Belle and Bob held a pow-wow with a group of friends and supporters at Maple Bluff Farm to discuss the creation of a national magazine. Charles R. Crane of Chicago, a wealthy plumbing manufacturer, offered financial support. He admired Bob's political philosophy.

Bob, who had always wanted his own weekly newspaper, was zealous in his enthusiasm and offered to take on the responsibilities of editor. He suggested Frederick MacKenzie as managing editor and Belle as associate editor. She would be responsible for coverage of women's issues, the home, nutrition, health and education in a weekly column.

Belle and Bob were not new to the world of publishing. Bob had owned and edited the *University Press* in Wisconsin. During the 1902 gubernatorial campaign they had published the *Voter's Hand-Book*, influential in achieving a Progressive majority in the Wisconsin state legislature. They were well aware a national Progressive magazine could be an effective force in presenting their programs to the people.

The new weekly journal was christened *La Follette's Magazine*. Its editorial offices were to be at 119 West Main Street in Madison. The first issue was scheduled to appear in January 1909.

Only Steffens seemed fearful of the burden Bob, in particular, would be undertaking. After the meeting he took Belle aside, whispered, "You mustn't let Bob take on this terrible load. It will kill him."

Belle wrote of this warning that she, too, "greatly dreaded the added burden and responsibility" but scoffed at Steffen's suggestion: "He knew Bob well enough not to expect me, or anyone else, to stop him when his mind was made up. Bob habitually overtaxed his strength, always keeping in harness until exhaustion or illness compelled him to stop work."

She found a new outlet for her ideas on health and mental development in her weekly column. The first issue, dated January 9, 1909, carried her column, headed "Home and Education." In it she wrote out of deepest conviction, "Good health and abounding vitality are the foundation of all excellence."

She continued: "Women especially are inclined to think that health is preserved by care. The only way to strengthen the body is by use. . . . And now one simple, homely exercise, for strength, beauty and usableness. Stretch and yawn; not a suppressed yawn but a great big natural yawn. Stretch as a cat stretches, gradually energize the whole body, stretching from the top of the head to the tip of the toes and at the same time opening the mouth wide, drawing in a great big long breath, filling the lungs full, getting a splendid sense of freedom; then relax and feel the perfect rest of letting go. . . . Repeat several times. And then repeat at least once each day of life thereafter. We can stretch and yawn away more small troubles in a minute than we can argue out of mind in a week."

In the January 23, 1909, issue she advised: "Unless we are lame or bedridden, we should make it a part of our life habit to go out for a walk every day. . . . A fit of depression can always be cured this way. We women are too much inclined to wrestle inwardly with a bad feeling. The same effort directed to putting the body in healthy action, will make the spirit normal."

The January 30 issue carried this advice: "There is no such good all-round exercise as running. It quickens the circulation, increases the respiration, starts the perspiration, stimulates the digestion, eliminates poisons that undermine health and destroy vitality. Running gives a delightful sense of lightness and youth to the body. Unfortunately it is not considered proper for women to run and there are few places where one can run without the depressing fear of being seen. . . . The standing run is a good substitute. Stand before a mirror—we should use our mirrors more for this purpose—take the running step over and over. Let the arms hang relaxed. Run at least 100 steps as a daily exercise. It will lighten the step and brighten the mind."

And on February 6: "Slower deep breathing means calmer, healthier thought; the exercise that expands the chest and strengthens the diaphragm strengthens the will; the elasticity of step gives youth and buoyancy of spirit."

Belle's basic philosophy extended to the expression of a table blessing she gave: "Humbly recognizing as one of the mysteries of life the fact that we have food, while others, even little children, starve or go hungry, we would learn to use effectively the strength of mind and body, obtained from this food, in the effort to secure a fairer distribution of life's material blessings."

Though Belle wrote primarily for women, increasingly her columns were valid for both sexes. The theme of a fairer division of material wealth ran through many of Belle's columns. An early one read: "Stated broadly, the aim of the Wisconsin Consumer's League is to assist in the recognition that the joys of labor are as important as the joys of owning and using. The whole world works together, day after day, and sometimes night after night, in youth and in age, in sickness and in health to produce food and clothing and house furnishings and ornaments. The more privileged enjoy the taste of the food, the warmth and beauty of the clothing, the protection from the elements that their houses afford and the sight of art objects. We are coming to believe, more and more, that this wealth should bring joy in the process of creation as well as joy in its consumption."

Belle was also strong in her belief that if a fairer division of labor and wealth, a better educated and healthy society—a better world—were to come about, it would happen only if women shared equally in the political process.

In the twelfth issue of *La Follette's Magazine*, dated March 27, she appealed to the women of Wisconsin: "Be sure to vote for state superintendent of public instruction on April 6, even if you cannot vote for other officers. Don't fold your talent in a napkin. If you vote when you have the opportunity, the opportunities will increase. If you have not been able to register, your vote is not lost. It can be sworn in on Election Day."

Over the years in her columns appeared eloquent proof of where her heart lay: gaining the vote for women, working for world peace, advancing civil rights, educating children and helping the labor movement, farmers, and the poor. She would always stand by her husband's side in his political battles but now she had the opportunity to spread the ideas she thought would help shape a more humanitarian world.

She also wrote occasionally in her column of the Washington scene. In her first column under a special heading, *Seeing Washington*, she told her readers: "I never go down F Street without seeing the alley through which Wilkes Booth escaped from Ford's Theater after the assassination of President Lincoln. And as I cross Tenth Street I always see, with a quickening heartbeat, the flag over the door of the house where Lincoln died the morning after he was carried there, from the theater across the way."

After the appearance of the first issue Steffens wrote Belle of his continued concern for Bob's ability to be both an effective Progressive senator and a magazine editor and writer. Steffens explained: "And I write to you, rather than to him, because I don't want this said to him till he is in the mood to take it all right. If he is worried, over-worked or, on the other hand, if he feels the same way himself, please say nothing to him except that which is also true—that he has made a better start than should be expected. . . . What worries me is the Senator's apparent illness. Isn't he overdoing? And isn't it the *Magazine* that is too much for him?"

Though there was a genuine openness within the La Follette family, one area was protected by a shroud of silence: Bob's health. Belle was keeper of the vital image, both publicly and privately, and this was why Steffens expressed his concern to her.

During this period Belle and Bob decided to rent a larger Washington home at 1804 Wyoming Avenue, a four-story house with a basement. Two large connecting rooms on the ground floor served as an office for Bob. On the second floor were the front and back parlors, the dining room and the kitchen. Bobbie, Phil, Mary and Nellie Dunn who, Phil said, "was almost like a sister," had rooms on the third floor. Belle and Bob occupied the top floor, "because it was more isolated." As Belle explained: "I preferred this, as I took my editorship of the 'Home and Education' department of *La Follette's Magazine* seriously and I felt I must have a quiet place to write."

They rented the house unfurnished but it still contained old mahogany pieces and Oriental rugs. This allowed Belle time to make new selections. She wrote, "I well remember the look Bob gave me and his tone of voice when he said one day: 'Belle, I want you to furnish this house completely and comfortably and in good taste. You don't need to skimp and economize. I am earning enough now so we can afford to spend what is needed for suitable furniture and belongings. We never yet have had a house that was furnished right. Let's make a good job of this while we are about it.' "

She commented, "Strange, I had never before observed that our commonplace furniture jarred on him. The only time I remembered being dissatisfied with it myself was when he was defeated for Congress and I had noted the deterioration and necessity of repairing all our household equipment. Whatever furniture I bought after that had been merely to meet the needs of our growing family and was adapted to the children's freedom from undue restraint in the home. When we moved from the executive residence to the farm, the furniture from the West Wilson Street house seemed good enough for the time being." She thought that "with the beautiful views of the lake and countryside, with the old fireplace either burning or ready to light, the farmhouse was always livable; I was content to get along with whatever furniture we had."

They had gradually accumulated a large collection of books, which soon overran the library at Maple Bluff farm. Books were stacked high in the living room and other areas of the house.

Belle accepted the mandate to furnish the Wyoming Avenue house less modestly and undertook the task with zeal. She "haunted the antique shops and attended Sloan's famous auction sales." She was pleased when the house was finally furnished to Bob's satisfaction and "our friends said it gave the impression of our having always lived there."

One of the children's teachers observed, "Life in this home was so rich that it was not surprising that the school activities took second place. They met at their table notables from all over the world and were up on politics and world affairs at an early age."

During this period Mary was described by her schoolteacher as looking "like a lovely blonde doll. Her interest was in art and not in the conventional academic course. She was prone to 'play hooky' when the grind became too boring, and Phil became her very strict guardian. She bore it unresentfully, but my feminist soul resented it for her!" With her paint box and crayons, however, Mary found complete happiness.

According to Phil, "Mother did not care for 'society,' but she always read the society columns in the Washington papers. She said you could get important leads to political affairs by watching 'who went where.'"

The family was now living on a grander scale. They had always entertained but now did so more often. Belle noted that during her life with Bob "many of our most precious and lasting friendships had their beginnings when Bob invited guests to lunch or to dine impromptu at our home." She described the four years at 1864 Wyoming

Avenue as "especially rich and happy." The dinners Bob gave, with a view to bring together Progressives of the Senate and House, created a closer personal and political understanding within the group. Belle tried, she said, "to make my receptions and other social functions contribute to the same end."

No longer was Bob "the lonely man in the Senate." He had staunch friends by his side who would work with him even though his proposals were at first defeated. On Sunday, February 13, 1909, a small group of senators met at the La Follette home for the first gathering of what Bob called the "so-called Progressives in the Senate for concerted action on legislation." Bob knew that to pass national legislation similar to that in Wisconsin, the Progressive Senate forces had to be organized. This could be accomplished only through team-work and by encouraging other members of the group to play more conspicuous roles. Belle commented about Bob, "As I watched him in his new role, I marveled at his faith, patience, skill and diplomacy."

In one column about President Roosevelt's New Year's reception at the White House, Belle wrote: "He was much more quiet, though no less cordial in his greetings than I had ever known him to be on any other social occasion. . . . He has been gaining repose these last years. . . . Or perhaps, the years of responsibility have tempered his nature. Perhaps it is a different Roosevelt who leaves the White House from he who entered it. We wish he were not going to Africa. America needs right now the influence of this strong man, matured and dis-ciplined by his great opportunity and experience."

A week after Congress adjourned that August, Bob, without taking any vacation, once again began his long lecture tour of the Chautauquas, traveling nonstop through Nebraska, Kansas and Mis-souri. He spoke day after day to large tent meetings under a hot sun. He wrote Belle: "This hot weather made me do some thinking, I tell you. My feet not only blistered but boiled to a turn. So I invested 2½ dollars in some white canvas shoes and I never knew such comfort before."

After one of his short visits home, Belle wrote: "I hardly know why the time seems so precious that we spend together and so vacant when separated. I realize the great value of your work and would not keep you at home but I have always the sense of waiting for your coming."

She also said the children's schoolwork was made difficult by the change of residence twice a year. Whereupon he wrote his sons: "The work in school is preparation for the battle of life, boys. So sweat and tug, no matter how hard it is, just remember you are at work on the armour and weapons with which to wage a great fight against the wrongs which oppress and the evils and ills which afflict the world in which you live."

He added, "I expect little Mary will have to be locked out of the lesson shop or she will be working on her armour and sword and shield all the while. She will be like her mama was as a little girl and a big girl too." Bob's expectations for Mary were as high as they were for Bobbie and Phil.

Belle and Bob were encouraged by the number of people who came up after Bob's meetings to tell him how much they liked his new magazine. "Always he regarded every subscriber to his magazine as a special friend," she commented.

Bob returned to Wisconsin for a few weeks in September to investigate the Menominee and other Indian reservations where, it was believed, the provisions of Bob's bill for protecting the Indians' forests were being violated. At that time the La Follettes met Elizabeth Glendower Evans of Boston, who was visiting Madison.

Mrs. Evans became a member of "the inner circle of our closest, most helpful and inspiring friends," Belle wrote. Mrs. Evans had recently attended a conference of the Women's Trade Union League in Chicago. Belle insisted she write a column describing the conference for La Follette's Magazine. Subsequently Mrs. Evans contributed other articles. Later, when the magazine was "in sore straits financially," Belle said, "she helped most generously to tide over the crisis—too generously, I thought."

During this visit to Madison, Mrs. Evans's lifelong interest in Bob's work and his family started. She wrote in one article her impression of Maple Bluff Farm and of her first meeting with Bob: "The house was a low brick structure with a wide vine-clad piazza standing a little way back from the lake. Between the house and the lake was a herd of Shetland ponies. Behind the house was a barn with horses and cows, the kitchen garden, and big orchards of apple, plum, and cherry trees. Across the sweep of the lake rose the great dome of the capitol.

"I became well acquainted with the children—Bobbie, a lad of fifteen, dark-browed, solid in his figure, serious; Phil, aged thirteen, volatile like quicksilver; Mary, aged eleven, blue-eyed and fair-haired, the only one of the children to resemble her father in features. The oldest daughter, Fola, was away from home.

"The first morning, as I sat on the piazza, the senator came and sat opposite me. His countenance was one to arrest attention in any gathering. But it was the expression of his eyes that compelled me. He looked out below level eyebrows with a directness that I felt I have never seen in other mortal gaze. . . . There was a solidarity about the La Follette family beyond that of any other I ever encountered. The children took part in every discussion and expressed their opinions freely. There was never an attempt to impose the opinion of the grown-ups upon them. Always they were treated as persons. The right government of the country was the very life of the household and they imbibed this feeling as the warp and woof of their being."

At this time Belle and Bob also met and became close friends with Louis D. Brandeis, whom the children called Uncle Louis. Belle later said their introduction to Brandeis and his wife by Elizabeth Evans, who lived next door to the judge in Boston, was "always a happy thought."

At the end of 1909 Brandeis became the legal mastermind of what was known as the Ballinger trial. In Belle's words: "Only those who witnessed the dramatic developments as they occurred could appreciate the obstacles [Brandeis] had to overcome and the genius he displayed in conducting the investigation. Arrayed against him was the entire Taft Administration, backed by the old guard forces in Congress."

During the Roosevelt Administration, conservation of natural resources was guarded by Gifford Pinchot, chief of the national forest service. He was a wealthy man with social position who chose to devote time and knowledge to public service. Taft suddenly appointed Richard A. Ballinger of Seattle as secretary of the interior. Ballinger at once restored to private ownership a large part of the 1,500,000 acres of public lands Roosevelt had withdrawn to safeguard valuable water power sites.

Belle attended a congressional investigation into Ballinger's policies, describing herself as "personally absorbed in the subject . . . among those who gathered every morning long before the committee-room door opened, standing in line to make sure of a seat." She listened attentively to every word uttered by Brandeis, lawyer for the conservationists.

He proved that fraud and deception had been used to suppress the truth and falsely clear Ballinger. Leading magazines and even newspapers that supported the Administration published Brandeis's disclosures, which had grave political consequences for the old guard Republicans. The Progressive movement was further strengthened in Congress and throughout the nation by Taft's underhanded action in this case, as well as his openly reactionary course on legislation during the first two sessions of Congress.

Brandeis had arrived in Washington on January 25, 1910, the day before the congressional hearings on the Ballinger case began. That evening he went to the La Follette home on Wyoming Avenue. Belle wrote: "Bob was impressed with the personality of Brandeis from the moment he grasped his hand and looked into his keen, thoughtful face. He came to love and admire him and always found him a genial and fascinating companion."

During this first visit, as they discussed government problems Brandeis considered confidential, Bobbie and Phil sat in the room, listening intently. Belle noted their presence seemed to trouble Brandeis. When they went to bed at nine he expressed relief. Bob assured him he need not worry as the boys were accustomed to hearing confidential political discussions and could be trusted. Years later, when Bobbie became a candidate to fill his father's unexpired senatorial term, some senators protested to Brandeis that Bobbie was too young and had no political experience. Brandeis replied, "Bob, Jr. and Phil have had more experience in politics than any boys since the days of the Roman senators."

Of Brandeis and his wife Alice, Belle said, "We met at the beginning on the basis of true comradeship and understanding which has ever since existed between the families. He had a standing invitation to join us at any time, and would often 'drop in' for dinner in the evening after the day's work was over."

Though the backgrounds of the Protestant Wisconsinite and the Jewish Bostonian differed, their values and methods were similar. "When confronted with a specific problem, they investigated it; sought first the facts; then devised instruments to deal with it," Belle wrote. "They never endeavored to solve social and economic problems from the blueprint of Utopian dreams. Neither was doctrinaire; but both had a deep conviction that industry, finance and government should be organized to serve the best interests of all the people of the country rather than the special interests of a privileged few."

Playwright George Middleton entered the family circle in 1910. Mid, as he was fondly called, had known Fola for some time in New York and, as a founder of The Dramatists Guild, was admiring of her efforts to create a similar organization for actors, Actor's Equity. As he recalled in his autobiography, *These Things Are Mine*, "From Fola's own experiences I well knew how some actors had been exploited. Once, on tour, neither she nor the other actors were paid for a performance missed because the property man got drunk and the costume trunks were put on the wrong train. Fola protested, as a matter of principle, since the stage hands got their pay. One told her, 'You see, *we've* got a union.' Fola related this experience when she spoke at the first public organization meeting for Equity, at the Little Theatre, New York, November 16, 1913. I could see some resented what they thought was her implication, that actors were laborers; though they worked for a salary, they thought they should be classed as artists. Yet to win, the actors had to join the American Federation of Labor."

The theatre had always been a part of Fola's family environment. Both Bob and Belle relished an evening at the theatre, attending whenever they could. One of Bob's standard Chautauqua lectures featured his analysis of *Hamlet*. John Barrymore, hearing from Mid that Bob had made a study of the character, asked to see it. After studying Bob's interpretation he wrote:

My dear Senator La Follette:

I have read with the greatest possible interest and intense satisfaction your extraordinarily illuminating essays on the subject of Hamlet and Iago. I am particularly pleased and intrigued by the fact that our ideas about the character of Hamlet—a thing critics have piled exhaustive and misleading Pelions upon Ossas for centuries—are in complete accord. And naturally from an intellect like your own this subconscious cooperation is a great and joyous stimulant. Thank you a thousand times for your great courtesy and kindliness in sending them to me. You must naturally know what a very great pleasure and honor it was to meet you. No one but myself has seen the manuscripts though indeed they are supremely worthy of wide attention.

Believe me, in the deepest gratitude,

JOHN BARRYMORE.

Fola had appeared in London on April 13, 1909, at the Royalty Theatre's production of *How the Vote was Won*, a farce on women's suffrage. The *London Star* reported, "Genuinely funny . . . The desolating effects of a general strike of woman workers are as significant as they are truly comic." The *New Age* commented: "It is the most rippling piece of fun which has been on the boards for a long time. Why not an invitation performance to cabinet ministers?"

The play was produced for the first time in America at the Criterion Theatre in New York on January 18, 1910. Fola was especially gratified to receive a letter on February 2nd from Anna H. Shaw, president of the National Woman Suffrage Association, telling of her pleasure after seeing the play: "It would be of excellent service to any suffrage club, or in any community where suffragists would desire to make propaganda."

Although Fola was making a bit of a name for herself, she was not yet earning much salary and wrote her father for help.

He sent a check for $25 on January 29, 1910, saying he would send more after filling speaking engagements. Then he wrote: "We are having a hard time just now. The bills here are very heavy. We lacked a couple of hundred of meeting last month's bills. . . . Now, dear, you understand this is only a temporary let-up. Your old Dad is with you until the stars melt and the universe rolls up. He believes in you more than ever and will play your game till you win, and then some. He just wants to spar lightly until he can get his wind. You understand, don't you?" He signed the letter, "With enduring love, Dad."

The year 1910 was a senatorial election year for Bob and in April he wrote Gilbert Roe, "I have not one dollar to begin a campaign. The farm is mortgaged. I have had to borrow $2,000 at the Capital City Bank to meet expenses here."

Two weeks before Congress was to adjourn on June 25, Belle was called to Baraboo by the serious illness of her father, Anson. She took Mary with her while Bobbie and Phil stayed in Washington with their father. Bob wrote Belle, "just a line to tell you how we all love you and how lonesome it is without you. . . . Three gentlemen present here at this moment join in worshipful adoration to the greatest woman in the world. In other words we love you with all our might and send a share to grandpa."

Phil wrote his mother every day in a large, slanting scrawl. He reported on June 18: "Papa will not let me order the meals anymore. I do not know why because my bills were under a dollar a day. Nellie is doing it now . . . I am very homesick for you, Mary and the farm. We received your letter telling us Grandpa was a little better." In another letter marked "personal," he wrote, "I have been crying all afternoon I am so homesick but never mind." Contributing to Phil's unhappiness was another of Bob's mysterious ailments that periodically sapped his strength and made him uncharacteristically irritable. It was during periods such as this that Phil's mercurial personality obviously grated Bob. That Belle was not there to act as a buffer must have been difficult for both father and son.

Belle wrote Bob on June 21, "Beloved Papa: I hope you are getting better and it seems to me as soon as Congress adjourns it would be wise for you to get out of Washington. If you do not feel equal to coming home, why not take the boys for a little trip, by the lakes or the mountains or some way that would make a change for you and be a pleasure to them always to remember. *Do not stay there [in Washington] and force yourself to do a lot of things that after you are refreshed you can do so much more easily and quickly.*"

She also counseled, "I think you will have to come home and get in touch with people here before you can make any plans for a campaign. I have the impression that there is a fight on. No one seems to doubt the result of the primary but understand the danger of the legislature." At this time senators were still chosen by state legislatures.

She signed the letter, "With very much love, Mamma."

Bobbie, now fifteen, wrote her on June 24 on stationery headed, "United States Senate, Washington D.C.", obviously taken from his father's desk. Obsessed, like the rest of the family, with his father's health he said, "I do so wish Dad would go home, he needs to get some rest." Bob had been suffering intense stomach pains and Bobbie reported, "He is feeling about the same and has some pain most of the time I think." He, too, missed his mother, adding, "I . . . hunger to get home."

Anson did not recover from his illness. Mid went with the rest of the family to Baraboo for the funeral. "There," he wrote, "I had my earliest glimpse of her 'folks' and their neighbors, so different from my city people. Outside the old farmhouse, I watched the passing line of men and women, whose forefathers had pioneered from different countries to escape poverty or religious persecution. Here near Devils Lake, the oldest of exposed geological formations, her mother's people had built their lives. These men and women had been the grass roots from which sprang the liberal movement her father led, to make Wisconsin a political experiment for social reform. I felt I was looking at the living pages of history."

While Belle had been in Baraboo tending her father, Bob was received by former President Roosevelt at his home in Oyster Bay, New York. It was the last week of June, just after Roosevelt had returned from his hunting trip in Africa. Bob wrote Belle that a Negro attendant showed him into the library, where he waited until Roosevelt "made his appearance, wearing linen knickerbockers, and after a cordial greeting said that he had just come in from pitching hay, confirming his statement by removing a rather liberal quantity of timothy from his person."

The visit, lasting almost two hours, was the last Bob had with Roosevelt, whom he had known for twenty-one years. In a letter written two weeks following the visit, Bob reported: "I had gone there upon a mission, and I sought to impress him with the fact that the Progressive cause had made great strides during his absence; that nothing could stop or sidetrack it. Also that T [Taft] had made a mess of things and that nothing short of a miracle could save the administration. Without quoting him [Roosevelt] I will venture to guess that he very much wants to be President again. He is not greatly changed. He will help some reactionaries on the one hand and some Progressives on the other, being cautious not to aid men who are regarded as ultra and extreme on either side. This has always been his idea of a square deal. He is not fundamentally democratic. His democracy is sentimental."

Roosevelt's only comment about Taft had been, "Sometimes a man makes a very good lieutenant but a poor captain."

After three days with the Roes in New York, Bob and his two sons left for Madison and "home," arriving July 6. There was "an outburst" of greetings to their mother and sister and "a rushing away to see the ponies with their new little colts, and the yearlings almost as large as their mothers, and Phil's calf twice as big as when he left," Belle wrote. At every homecoming Bob first gave attention to the farm, inspecting the stock, fields, orchard and woods, sharing with Belle and the children plans for work to be done.

Many Progressives in all parts of the country were contributing to Bob's senatorial campaign fund. He had expected to "camp in the field, to speak throughout Wisconsin during the summer." But he suffered such agonizing attacks of indigestion and pain that Dr. Fox, after examining him, warned he was not well enough to launch the rigorous campaign. For the first time Bob did not make a single speech in a primary campaign.

Belle wrote Bob the day before the primary, on September 5, "I do not feel any anxiety about the election although I am quite prepared for anything in the way of result. It seems to me that personally we have nothing to fear or dread or be disappointed about. We have so much of the best of life."

The primary, on September 6, brought an overwhelming victory for the entire Progressive Republican state ticket. Bob was renominated by almost three to one, receiving 102,187 votes more than his reactionary "Taft-Republican" opponent, Samuel A. Cook.

On the first of October Bob's abdominal pains became so excruciating that Dr. Fox took him to the Mayo Clinic for an examination. Belle received a letter from Dr. Fox recommending "the gall bladder be drained and the appendix possibly removed. When this is done, the indications are that he will be in better health than he has been for years. If it is not done the conclusions are that he will break down before long and possibly not recover, at least perfectly."

Bob underwent the operation on October 4 and three days later Belle wrote the children in Washington: "I think the doctors believe that practically all danger is passed. Dr. Fox gave out a statement last night. It seemed necessary to make it because people were already beginning to ask and plan for Papa to go into the campaign. They do not seem to realize that time for recuperation is as necessary as time for the operation. And this is what we must impress on Papa."

Bob's family and friends knew it would be difficult to slow him down enough so he would recuperate properly. Two days after the operation, Steffens wrote Fola that her father "owes it to all of us to take all the time there is to get strong and perfectly well. I make this appeal to him personally because I think that he will respond more to this view than to that of love. And to bring it home to him, I should like to remind him that as things go on, our other leaders, one by one, show weaknesses that point more and more to the likelihood that some day we shall have only the one man to head this movement."

Bob's condition was given so much negative publicity that Belle issued a statement saying the newspaper accounts of his illness had been "greatly exaggerated and distorted." She explained that after "an exhaustive examination by the Drs. Mayo and Dr. Fox, his family physician, an operation was deemed advisable, not because of any acutely dangerous condition requiring immediate attention but because it was felt that an operation would ultimately be necessary, and to perform it now gave every expectation of returning to perfect health."

Belle wrote the children from the Mayo Clinic on October 11: "Dear Ones All, Mary's letter gave us a lot of pleasure. Papa was so gratified and said it was a nice letter. He has not said so, but I know he feels it that Robert doesn't write. You children were all so good when Grandpa was sick. It was a great comfort and I shall never forget it. I did not expect it and the bunch of letters that came made my heart glad. Because you were so good then, I have expected each day to get a bunch for Papa. . . . He has a great heart hunger for you children. I know you have for him but you must not depend on Fola to express it for you. Write yourselves. Do you not remember the dear beautiful letters he used to write us on his long hot wearisome trips?"

She concluded, "Fola says in each letter you have all been fine and shown a lovely spirit and been helpful, each one carrying each one's responsibility. It makes Papa and me very glad and relieves us of all anxiety for now and helps us to look into the future without fear. It has always been my thought that the most we can do for our children is to fit them to care for themselves."

As soon as the operation was reported in the papers, letters and telegrams from all parts of the country arrived at the hospital, messages from unknown men and women who thought of Bob as their friend. William Allen White, who had written articles for *La Follette's Magazine* from his editor's office in Emporia, Kansas, sent Belle a telegram on October 1, when Bob first fell ill: "Tell Robert to hang on to the willows, don't let go. He is needed more than any other American leader for the work now in hand. Let me know how he is progressing *day* to *day*. All Kansas is anxious for the best news."

Bob and Belle returned to Madison October 26. Both were convinced his reelection represented the defeat of reactionary Republicanism and condemnation of the Taft Administration. They hoped the Progressive forces might ultimately capture the Republican party and make it the instrument to achieve nationally what they had accomplished through years of work in Wisconsin. The 1910 elections placed Bob in the strongest position he had ever held in the Republican party and newspapers and magazines predicted he would be an important factor in the 1912 presidential campaign.

Belle and Bob took time out from politics in January, 1911 to travel to New York to see *The Scarecrow*, a play by Percy MacKay, a friend of Steffens, in which Fola was appearing at the Garrick Theater. Steffens, who also saw the play, wrote MacKay, "It is beautiful, that play. It is a rare combination of whimsical humor and profound philosophy. And Fola has the key to the whole conception: simple, pure, young, curious, honest. It was a perfect play of a lovely part. I was delighted with her, and proud—I was as proud as if she were a relative, a very near relative."

A special session of the Sixty-second Congress met on April 4, 1911, and, as the newly elected senators took the oath of office, some observers recalled the prophecy Bob had made on the Senate floor on April 19, 1906: "Unless this important question is rightly settled, seats now temporarily vacant may be permanently vacated by those who have the right to occupy them at this time." He was referring to how the voters would react to his publicizing the roll calls on the question of railroad regulations. Ray Stannard Baker, like Steffans, a muck-raking journalist and biographer, observed as this new Congress began its work, "That prophecy has become almost literally true. The old guard has vanished utterly before that puff of applause in the people's gallery." He was reminding his readers of the gallery applause Bob had received on his original remark.

Former President Roosevelt sent word to Bob that in the coming Presidential election of 1912 he believed the Progressives should put him forward as a candidate for President. He urged Bob to get into the fight at once. Roosevelt also said he believed Taft could be beaten but that he, Roosevelt, could not openly oppose him because he had made Taft the President.

As Bob achieved his role of Progressive leader in the Senate, Belle's weekly columns in *La Follette's Magazine*, now read by thousands of women, were hailed as "a new sort of woman's page" by the *Cincinnati Enquirer*. Instead of writing recipes for food or beauty preparations, as did the typical woman columnist of the day, Belle gave her readers news of women's fight for political, economic and social equality. No woman at this time was writing so consistently, if at all, about woman suffrage, international disarmament and peace, education of children, prison reform and segregation.

In her columns Belle described the role of prominent women such as Jane Addams and her work at Hull House in Chicago to help deprived women and children. Belle publicized a report by the General Federation of Women's Clubs stating there were over eight million women "who want woman suffrage and peace in the world." Belle also described the work of Mary Connor, a librarian in Cleveland, who established a "traveling library" to make books available to those who otherwise might not read.

Belle also wrote of Professor John Dewey's ideas of progressive education and the need for coeducation. She urged her readers to support bill 241-A in the Wisconsin legislature, which provided that "students of both sexes" be admitted to all schools and colleges of the University of Wisconsin. Belle commented, "It will doubtless be a surprise to many to know that this is not already the law."

Sometimes her columns were of a more personal nature. On April 17 she wrote on the subject of "poise," pointing out the importance of "standing straight" and advising, "The poise of the body should not be merely mechanically correct. It should be light, free, ready for action like a little child at play, moving in easy opposition, an expressive agent of inner thought."

A month later she wrote of spiritual poise: "Blessed are the mothers who bring comfort and repose instead of fretful irritation to their homes. . . . Blessed are the teachers who do not nag or frighten or goad; who encourage, strengthen, and help to unfold."

In another column Belle gave her thoughts on the then taboo subject of sex education: "It sometimes happens that the dearest of mothers dread unfolding the genesis of life to their girls, often because they themselves were not wisely told. Blessed are girls with mothers like mine, who from earliest childhood had the absolute confidence of her children. We never feared to ask her questions and she never feared to answer them truthfully.

"The knowledge of sex should never be regarded as a subject of awesome revelation to be made to children all at one time and avoided ever after. There is never any danger of disclosing gradually the mystery of life to our girls as one of nature's phenomena. The function of motherhood should be told a girl as early as she has any understanding, not later than six or eight years and after that much that she should know may be taught indirectly without making her fearful or self-conscious."

Concluding the column in her consistently forthright manner, she advised, "From infancy we parents should guard against any sense of ownership of our children. We are trustees, not proprietors."

Belle once summed up the philosophy behind her columns: "I have written upon the supposition that no subject is too broad, too dignified, too advanced for women readers. Time was, perhaps, when a woman could succeed socially, and as a wife and mother, by being merely sweet and pretty. Now she cannot; an alert and trained intelligence is the essential requirement which modern society makes of its women."

La Follette for President

[1911–1912]

Throughout the spring and summer of 1911 articles in newspapers and magazines reflected the growth of the Progressive movement. They cited the importance of Bob's leadership in Congress in opposition to Taft and the reactionaries.

The Saturday Evening Post of June 10, in its leading article entitled *The Lonely Man of the Senate* by Samuel G. Blythe, described the change in Bob's position from "lone crusader" to "leader." An illustrated article by Henry Beach Needham entitled *La Follette's Ideas, An Interview With the Leader of the Progressives*, appeared in the *Post's* July 8 issue with a photograph of Maple Bluff Farm and pictures of the ponies.

Belle wrote Phil, "Don't you think it fine that *The Saturday Evening Post* published the picture of your ponies? It ought to advance the market value." The family talked of the money they would make from the sale of ponies, knowing full well they would never sell one of their beloved animals.

The magazine *World's Work*, edited by Walter Hines Page, who later became the United States ambassador to Great Britain, in July carried a ten-page illustrated article by William Bayard Hale, entitled *La Follette, Pioneer Progressive, The Story of 'Fighting Bob,' The New Master of the Senate and Candidate for the Presidency*.

Issues of the coming year's campaign for the presidency were clearly defined by the fall of 1911. Governor Woodrow Wilson of New Jersey went on speaking trips through the Northern states, appearing the most likely candidate for the Democratic party. A number of Progressive Democrats rallied to his support, diminishing Bob's ranks.

A conference of Progressive Republican political leaders met in

Chicago on October 16 and endorsed Bob's candidacy. Taft, after an unsuccessful tour through the Western states, gained support only from the corporate East and the conservative South. In November there were even some Progressive victories in local elections in Taft's home state, Ohio.

Bob's star seemed rising. But then a number of prominent Republicans suggested the only way to heal the breach in the Republican party was to nominate Roosevelt. Reports were leaked to the press that Bob was withdrawing in favor of Roosevelt. Bob had to keep making denials. To Belle he remarked, "Make no mistake about it. The Great Hunter is playing the game."

Meanwhile, Belle was actively involved in the operation of Bob's Washington headquarters. She and Bob had been preparing an important campaign document, a complete review of his record as congressman, as governor and as senator. It was Bob's personal roll call, intended to prove he was the originator of the Progressive ideal and the logical choice to be leader of the Progressive wing of the Republican party. Roosevelt's name was not mentioned.

As the manuscript was about to go to press, one of the workers noticed some changes in the draft and showed them to Belle. Additional material had been added implying if Roosevelt entered the race, Bob would support his candidacy. Belle immediately deleted this new material, restored the original sense of the document and rushed it to the printer's.

At this time a number of Progressives who would have been for Roosevelt if he were a declared candidate, were backing Bob. It was revealed that one of them, Mendil McCormick, had seized the opportunity to "edit" the text and promote his preferred candidate.

Bob and Belle put aside the presidential race for a moment while the family took time out for a wedding. One year and nine months after they met, Fola and George Middleton were married on October 29, 1911, at the La Follette home in Washington. The Senate chaplain, Reverend Ulysses G. B. Pierce, officiated. Mary was bridesmaid and Paul Kester, with whom Middleton had collaborated on a play for Julia Marlowe, was best man.

Mid became literary editor of the *Magazine*, writing a column about books and plays under the headline *Snap Shots*. Over the years Belle and Bob followed the production of their son-in-law's plays with as keen an interest as Mid showed in his father-in-law's work as senator.

Belle (circa 1863), wearing a woolen dress spun, woven, and sewn by her grandmother, Lucetta Moore Case.

Belle's graduation picture (1879).

Bob La Follette, the fighting district attorney of Dane County (1881).

Mary and Phil at Maple Bluff Farm with their string of ponies (1907).

The cover of the first edition
of *La Follette's Magazine*,
which became *The Progressive*.

Belle at Maple Bluff Farm
in the summer of 1910.

The La Follette family in Washington, D.C., 1910.
Clockwise from upper left: Fola, Bob, Belle, Bobbie, Phil, and Mary.

A cartoon from the December 29, 1911, edition of the *Chicago Daily Tribune*, when Bob was becoming a serious contender in the presidential campaign.
Cartoon by John T. McCutcheon.

This cartoon from the February 17, 1912, *New York Globe* illustrates the pressure put on Bob to withdraw from the presidential race.
Cartoon by J.N.Darling.

A rare photograph of Belle speaking for suffrage (Blue Mounds, Wisconsin, circa 1915).

Bob, vilified for his stand against America's entry into World War I in this cartoon from a 1917 issue of *Life*.

The La Follette family in the summer of 1918. At this time, Bob faced possible expulsion from the Senate for his anti-war stance.

Belle and Bob relaxing at Maple Bluff Farm
before the arduous 1924 presidential campaign.

From the private collection of Gordon Sinykan

ROBERT M. LAFOLLETTE
THE IDOL OF WISC⋯

BOB JR.
U.S. SENATOR
FROM WISCONSIN

PHIL
GOVERNOR-APPARENT
OF WISCONSIN

WISCONSIN

This cartoon by
John T. McCutcheon
appeared in the
Chicago Tribune in 1930,
a convincing illustration that
the La Follette political dynasty
would continue to flourish.

Ray Stannard Baker and Louis Brandeis dined at the La Follette home on November 25. They told Belle and Bob that in a recent interview Roosevelt had said, "I am not a candidate," but had refused to say, "I will not be a candidate." Baker noted that if Roosevelt chose to run for a third term he could steal the Progressive votes from La Follette while Bob bore the brunt of the fight.

In spite of Roosevelt's public denials, rumors persisted he would be a candidate, creating much confusion among the Progressives. After Bob's experiences with Roosevelt as President, he never counted on the Rough Rider's promises. He realized that if it suited Roosevelt's purposes he would swiftly "change his mind."

Just before Christmas 1911 Bob and Louis Brandeis, on separate schedules, started touring the critical states of Ohio, Minnesota, Wisconsin and Illinois. Urging Bob's nomination for the presidency, Brandeis said, "What he has done in his state and what he has done in Congress he would do in every position of trust in which he may be placed, and no position, in my opinion, can be too high for a man who understands, as he does, the needs of the American people, who feels as he does brotherhood with them, and the great brotherhood of them in a way that I believe no American has done since Abraham Lincoln."

Though on tour, Bob did not forget December 31, his wedding anniversary. He telegraphed Belle: "Dear Girl, My heart is with you and the dear ones on this our anniversary day. Blessings on you all. It seems an age since I left. Hope for some word from you tonight. Trip has been remarkable. Great meetings both day and night and great enthusiasm everywhere. Am tired but standing work in the same old way."

Belle kept up her columns in behalf of woman suffrage and allied subjects. On December 7 she wrote in praise of the work of Maria Montessori, the famous child educator, saying, "What would I not give to have had at the beginning of my children's upbringing such a guide to the fundamental principle underlying their best growth and development." Belle explained the central idea of the Montessori method of schooling was "that no one can be educated by anyone else, he must do it himself, or it is never done. A teacher gives guidance. . . . Whatever its merits, there is something radically wrong in our system of education which, from kindergarten through the professional course, keeps the young under continuous strain without keeping them really interested from within; which absorbs the richest part of their lives without making them productive or creative. There is also something wrong with our home training, which fails to develop joy in work or repose in leisure, which fosters a constant craving for amusement and does not develop a true sense of responsibility."

Her column of January 6, 1912, carried her editorial, "Women's Work," in which she predicted "the trends of events is that women, both before and after marriage, shall continue in gainful and stable occupations, consistent with their inherent responsibilities. This will not result in the destruction of the home, but will lead to its read-justment on a more economical and efficient basis which will place higher value on women's time, labor and development."

Belle wrote in favor of establishing a federal Children's Bureau in her column of February 2, 1912. She said she would like to see the Senate "correlate its humanitarian work and bring the isolated bureaus together into a Department of Health and Education." She concluded, "The name is not important so the thing is done." In another column she focused on "Planning a Slumless City." In another, "The Vital Importance of the Early Recognition of Cancer."

Bob returned bone tired from his heavy schedule of speaking in the West but in a few days felt himself again. Belle commented, "It always gives him new strength to go among the people and find how much in earnest they are." Roosevelt, evidently impressed by Taft's relative weakness and by the ease with which Bob was stealing votes from him, felt encouraged in his own behalf. He made a statement to the effect that he would accept the nomination for the presidency if it came as the result of a popular demand.

On January 22, Bob gave a speech at Carnegie Hall in New York, talking for two hours to an enthusiastic full house. At a meeting with Steffens the next day at the Roe apartment, "Steff," as Bob called him, told him "it looks bad at the moment. The Colonel [Roosevelt] is mussing up the whole Progressive situation with his 'to be or not to be.' And he won't make a statement. He talks to us privately, but not convincingly, at least not to all of us."

At the same time Bob was carrying on his arduous Senate duties, he was trying to complete a series of articles for *American Magazine*. He worked late at night and, often finding it impossible to sleep, would return to writing at his desk until early morning. To add to his anxieties, some of his staff informed him at a meeting in his office on January 29 that Roosevelt was now actively seeking the nomination and they could no longer support Bob.

That same day Bob and Belle learned that Mary, now thirteen, had to undergo a critical operation. A gland close to her jugular vein was tubercular and had to be removed at once. The operation was set for the morning of February 3 at Providence Hospital in Washington.

Bob wanted to cancel a speaking engagement on February 2 in Philadelphia at the annual banquet of the Periodical Publishers' Association of which he was a member as publisher of *La Follette's Magazine*. In his heart Bob wanted to be with Mary, knowing how dangerous was the operation. But he yielded to the advice of Belle and others, who insisted that a failure on his part to appear would be interpreted as confirmation of reports he intended to retire in favor of Roosevelt. He planned to leave Philadelphia after his last words and catch a train back to Washington.

Bob and Belle took Mary to the hospital the day before the operation, February 2. Belle remained with Mary to hold her hand, read some of her favorite stories to her and assure her all would be well. Belle worried about Bob as she always did when he was under stress and had a critical speech to deliver.

That evening Bob left for Philadelphia by train, working en route on the forty-minute speech he planned to deliver. He was disturbed to find the material had to be cut in many places. There was no time to have the final text retyped. He would have to carry the entire manuscript into the hall.

Bob intended to emphasize the educational importance of magazines and to stress the danger of increasingly subtle domination by advertising. He planned to contrast the subservience of some of the larger newspapers to special interests with the independence of the smaller weekly and monthly periodicals. He was unaware the Association had invited many prominent newspaper publishers to the banquet. He saw himself as a magazine publisher speaking to other magazine publishers.

Mid met him at the Bellevue Stratford Hotel where the Publishers' Association had reserved his room. During the day Bob had suffered an attack of indigestion and had eaten no lunch. He ordered a hot chocolate as he dressed for the dinner. He commented to Mid as he drank the chocolate that it was "lukewarm and nauseating." Before leaving the room he also took a drink of whiskey, as he sometimes did when fatigued, before going on the platform. He walked with Mid to the banquet hall, where the dinner had been in progress since eight. It was now eleven.

Among the six hundred guests were the nation's leading magazine and newspaper publishers, writers, editors, correspondents and other distinguished men of the day—Alexander Graham Bell, Rear Admiral Robert E. Peary, Amos Pinchot, Steffens and a few of Bob's friends in the Senate. A place between the toastmaster, Don Seitz, publisher of the *New York World*, and Mayor Rudolph Blankenburg of Philadelphia had been reserved for Bob.

As Bob entered the hall Governor Wilson was just ending his address so Bob stood quietly in the back. Adapting to the late hour, the governor had handed his prepared speech to the press and improvised a shorter talk. When Wilson finished speaking, Bob walked to the speakers' table where he and Wilson shook hands.

The Philadelphia *North American* reported the next day: "The fighting Senator got a heartening reception. His opening was good-humored and graceful and gave no hint of the painful scenes that were to follow. When he remarked that if a Democrat were to be elected President he hoped it would be Governor Wilson, there were appreciative cheers for the handsome compliment to a political rival."

The "painful scenes" occurred as Bob picked up the pages of his prepared speech. Something, perhaps the unhappy expression on Seitz's face, made Bob realize his manuscript appeared a formidable document at this late hour. To explain to the audience why he had to read from the manuscript, he said, "For fear there may be some here who will not report what I say correctly, and because I am going to say some things I consider important, I want to have a record of them." He held in his hand what Seitz later estimated as sixty closely-written pages, commenting, "I looked aghast when I saw he intended going through them all."

The unfortunate phrasing by Bob of his apology for use of the manuscript at once lost the sympathy of his audience. Because so many of the guests were newspaper editors and publishers, they felt unjustly accused by his words, "For fear there may be some here who will not report what I say correctly." He got off on the wrong foot and never regained a hold on his audience.

He finally put down his manuscript, which he had started to read in its deleted form, and tried to talk extemporaneously. He was suffering not only from acute indigestion but fatigue and worry. Mary's illness was the first serious physical ailment to strike one of his children.

Whenever Bob sensed a restless audience in the Senate or on the lecture platform he would put aside his manuscript and drive home a point in brief summary. Aware he was losing his audience, he tried this now, to no avail. Angry at the listeners and at himself, he returned to reading parts of his hastily cut manuscript, elaborating thoughts he had already covered and losing all sense of time. At one point, picturing the evils of corporate control over newspapers, he asked rhetorically, "Is there a way out?" A man in the audience shouted, "We hope so!" and headed for an exit.

Bob's speech lasted an hour and a half and to his weary listeners his tone was strident and his message a personal attack on newspaper publishers who were guests at a dinner arranged to bring together the newspaper and magazine worlds.

Some said later in joy, others in sorrow, this speech would end Bob's chances for the presidency. When he finally sat down, Seitz rose to his feet. Slowly and distinctly, he said "I want to apologize to the newspaper press of the country in general for the foolish, wicked and untruthful attack that has just been made on it."

It was one a.m. by the time the meeting ended and Mid raced up to his father-in-law. Mid later recalled, "Hardly anyone spoke to him. I walked with him to the elevator. When we entered our room he went immediately to the bathroom and vomited. . . . Steffens came in. But the senator made no comment. He hardly spoke. I went with him and John Hannan to the station, where he caught the last train for Washington in order to get back in time for Mary's operation."

Bob was at the hospital early the next morning, joining Belle, who had stayed overnight. Mary was on the operating table for two hours and twenty minutes. Not one but three glands near the jugular vein contained tubercular growths and had to be removed, a protracted and delicate operation. Belle and Bob stayed at the side of their daughter throughout the day.

That morning the newspapers reported on the publishers' dinner in Philadelphia. The Philadelphia *Public Ledger* foreshadowed the ominous blasts to follow. It quoted extensively from Wilson's address, compared the two principal speakers noting they "were both applauded before their speeches, and Governor Wilson was applauded after his speech. . . . They both in a sense went after the same thing, but Wilson was a rapier and La Follette a club." In an interview Seitz attributed the length of Bob's speech to his "broken-down mental condition."

For days after Seitz's interview newspapers from coast to coast headlined stories of Bob's "collapse" and "mental breakdown," coupled with announcements of his withdrawal from the race for President. Rumors that he had frothed at the mouth, wandered incoherently and spoken in a drunken condition were circulated in whispering campaigns throughout the 1912 campaign for the presidential nomination.

Traveling in the West, Brandeis read the newspapers and on the train from St. Louis to New York wrote Belle on February 7, "My thoughts have been much with you and Bob and the children and I long to be East where I may hear something authentic. Only make Bob take the rest he needs and make a pleasure trip out of this necessity. When he comes back we will take up the good fight again together. With much love, Louis."

At no time before or after the Philadelphia fiasco did Bob either contemplate or sanction the withdrawal of his candidacy. But because he knew his failure in Philadelphia was due to extreme fatigue and nervous exhaustion, as well as worry over Mary, he cancelled all immediate speaking dates.

Belle prepared a statement Bob's office issued: "Mr. La Follette became a candidate at a time when it was generally believed Taft could not be beaten; yet it was important for the Progressive movement that someone assume the leadership. When the Progressive campaign disclosed that the movement had a deep hold on the people, pressure was brought to bear to force Mr. La Follette either to combine with Roosevelt or get out of the field altogether. This he refused to do, because he never enters into any deals or compromises, which might confuse the issue, or sacrifice fundamental principles. The persistent reports that he has withdrawn and misrepresentation as to his health are part of the plan to make him yield."

Some of Bob's campaign staff felt that with Roosevelt now actively in the field it was foolhardy for Bob to continue his campaign. A group drew up a formal statement to this effect, showed it to Bob on February 5, and asked him to sign. He said he would sign no statement without consulting Belle.

Three members of the group, Congressman Irvine Lenroot, Walter Houser, the Wisconsin Secretary of State, and John Hannan, Bob's secretary and campaign manager, went to the La Follette home that night, where they submitted the statement to Belle. She read it, then said she would rather "see Bob in his grave" than have him sign it.

The following day she recorded her reactions in a longhand letter to Roe in New York: "When I learned of the humiliation Bob had suffered in Philadelphia, I longed for you, Gilbert. And it is you and Alf [Rogers] who are needed here or men like you—if there are any. The impression Bob made must have been pretty bad. I should judge it was pitiful and yet the way Hannan, Lenroot and Houser have been willing to make a funeral of it, rouses my ire. They are telling how slowly he works, how he has not done anything new for a long time. Lenroot is particularly aggravating along this line . . . I know Bob suffers from brain fag all the time because he will not try to rest, but to hear these men talk you would think he had been a dead man for several years instead of carrying the whole load of the Progressive movement. It needs a man to talk back to them."

To a friend in Chicago, William Byron Colver of the Scripps newspapers, Bob sent a night letter: "No change. Always remember, I never quit. But I find I must have a few weeks of sleep in order to catch up. Didn't know I was really in need of it. There won't be any funeral unless it's the real one with music and flowers."

Belle wrote Emily Bishop on February 3: "In some way I always assume that you understand all that is going on in our household through intuition. The last few weeks have been difficult, but Mary is almost well; even the scar on her neck hardly shows. In spite of all that she suffered . . . [and] the anxiety we felt . . . I am rejoiced that it is over and that we did not delay longer. Bob, too, is strong in spirit, and though very much worn and in need of rest, he is not as ill as I have known him to be at other times in his life. I feel satisfied that if he could have a complete rest of even a few weeks he would be well as ever.

"The Presidential election is grievous. Not one of the Progressive senators, unless perhaps [Joseph L.] Bristow, has stood the Roosevelt stampede. Even Bob's closest friends have advised him to retire from the race and endorse Roosevelt. This he could not do, and will not; so he is again a lonely man. I think the breaking down of the Progressive alliance, which as you know took him so long to build up, is the hardest part of the situation."

Support for Bob's refusal to withdraw appeared in telegrams from "many people who would have felt they were betrayed if he had taken any other stand," Belle wrote. A few days after the Philadelphia dinner Charles Crane sent word he would continue his support, as did Elizabeth Evans, Rudolph Spreckels, the Chicago sugar heir, and others who had helped support the campaign financially.

Belle drafted another statement about Bob's illness, recovery and desire to continue in the race against Roosevelt, which was sent to many who had written to support him. It read: "We thank you for your strong letter. Like messages from over the country evidence deepfelt and widespread approval of Senator La Follette's announcement that he will remain a candidate and fight for the nomination and a Progressive platform to the finish.

"While he is obliged, because of overwork, to cancel for the present all speaking engagements and to take some time for rest, he himself is certain, and so are we, that it will not be long before he is ready to take up work again. On two or three other occasions during his twenty years' war against Privilege, when his zeal to meet conditions has overtaxed his strength, he has had to stop, but he has recuperated quickly and returned to the field, with renewed vigor and power. We who know him realize that he will never relinquish the fight as long as he lives."

The first presidential primary in the United States was to take place March 20 in Valley City, North Dakota. On March 12 Bob left for North Dakota at the urging of North Dakota's Senator Asle Jorgenson Gronna. This was Roosevelt territory. As a young man, the former President had lived on a ranch nearby, where he learned to ride and hunt. So sure was he of winning the primary here that he did not plan to campaign at all but sent Pinchot in his place. The fight for delegates was now between Roosevelt and Bob, for the old-line Republican organization had practically abandoned Taft and was backing the wild-game hunter.

Belle wrote Fola on March 11, the day before Bob left for North Dakota, that she had encouraged him to go because it was "the best way to give the lie to these deserters who are going about claiming they left him because he was so disabled."

Pinchot had publicly announced his switch from Bob to Roosevelt, claiming Bob was "mentally and physically incapacitated." Pinchot described Bob as "a disabled steam engine" that could no longer "take the Progressive train to the terminal."

Bob's first speech was in Valley City, where, he said, he had recently been labeled "a disabled steam engine" and was there to demonstrate "my fire box is all right, my drive wheels strong, and my sand box isn't empty." He discussed what he believed were the important issues of the campaign. He reviewed both Taft's and Roosevelt's legislative records on the economic and political problems that had to be solved if representative government was to survive.

Later, the Washington correspondent of the *Minneapolis Tribune* who covered the trip, wrote of Bob, "He is unique. Supposedly coming from a sickbed, the Wisconsin senator looks anything but a sick man. He is tense, vigorous and full of fighting ire . . . He is apparently unafraid. There is no shrinking in his manner. . . . There is an indomitable something in this fighting man that evokes admiration whether willing or unwilling."

In the North Dakota primary election Bob received 28,620 votes, Roosevelt, 19,101 and Taft, 1,543. In the Wisconsin primary on April 2, Bob's ticket carried the state by almost three to one over Taft. There was no Roosevelt slate. The Colonel had stayed out of Bob's territory and received only 628 votes.

With North Dakota and Wisconsin behind him, Bob, accompanied by Belle, started out early in April on a whirlwind campaign that took him into states where prominent Progressive governors, senators and congressmen had shifted their support to Roosevelt. Belle wrote the children from Nebraska: "Papa is having great meetings. Crowds everywhere. And yet there is something different from North Dakota. It may be the management or it may be that the politicians are tied up. No one seems confident of the result. And yet neither Taft nor Roosevelt seem to have much doing. I am puzzled by the situation."

On this trip Belle spoke on behalf of woman suffrage. She made the point that political equality would create closer comradeship between husband and wife and therefore better marriages and better homes—that "equality and partnership in marriage" would result from suffrage.

Fola joined her parents to add her voice for the women's vote. The night her father addressed a large crowd at the Omaha auditorium she was "expounding the doctrines of woman suffrage," as the *Sunday World Herald* of Omaha put it, to another audience.

Bob spoke in Salem, Oregon's capital, where hundreds who came to hear him had to be turned away from the Grand Opera House. Then Belle, Fola and he traveled to Portland where he announced, "I shall continue to be a candidate for President until our government is entirely restored to the people. I would rather have the place in history as the man who led such a fight than to have been one of a score of Presidents whose names you can not remember tonight."

Bob and Belle left for California on the night of April 18, expecting Bob would carry the Nebraska primaries the following day.

They were shocked to learn in San Francisco that Roosevelt had not only swept Nebraska but run 6,000 ahead of Bob in Oregon. Belle wrote Elizabeth Evans on April 20: "It was a body blow to get the news from Nebraska and Oregon this morning. In spite of all my experience in politics it took me, and the rest of us too, entirely by surprise."

Belle wrote Netha Roe in New York on April 23: "Nothing has been so hard as coming here to San Francisco after Oregon and Nebraska. No time to gather ourselves up and get ready to go on. I will try to think of our mercies, which are many. Bob's voice is getting better and he is well otherwise. Rudolph Spreckels is doing the princely act [paying for the trip]. While I do not see any earthly chance here, judged by all ordinary political standards, still we are relieved of the financial burden and are glad to make the fight, win or lose.

"I long for the children and wonder how they are. I wish we could all meet at Maple Bluff Farm and have a summer colony. I love you all. Hastily, Belle."

Bob drew large crowds in California, as he later did in Ohio, New Jersey and South Dakota, speaking a few days in each state. He predicted that Roosevelt and Taft would go into the Republican National Convention so evenly matched that a handful of delegates would have the balance of power. He believed he could win, for there was now animosity between Roosevelt and Taft. Supposed Roosevelt adherents on the Republican National Committee had agreed to seat Taft delegates. Whereupon the Colonel's roar rose from Oyster Bay, denouncing this decision with charges of fraud and treason. He promptly boarded a train to Chicago, where the committee was meeting, to personally direct the fight against the man he had made President in 1908.

Roosevelt also had become alarmed at the revived La Follette bid for the presidency and spent large amounts of money to halt it. Bob described the activity: "Headquarters were established, East and West, North and South, and an army of men employed and put into the field. Special trains, private cars, literary bureaus, newspapers, documents, special dailies—the whole conduct of the campaign itself was proof overwhelming that big finance was behind Roosevelt."

Bob went to the Republican national convention, which began on June 18 at the Coliseum in Chicago, with only two states behind him—North Dakota and Wisconsin. When the roll was called, the result was: Taft, 561; Roosevelt, 107; La Follette, 41. Roosevelt promptly announced he was forming a third party, the Bull Moose. On July 2 at the Democratic national convention in Baltimore Woodrow Wilson was nominated on the forty-eighth ballot.

The summer saw Senator William Lorimer from Illinois evicted from the Senate, charged with getting elected through bribery and corruption of the Illinois legislature. Bob was one of those who opposed seating Lorimer and worked for a constitutional amendment providing for direct election of senators, which the Senate passed. Bob used the Lorimer case to achieve his larger goal—the direct election of senators.

In September, with the election campaign well underway, Belle and Elizabeth Evans spoke for a week at county fairs, advocating the passage of a state referendum to give women in Wisconsin the right to vote.

Though Bob did not publicly endorse any presidential candidate, his widely reported speeches were interpreted as pro-Wilson. In return, Wilson in several speeches digressed from criticism of the Republican record to praise Robert La Follette.

Through his *Magazine* and on the lecture platform, Bob planned to give all the help he could to Republican candidates for Congress and for state offices in those states that had Progressive programs. He thought this would help strengthen the small band of Progressives in the next Congress. If Wilson, as President, proved Progressive, then these Progressive Republicans could be of service to him.

The night before Election Day Bob ended his speaking campaign at the gymnasium of the university from which he graduated. It was the first time he spoke there since introducing Taft in 1908. Now, on the last night of this bitter 1912 campaign, the huge auditorium was packed to the doors, as it had been when in 1904 he was renominated as a candidate for governor.

Before Bob spoke, Belle gave a half-hour speech for the woman suffrage referendum, on the ballot in Wisconsin. She had campaigned for suffrage at most of Bob's other meetings in the state. Throughout the campaign Bob supported the referendum and the hometown audience applauded the tribute he now paid Belle at the close of her speech. They laughed when he referred to a tall tale told by his enemies who claimed the reason he allowed Belle only thirty minutes was because the audience might find out who was really the author of the speeches he had delivered over the past twenty-five years.

The following morning Belle and Bob arrived at 9:35 at their Madison polling place in Wingra Park. Bob entered the booth, cast his vote, then went to his law office where his partner, Alf Rogers, practiced. Belle remained at the required legal distance from the voting booth, trying all day to persuade men to vote for the referendum giving Wisconsin women the right to vote.

That night she, the children and Bob, along with a few close friends, gathered around the fireplace at Maple Bluff Farm to await the returns. Before eleven, they knew that, as expected, the split in the Republican party had elected Wilson by 33,634 over Taft. Roosevelt blamed Bob for the loss of the presidency, Bob blamed Roosevelt for his own lost chance and they never made peace. Women did not win their right to vote in Wisconsin that year. Bob returned to the Senate and Belle, to her typewriter.

In her column entitled "A Question of Democracy," she wrote: "The real issue in this struggle for equal suffrage is . . . a question of democracy . . . My basic reason for believing in equal suffrage is that it will make better homes. The home is the foundation of society. Government exists for society. Home, society, government are best when men and women keep together intellectually and spiritually; where they have the widest range of common interests; the most to think about, to talk about; where they share with each other the solution of their common problems."

She concluded: "Government is not alone a man's nor a woman's problem. It is their mutual problem. And only when women are given their share of responsibility in the solution of public questions will the affairs of government be brought into the home for discussion. Not until then will government be an intimate part of family life, loved and understood as it must be if democracy in its best form is to endure."

CHAPTER
10
....

Belle Battles
for Her Own Causes

[1912–1914]

Belle marched in the first major parade for woman suffrage on May 6, 1911, on Fifth Avenue in New York City. Beside her walked Fola, carrying the banner for the Actresses Division of the National Woman Suffrage Association. Beside her walked Mid. He and Gilbert Roe were among the few men who joined the historic march.

Belle used every opportunity to present the case for suffrage in the *Magazine*. In her column of August 10, 1912, she quoted remarks by Dr. Luther Gulick, director of the Russell Sage Foundation, before the National Education Association. He expressed a fresh view of the value of equal voting rights: "Woman is as sure to have suffrage as the tide is to rise, not because she is as wise or as skillful as man, nor for any reason of likeness at all, but because she is different, because she can do what he cannot, because the world needs her peculiar and special abilities. She is making healthier conditions in schools, fairer conditions for the work of men, women and children in farm, store, factory, shop and mine. She is beginning to see that she is responsible for much of the municipal housekeeping. It is because she is different and because these differences are fundamental to world needs, that it is necessary that she bring these differences to the service of the world."

Belle was an avid writer but a reluctant speaker. During their college years together, Bob had trained her in the platform arts and once she found herself in front of an audience, she spoke clearly and effectively in spite of her nervousness. But as she confessed, "I suffer with anxiety . . . I dread to go on that train and be obliged to talk to people." The only force that could overcome this fear was her determination to fight for the causes she championed and her knowledge that Bob believed she could speak convincingly.

In her column she wrote of her suffrage talks as she traveled with Bob during the presidential primaries: "Accompanying Mr. La Follette in his campaign of North Dakota, Nebraska, Oregon and California gave me the opportunity to get in touch with the suffrage sentiment of those states. . . . Although Mr. La Follette in all of his addresses spoke for equal suffrage as a fundamental principle in democracy, the women were anxious that I should also say something. . . . It was with grave doubts that I first addressed a great outdoor audience at Pendleton [Oregon] from the courthouse steps, but the respectful, interested attention and good will of that large mixed crowd was the best argument that could be made for the co-operating of men and women in public affairs. In every place I spoke it was just the same."

She wrote further: "Leaving a banquet hall loaded with flowers to visit the bedside of a pioneer suffragist, I shall never forget the half humorous, half earnest way this noble woman, who had suffered for the cause with Susan B. Anthony and Elizabeth Cady Stanton, said, 'It was very different forty years ago. There were no flowers then. My bouquets were cabbages and brickbats and—eggs.' "

She recounted another anecdote: "One prominent society woman in Portland [Oregon], whose influence was very much desired by the suffragists, was at a tea given for me. She was very much in doubt about taking a stand for suffrage although her husband actively favored it. I asked her this question: 'If the passage of the amendment next fall depended on your support of it, what would you do?' Without hesitation, she replied, 'If the responsibility of really deciding it was on me, I should be for it, because I know it is right and just and bound to come, only I dread it, and would rather not vote myself.' Then and there she was surrounded and converted and made to see that her duty was just the same as though she knew that she held that balance of power. For no woman knows but that her influence may settle a question."

Belle cited yet another example. "An Oregon farmer avowed that the old antisuffrage argument that women would vote just like the men had really converted him to the cause. 'You see,' he said, 'I got to thinking about it, and it occurred to me that if that is so it will double the vote of the stable population. There are thousands of floating votes here in Oregon among men—unmarried men—who come and go and have no responsibilities and no real interest in the state. If women vote, it will double the representation of the family, and will tend to increase the influence of the country people over that of city folks.' "

In her column of August 31 Belle came out for prison reform and against capital punishment: "Investigation and experience have proved what common sense ought always to have told us, that solitary confinement, or worse, promiscuous herding of criminals in idleness and under harsh conditions, makes the savage more savage, and destroys the hope of improving those not wholly degraded . . . Capital punishment is a survival of barbarism and its existence is contrary to the best thought and practice of modern civilization."

Belle used her column to stimulate other women to take action on a variety of issues. Typhoid fever was still a dangerous, often fatal disease. Belle wrote numerous columns on various techniques to combat the "typhoid fly" in the home, on the farm and in the workplace. She also alerted readers to the dangers of lead poisoning in the workplace and in food preparation. She was constantly concerned about good nutrition and healthy food preparation. She wrote on April 19, "Imagine the effect upon your child's stomach of a bakery jelly roll in which the jelly is a mixture of glucose colored with coal tar dyes and flavored with synthetic ether! This is not uncommon and (unfortunately) the roll tastes particularly good."

She also wrote of a packing house scandal: "The public was horrified by tales of ancient and odoriferous scraps of flesh rejuvenated by dyes and deodorizers to serve as sausage and potted ham. The meat inspection law must be strengthened and corrected so that it can never be interpreted to serve the packer's interests rather than the people's. American consumers must keep after their representatives in Congress. It is especially up to the women of the United States to bring this about."

She alerted readers in her column of September 7 to a revision of the Food and Drug Act making it a punishable offense "if a package or label shall bear or contain any statement, design or device regarding the curative or therapeutic effect of any ingredients therein which is false or fraudulent." Then she commented, "The Law should go a step further and forbid all fraudulent claims in advertising as well as labeling of drugs. I am told that in Germany the government forbids false advertising of any kind and the law is strictly enforced."

One of her long-term goals had been the formation of a Federal Children's Bureau. She stated in her column of October 5, 1912, "For years the federal government has spent enormous sums of money annually gathering and disseminating information about the diseases of cattle, hogs and horses, but has done nothing to prevent the great waste of child life."

She pointed out "twenty percent of all deaths are children under one year. One quarter of all blindness in children can be prevented. The greatest cause of injury to children in factories is because of their inability to read instructions. Critics say the Children's Bureau will interfere with the personal management of children and infringe on the liberty of parents but the Children's Bureau is designed simply to give information on subjects pertaining to child welfare."

She reported that "after months of waiting for the necessary appropriations, the Children's Bureau, created by Congress last April, has at last begun its work. The director is Miss Julia Lathrop, long a co-worker with Miss Jane Addams at Hull House. Miss Lathrop is charged by the law with the task of investigating and reporting upon all matters pertaining to the welfare of children, especially the questions of infant mortality, the birth rate, orphanages, juvenile courts, desertion, dangerous occupations, accidents, disease, employment and legislation affecting children. Realizing the increasing problems affecting child life arising out of the growth of industrial centers and the overcrowding in cities, with their attendent ills, earnest-hearted men and women have for a long time urged the establishment of such a bureau."

At this time Belle undertook with Elizabeth Evans a twelve-day tour of Wisconsin, campaigning for woman suffrage. This pioneering venture was described in a column on Belle's page written by Elizabeth. Her article started with the note that during a twelve-day tour of the state, Belle spoke thirty-one times in fourteen different counties.

Elizabeth described one stop at a county where a torrential rainstorm occurred as Belle started her talk: "The speaker had gotten but a little way when the flood gates of Heaven were opened and all its waters were let loose! So fiercely did the rain beat upon the roof of the grandstand and upon the umbrellas, that the speaker's voice could not be heard. So she seized the secretary's megaphone and spoke through that, sometimes to the throng on the grandstand and sometimes to the circle of men who stood there on the race track soaking in the downpour, and ankle deep in mud and water.

"How they listened! And how they applauded! Mrs. La Follette gave her full talk without abridgment, speaking living words right out of the experience of her whole life. She pleaded for the home—for the better understanding, the closer comradeship and the fuller sympathy between husband and wife when they have public as well as private interests in common. 'Where do we find strife and division?' she asked. 'Why, in homes where the husband and wife have not had mutual interests, where they have grown apart and one has outstripped the other in development and is forced to seek companionship outside the house.' Then she pled for the children, for their education in citizenship when they heard public affairs discussed by their father and mother around the family board, saying the training of children is the peculiar province of women."

Then Belle asked, "But how can their mothers teach them to be good citizens when they have no knowledge themselves of public affairs? My boys often come to me to ask about this or that when they can't get at their father, and if I am able to answer their questions intelligently, is not that a good thing for them? Are they not so much the better prepared for citizenship?"

She concluded by pleading for the women themselves and "for the enrichment that comes into their lives when they think of their own homes as related to their larger home—the township, the state and the nation." She pointed out, "It is less than two generations that our universities and even our high schools have been open to women upon the same terms as men . . . Government is considered as men's exclusive province—a limitation that has narrowed the lives of the women, that has robbed the children, and that has reacted most injuriously upon the state."

Elizabeth ended the column by quoting Belle's plea to the men to support suffrage: "And, men of Wisconsin, don't you go back on me! If you should, I should be so disappointed, and so humiliated for our state!"

Then, Elizabeth wrote, Belle "reached out her hands to them beyond the dripping umbrellas and the men and women together burst into a great cheer."

At the start of 1913 the suffrage organization worked hard to pass a bill before the Senate Committee on Woman Suffrage. During January and February, Belle, Elizabeth and other women spoke at meetings in Washington and Baltimore. When Congress met in special session to discuss the bill, Belle had expected to head the homemaker's section of a parade on April 7. But Mary fell ill with scarlet fever and both she and Belle were quarantined in the top bedroom floor of their Washington home. Bob had to remain downstairs. Belle brought Mary all her meals, washed her, combed her hair. Mary admitted feeling "exceedingly happy" to have her mother all to herself.

Belle read to Mary during the day "with great feeling," from such classics as *The Mill on the Floss* and *Little Women* ("We both cried and cried," said Mary) and the novels of George Sand, Belle's favorite author. She also read the poems of Robert Burns, one of her favorite poets, "in a Scottish accent," though she was not as proficient as Bob, who with his keen dramatic sense read the poems as though a born Scotsman.

Since Belle could not appear for woman suffrage, she was represented by her two sons, who marched up Pennsylvania Avenue to the Capitol in a parade that included 531 women, two from each state and one from each congressional district. They carried petitions asking Congress to pass the suffrage amendment—Fola held the Wisconsin petition (she was such a feminist she used her maiden name her entire life). A group of senators and congressmen met them in the rotunda of the Capitol, where Bob was present to greet his daughter.

Senator George E. Chamberlain of Oregon presented a joint resolution proposing a constitutional amendment, known as the Susan B. Anthony Amendment, extending suffrage to women. It was referred to the Senate Committee on Woman Suffrage. When this committee granted a hearing on April 26, Belle was among the prominent speakers introduced by Dr. Anna Howard Shaw, president of the National Woman Suffrage Association. Belle's speech was recorded by the senate committee, giving it a place in senate annals.

She started by saying, "In this struggle for equal suffrage the real issue is not, it seems to me, whether all women are asking for the vote or whether all men are demanding it; but whether it is in the interest of the home, of society, of government, that the people as a whole shall participate in making the laws that govern them as a whole."

She pointed out that in "modern complex life government touches its every phase" and "roads, schools, streetcar service, gas, electric lights, markets, are all questions in which women primarily should be interested at least equally with men." She declared that when it came to national affairs, "I cannot think of a single important question that has been before the Congress of the United States in the last twenty-five years in which women have not been equally concerned with men," mentioning the pure-food law, the conservation of national forests, child-labor legislation and children's bureaus.

She stated: "Women should be interested and should understand the great economic questions. If the tariff in any way affects the cost of what we wear and what we eat, if the trusts and combinations have anything to do with the high cost of living, in that the price of the great staples like beef and sugar and oil and woolens and silks are fixed by monopoly, then women should know about it, because if that is true, the only way to remedy those wrongs radically is through national legislation . . . women's direct influence in legislation would supplement the work of men and make our government more regardful of the general human welfare."

She reported women do most of the buying, that the ninety percent of the $10,000,000,000 spent in the United States for food, clothing and shelter is spent by women. She said to the senators, "When we buy a gallon of oil, a yard of cloth, a pound of sugar, we are up against an economic problem the same as when those questions are considered by you in the United States Senate."

She said she did not expect any "great radical change because of equal suffrage—that is, any great radical, immediate change. It has always seemed to me very natural that women and men of the same family should have somewhat similar views on political questions, much as fathers and sons and brothers now do."

She pointed out that equal opportunities to women in education, which "met with much the same bitter opposition," did not suddenly change the status of society, "but who questions the powerful influence upon society today of the liberal education of women?"

These words brought applause from the gallery as did most of her points, including her concluding remarks in which she referred to Lincoln's definition of government in his Gettysburg Address, "that this nation shall have a new birth of freedom, and that government of the people, by the people, for the people, shall not perish from the earth."

She then asked: "And are not women people? Government is not a man's problem nor a woman's problem alone. It is their mutual problem. And it is only when women are given their share of responsibility in the solution of public questions that the affairs of government will be brought into the home for discussion. Not until then will government become a familiar subject, interwoven in the family life and understood as it must be if democracy in its best form is to endure."

The Senate Committee on Woman Suffrage unanimously recommended passage of the amendment on June 13. Suffragists, bringing petitions from every state bearing signatures representing almost 200,000 women and men converged on the capital July 31. The procession wound its way up Pennsylvania Avenue with members of the senate committee in one car. The women delivered their petitions to the senators at the Capitol, then went to the Senate galleries to hear the session.

The petitions were referred to the senate committee but no further action was taken. Belle expressed her frustration in her column: "This business of being a woman is, in many ways, much like the business of belonging to a despised race. Many a woman, finding intolerable the restrictions placed upon her by society, has obtained relief only in joining other women to set their sex free . . . in working with other women *for* women. In the suffrage movement many a discontented and unhappy woman has found peace and spiritual health. There is no tonic like loyalty."

Organizing women for political, social and economic action was a theme that ran throughout Belle's columns. On August 12, 1914, she reported that 1,000 telephone operators in Boston had formed a union. The women were asking for an eight-hour day, a full hour for lunch, a fifteen-minute rest every four hours of work and compensation at the rate of one and a half for overtime, including Sunday and holiday work. The wage scale was listed as six dollars a week for the first six months, eight dollars a week for the second year, and a dollar a week raise for each succeeding year. Belle pointed out the minimum living wage in Boston was between nine and twelve dollars a week.

A machine was revolutionizing office procedures in 1912—the typewriter. Belle realized the typewriter could be an economic plus for women. But there was considerable resistance to this expensive, noisy piece of equipment. Belle wrote: "Handwriting has always been hard for me. I remember my early struggle with my copy book. Try as I would, I could not make my letters neat and even. If I had my way, typewriters would be as common as sewing machines and cheaper, so as to be more available. Anyone can learn to use a typewriter and can acquire the up-to-date touch method with exercise and patience. If the thoughts of poets, novelists, scientists are made to reach our brain through the printed page, why not accept the typewriter?"

The La Follette family had to give up their home at 1864 Wyoming Avenue in 1913 because the owner wanted to live in it. They found a larger house at 3320 Sixteenth Street for $100 a month and this became their home for the next ten years. It had several spacious rooms for entertaining and Belle and Bob enjoyed the informal dances and parties the children held on weekends and during the holiday season.

Belle wrote Netha Roe on August 23 about Bob's failure to win the Republican nomination the year before: "In spite of the odds, I looked for a change and thought luck might be on our side just once. But the fight for better things is all uphill and luck is the other way. And what appalls me most is the thought that perhaps the results of these political movements just about measure the standards of the average man when put to the *test*. Bob never loses faith in the people—and I'm glad he does not. I wish I didn't. Like you, my faith in a *few* is what sustains me in these crises, which are such a strain on one's faith in humanity."

She described the anticipated move: "I am scurrying around trying to make the 'allowance' for papering over the cost of the move. We have decided not to put so much in another house as we have put into this one at our own expense. And we are likely to stick to this good resolution because of the *necessity*. Yours always, Belle."

Another financial burden was added when Bobbie left home to attend the University of Wisconsin. That night, September 19, his father wrote him in Madison, "No one wanted to go back to the house, so we drove until bedtime to drive away the 'lonesome devils.' You are close to our hearts, laddie." When Bobbie was elected president of his class, his father telegraphed, "Congratulations from Dad. Be nice to the fellows who were beaten and now remember what your real job is. With worlds of love I am yours to count on."

Following passage of the Wilson administration tariff bill in the fall, which reduced rates and which Bob supported, he felt free to arrange a brief speaking trip through the South and Midwest to earn money to pay for the move to the new house and to cover the *Magazine's* bills. A few hours before leaving he wrote Belle, in Boston speaking for suffrage: "Dear heart, I shall not see you till I come back about the tenth of November. By that time I'll have earned enough to beat the wolf for a while anyway. The big house seems lonesome without you."

While Bob was brooding alone in Washington, Bobbie was partying at the university in Madison. Though he knew Bob and Belle disapproved of fraternities, Bobbie wrote home about the joys of joining Beta Theta Pi. He described the late night dances where "everybody is doing the grapevine," his need for some "classy ties" from the "Young Men's Shop" in Washington and the agony of eight a.m. classes. He also failed a number of his examinations at the end of the semester. When this news reached Washington, Belle responded with a letter dated January 23, 1914:

"My beloved Robert, we were glad to hear from you. Mother's heart ached for her baby boy. She knew exactly how he felt over his exams. It was just the kind of fever she used to have and still has at times. But seriously, Robert dear, I do not see why you need suffer this way. You have on all other occasions such perfect command of your powers. I was ever a bashful young person and had to gain by slow degrees the confidence that you seem to have been born with. Do you not think you could rise above the fear that possesses you at the thought of an examination? Do try a few mental gymnastics and see if you can not be calm and clearheaded. That control would be a greater gain than to pass the examination.

"Mary has to go over her German again. But I think it is just as well. Miss Ruplee says it is the declensions that hold her back. She would pass her otherwise. She has a Good in History and English and her drawing teacher says Mary has real talent. She takes an hour a day in drawing. I think Mary has done very well on the whole and she has been happy in the high school group.

"I must dress for dinner. Wish you were going to eat with us. Remember us to all inquiring friends. Love ever, Mama."

Belle, in her January 17, 1914, column, deplored how "the suffrage jokes—cheap ones too—are received with laughter and applause in the House of Representatives." But suffrage was not the only cause she espoused. She started speaking out against the segregation of Negroes in the nation's capital. She took up cudgels in the case of a black woman employee of the treasury department, fired for sitting at a table assigned to white women employees.

Belle started her own investigation of the incident. She asked for a statement from treasury secretary William McAdoo. Instead, the director of the Bureau of Printing and Engraving responded: "It is a fact that in the lunch room there are six tables. Two of the tables were assigned especially for the use of colored girls for the reason that it would be better for them to associate together while eating their lunch. There had been no objection on the part of the colored girls, except for three who persisted in sitting at the tables occupied by white girls. After two of the white girls objected, a kindly suggestion was made that it would be best for them to occupy tables with girls of their own race. But as they persisted in disregarding the suggestion, it was necessary for me to give them positive directions to use tables assigned to colored girls."

Subsequently, one of the "colored" girls, Rosebud Murraye, was fired on the charge of insubordinate conduct. Belle then invited the girls to her house to hear their side of the story and wrote: "They had all obtained their positions under Civil Service examinations. Appointments are secured by merit only. Two had been employed by the Bureau of Engraving and Printing for eleven years, one for nine years. They had always eaten wherever they wanted."

The new lunchroom rules had been initiated by the Wilson administration. It was the first Democratic administration in sixteen years and Belle was certain that conservatives from the segregated South were responsible for the new rules. She wrote directly to both Secretary of the Treasury McAdoo and President Wilson appealing for a review of the charges against Miss Murraye. In her letter Belle reviewed the facts, then ended, "I should not presume to take your time for considering an individual wrong if the record did not appear to involve the larger question of human rights." President Wilson responded, through his secretary, that this was a treasury department matter. Treasury Secretary McAdoo refused to review the case.

Frustrated in her attempt to move the bureaucracy, Belle took to the speakers platform. At this time street cars in Washington were segregated. Belle addressed one meeting sponsored by the YMCA in Washington and another at the NAACP annual convention in New York. She reported in her column, "I called attention to the proof of enforced segregation in government service. I said that Negroes had submitted to discrimination in travel, in hotels, in public entertainments, in schools and in churches. That under conservative leaders they had remained silent when deprived of the ballot, depending on their economic and educational progress to bring them justice and recognition through a gradual evolution of public sentiment. But to have the United States government take a backward step, to have the colored line drawn in places that they have won on their own merit, to be humiliated, repressed and degraded at the capital of the nation by their own government is a body blow to hope, pride and incentive."

She summed up: "Continued violation of the fundamental human rights, touching a race that constitutes one-tenth of our citizenship, must ultimately degrade our standards, corrupt our ideas and destroy our sense of democracy. Equality is in no way a matter of social privilege. It is a matter of civic right."

Following these two meetings Belle received a flurry of hate mail. One letter castigated her: "This does not raise you very much in the estimation of decent white people. Don't do this again. For a white lady to address a Negro audience is out of place." Another: "You may call race segregation a disgrace, but it is not half as disgraceful to the white race as you are. It may be that you do not belong to the white race, just happened that you are a little light in color. [This is] Written by a real white person with no black stripe down the back like you." She received only a few letters commending her stand. Nonetheless she continued to speak out for equality and human rights both on the platform and in her column.

Belle wrote Bobbie at the university in Madison on January 30, 1914: "My dear Boy, Susan Brandeis came this afternoon and the children are having a rough house party for her, playing in the attic and dancing down the stairs. Another good letter from Fola this morning. She has not secured any platform work yet [speaking for suffrage] but she could hardly expect much response at first. I think it will come in spite of the slack times. Mid sent me his new book. It looks very good and with the other two makes quite a showing.

"Yesterday I went to Beltsville, Maryland, to speak to the Montgomery County Grange. It was a quarterly meeting and a fine crowd, chicken dinner and lots of good things to eat. I never enjoyed talking to any audience better. After the strain of New York and Philadelphia, I felt as though I had come home to my own kind and made the best speech I know how. I think I made a lot of converts. Phil met me at the train. He came out with two G's and two F's. 'Good' and 'Fair.' He has not had any coaching or coaxing and so I think he has carried his responsibility mighty well [Phil was in high school].

"Sunday evening I speak at a colored Methodist church. I have promised one more 'color line' talk in February. I like to get the practice. It gives me confidence for my next summer's work.

"Papa thinks he is better each day. But he does not feel equal to going to the Senate yet. He has a pain in his side, which is the result, the doctor says, of the effect of the poison in his system on the nerves. Your Papa watches the mail and wonders why we do not hear from Bobbie. His thought is ever with you and I hope that we hear from you soon. Heart full of love. Mother.''

"Boston Mother" Elizabeth Evans by now was an active participant in Belle's battle for racial and sexual equality. She was an associate editor of *La Follette's Magazine* and often contributed articles. She wrote, on February 2, 1914, of heading a delegation of working women to plead their case before President Wilson for receiving the same wages as men for the same work. She reported she said to the President, "You know very well there is no chivalry in industry. You must know that working women, because they are weaker than men, need the defense of the ballot even more."

She quoted him as replying, "Mrs. Evans, I have before stated my position. I am not free to act as an individual. I can only act with my party."

"Can you do nothing for us?" she asked.

"I cannot speak for my party," he said.

"Mr. President, we don't ask you to speak for your party," she said. "We ask you to speak to your party."

President Wilson did not answer.

Bob now persuaded Belle to take a month's cruise in the Caribbean as the guest of Elizabeth. For months he and Belle's close friends had been worrying about her heavy work load—speaking in the suffrage campaign, writing her weekly column and redoing an entire house. Efforts to persuade her to go away for a vacation failed until Bob offered to be with her for a few days in Atlantic City before she left on the cruise. Fola and the Roe family also joined them.

After Belle sailed from New York with Elizabeth, Fola wrote her father on April 13: "It was a pull for Mother to push off from the shore where her beloveds were." Four days before Belle had written a good-bye note to Bob, saying she did not fear the trip but that "if anything *should* happen I want you all to get the largest happiness out of life possible and whenever or whatsoever befalls me I know you will make up to each other what I should do for you."

She wrote of the start of her trip: "For six days we have had a perfectly glorious yet uneventful trip. How strange that life's joy and good fortune is so much less dramatic than its tragedies." They spent Easter Sunday off Cape Hatteras, then Monday, off St. Augustine. On Tuesday the Bahamas were "on our right," and early Wednesday they saw "the mountainous side of Cuba looming up in the distance." She marveled at the flying fishes: "At first glance they look like flocks of birds skipping over the waves. In the sunlight they shine like silver."

Then on to Jamaica: "A beautiful sight—the mountains looming up back of the crescent-shaped bay." They stayed in Kingston, "a strange city in a tropical island." She described the outskirts, where women, who lived in primitive dwellings with thatched roofs, "crushed the rock with hammers into small pieces suitable for the foundation of the fine macadam roads of which there are said to be 3,000 miles on the island. These women labor from seven to five at this work for twenty-five cents a day. And yet in some way I could not help thinking it was out of doors and more wholesome than the work of whirring factories."

Elizabeth, in a column for the *Magazine*, described the charm of San José, capital of Costa Rica—no sign of child labor, no drunken beggars in the street. She told how she and Belle decided to take a trip on horseback, led by a guide, up Mt. Irazu in Cartago, twelve miles to the east of San José. Mt. Irazu stood on the continental divide, 5,000 feet above sea level. Tourists were told that from its top they could see both the Pacific and Atlantic oceans.

Elizabeth praised Belle, who had been on a horse since childhood, as being "at her topmost mark throughout our whole strenuous undertaking, while I was so spent before we reached the summit that several times I was fain to lie down and die. I was so impracticed in the saddle that I could only cling on by the aid as it were of fingers and toenails. Probably it was fatigue and the high altitude combined that chilled me *inside* as if my very life were ebbing.

"And I think I could not have kept up but that Mrs. La Follette forced me to put on her sweater, and once we were on top of the mountain, gathered fagots and built a fire which warmed me back to life. Our guide, who had no more notion of waiting on womenfolk than of treating the horses as if they were made of flesh and blood, seemed to think his duties discharged when he had flogged and finally dragged our starved little beasts to the summit. Such inhumanity to dumb creatures I hope never to witness again.

"It was dark almost all the way up the mountain. The trees loomed black against the sky. It was 6:30 when we reached the edge of the crater. Its hollow was filled with a drenching cloud which obscured the outlook. But presently the mist shifted and we could look down into the awful chasm; while far away to the west across a fleecy ocean of cloud, was a line of dark blue mountain peaks, and

the pale glassy waters of the Pacific. We did not see the *two* oceans.
But it did not matter. What we did see was enough."

Belle described the next leg of the voyage, "The Canal Zone—A
Health Resort," in one of her columns. She wrote: "Today for the
first time in our touring trip Elizabeth and I have parted company.
She credited me with greater endurance in climbing Mt. Irazu. It is
only fair that I should confess she has far outstripped me in energy
and zest in this less invigorating climate. While I am lazily fanned by
Atlantic breezes, she is doing the island of Taboga, twelve miles from
the mainland in the Pacific, where Pizarro organized his famous ex-
pedition to Peru. . . . I know Elizabeth will come home with wonderful tales of what she has seen, but while I may allow I've been a
bit lonesome, I shall not admit that anything would compensate for
this day of leisure."

On arriving home Belle found Bob "in good spirits and in good
physical condition." He had taken a two- or three-mile walk every
night before going to bed and vigorous exercise in the morning. So
it came as a shock to her when he suddenly collapsed with a digestive
disturbance during an intense heat wave in June. For a few weeks his
doctors did not allow him to go to the Senate. They told him his
illness was due to overwork and predicted he would completely recover if he took care of himself.

While he was recovering, Belle left with Elizabeth to fulfill a
contract for a two-month trip on a midwestern Chautauqua circuit
to debate with antisuffragists the question of granting votes to women.
Bob wrote Fola, also away from home on a speaking trip for the
suffrage cause, "Mama found it hard to go—but she could not cancel
without giving some *big* reason and she smothered her feeling and
went out because it was necessary to protect me from publicity on
this—and publicity would of course come—if at all—in its worst and
most sensational form."

In the same letter, written in pencil on scratch paper, he said:
"Now dear, a word to *you* about myself—and this I feel so sensitive
about that you must not mention it to Mid, Gilbert or anyone else.
I *think* my trouble is due to toxic poisoning—I *believe* the doctors
think so. I am *certain* that I shall be my normal self in a few
weeks—but just now I am somewhat knocked out—partial loss of
feeling on one side—a little impaired motion on the other. I cannot
quite walk right—that is my left leg is a little off. Now these conditions
have improved vastly in the week since they first came on. Should

the use of my left leg improve as much in another week I don't think *it would be noticeable in my walk.*"

He went on to say the doctors told him his arteries were not hardened but soft and that the large area affected argued for poisoning "rather than some spot of *pressure.*" He concluded: "Beloved one, I have given it to you straight. . . . You are my girl and you will meet it whatever it is. But I feel it so keenly that I don't want anyone to know except the bone of my bone and the flesh of my flesh. I have had a half dozen of the best specialists and they all agree with what I have given you. Also they all agree that it will disappear in a few weeks or months at most. They say I have twenty years of reasonable work in me yet."

That summer he remained in the large house in Washington with Bobbie, who had desperately wanted to come home for Easter. He had written his father, "I *miss* home. I miss you, each one. I don't think I will ever be content except at home. I miss politics and the big men that come to the house. I got more out of one conference with Mr. Brandeis and John Commons than I will ever get out of a year's work in geology."

Bob had written his son there was no money to spend on transportation for vacations and Bobbie should send him brief daily reports on how he was doing at the university. But now, with Belle on tour, Bob welcomed his older son as company. Mary was spending the summer at Maple Bluff Farm and Phil was in England, thanks to the "butter and egg" money set aside by Grandma Case. She had bequeathed $300 to each of her grandchildren. Belle urged Phil to use the money for this trip. Bobbie had bought a Harley-Davidson motorcycle with his share.

On August 22 Bob wrote Belle it was "so lonesome" you could hear it "without whispering" and reported he lived on buttermilk, bran bread and Granola, per her advice. Bobbie answered the telephone, marketed and counseled with his father on important political decisions. Bob wrote Belle their older son was "one fine manly fellow, with a great head on him. He would make a smashing good writer and I think is a natural orator. . . . I wouldn't take anything for this summer with Bobbie."

In his letters Bob described his opinions on pending legislation, the political turns in Congress, the financial problems of the *Magazine*, the small events at home. He eagerly awaited the almost daily letters from Belle and the children. He worried over the hardships Belle endured on her long Chautauqua tour through a dozen states, speaking on hot days in crowded halls, as she reported in her column.

He wrote, "Poor Girl, this has been one awfully grueling summer. How you have stood up under it I don't understand. . . . My, but you are a great woman. I love you." He kept all of her and Fola's letters, which recorded the conditions of campaigning for women's suffrage on the Chautauqua circuit. He wrote Fola, "I cannot destroy letters that are a part of someone I love."

Bob's illness forced him to cancel a sorely needed $8,000 worth of speaking engagements in the vicinity of Washington. Thus further financial difficulty was added to his despair. He wrote Belle on August 2nd, "I'm so hard up that it doesn't make any difference any more. But I'm going to get strong and sound so I can work off my debts when I do." Frightened as much by his precarious financial condition as his physical one, Bob did try to follow his doctors' regime by limiting his activities to writing for the *Magazine*, taking his favorite drives in Rock Creek Park, and seeing only a few close friends like Brandeis, Roe, and Alf Rogers.

When Brandeis came to dinner on August 1 they had "a good old talk," he wrote Belle the next day. They discussed the "old reactionary crowd" now returning to power. Bob told Belle the President's "clearness of mind makes him cocksure and stubborn while his inexperience and ignorance of more than the merest smattering on the problems and his intense political partisan feeling renders him almost impossible. It just breaks one's heart to see him throw away chances for good things and swallow bad things with good labels, while the old Republican and old Democratic devils chuckle."

He said his talk with Brandeis confirmed his own views about the unsatisfactory situation in the Senate on the bill regulating the financial operation of railroads: "It makes me 'have' to get into the fight; and nothing but the fear of the Lord keeps me back—and I don't know how long that will be."

But the doctors were adamant in their orders that he not return to the Senate until fall. He was deeply disappointed he could not contribute directly to the pending legislation dealing with the trusts, railroads and other economic problems he had worked on for so many years. But he followed the proceedings closely, commenting on them in the *Magazine*.

Belle realized the money from her speaking tour was more important than ever, though she felt tired and often wished to give up and return home. She wrote Bob on July 2 from Troy, Ohio: "I often wonder if the nerve I have comes from long association with you or if it comes from within. Certainly I should not have believed I had it in myself alone to rise to the occasion as I have. I think the inner conviction that I am as nearly equal to the situation as almost anyone could be makes me calm and, if need be, *hard*."

She wrote to Bob and Bobbie from Mt. Gilead, Ohio, on August 1, "Beloved Boys," then "Burn this letter." She said: "I am tired and had started to bed thinking I would write you tomorrow but concluded I could not rest until I had written." She explained the manager of the Chautauqua tour wanted Elizabeth and her to let up "on suffrage debate," complaining there was "too much suffrage" in their speeches. She was furious at his open opposition to suffrage.

Belle sent Mary a four-page telegram on Mary's birthday, August 4, that ended, "I wish we might all be together for your birthday. But we all enjoy it in spirit. We are getting on very well now. We are up all night tonight and we have many bad schedules ahead. But I do not mind that part very much. My concerns are about you. Hugs and Kisses. Mamma."

On Belle's return, her column told how she felt after the two grueling months: "Oh, how glad I was to get home after filling sixty-four Chautauqua dates! We began at Blairstown, Pennsylvania, Saturday, June 27, finished at Lebanon, Indiana, Saturday, August 29." Exhausted but satisfied she had been effective, Belle returned to the open arms of her family.

CHAPTER

11

....

A Husband
Hung in Effigy

[1914–1917]

Belle read with anxiety the last week in July, 1914, newspaper stories reporting diplomatic tensions between Austria and Serbia, following the assassination of Archduke Franz Ferdinand at Sarajevo. During her lecture trip Bob wrote her, "The outlook for general European war is very black at this time. . . . We are all cavemen under the surface I guess."

Even Bobbie at the university wrote his mother on July 31, "The trouble in Europe is the absorbing topic at our little table," meaning at the fraternity house.

Phil was still in England as the war clouds gathered. Bob wrote his second son on August 4 that no one could "forecast the outcome of this thing" and commented it would be difficult for Phil "to do ancient towns and castles and highways and scenes of historic interest when you are in full view of the stage where with lightning-like rapidity is being performed the world's greatest drama." As Bob predicted, Phil deserted the tour of antiquities and instead managed to be admitted to a closed session of Parliament, then cut short his trip and took the first ship home.

Germany and England exchanged declarations of war on August 4 as the Kaiser's armies marched into Belgium. President Wilson proclaimed the neutrality of the United States. As official head of one of the powers that had signed the Hague Convention, established to keep peace, he offered to act in the interest of European peace.

Belle wrote Bob on August 8 from Michigan, where she was speaking on suffrage, "I suppose Washington is in mourning . . . What a shock Mrs. Wilson's death must be. How terrible this war. It does *seem* as though all this peace sentiment ought to avail us in some way. . . . I hear only praise for the President because he kept us out of war. Roosevelt's day is done, men say. It is strange how things work out."

La Follette's Magazine had an article in which Bob supported Wilson's stand on neutrality, calling the President's course "high statesmanship and splendid patriotism." Bob was convinced that if the United States were drawn into the war, special interests in banking and manufacturing would seize the opportunity to bypass Progressive legislation and set the struggle for democracy back at least a generation. President Wilson himself had stated, "Every reform we have won will be lost if we go into this war."

Both Bob and Belle were heartened by the belief that Wilson, the Democratic reformer, would keep America out of war. But the reports they had been receiving on the political situation in Wisconsin were upsetting. The Progressive Republicans had not been able to unite on candidates for the September primary, when candidates for governor, senator and various state officers were to be nominated. As a result, the Progressive candidates lost the primary race for governor.

This defeat was interpreted in the newspapers as a major one for Bob and the end of the Progressive movement in Wisconsin. Progressive leaders pleaded with Bob to come home and run for governor on a separate Progressive ticket. This he refused to do, heeding his doctor's advice to take a "rest cure" and follow a careful diet. He was also anxious about the *Magazine*, now over $10,000 in debt. He feared he might have to give it up if he had to cancel any lectures and curtail his income.

Now in its sixth year, with a circulation of almost 40,000, the *Magazine's* debt seemed impossible to meet. Maple Bluff Farm was mortgaged to the limit and Bob had no other personal security to borrow against except his life insurance. Brandeis thought he should give up the *Magazine* and concentrate all his energy on legislative work in the Senate. But Bob could not accept this. He believed his magazine made an important contribution to his work in the Senate through his editorials, which were quoted in many other publications. He knew over the years that publishing the roll calls on the nation's legislators had played a part in the defeat of reactionary candidates and the election of Progressive senators and representatives to Congress.

Belle suggested Bob should borrow enough on his life insurance to persuade his creditors to wait and let him pay the rest as quickly as he could earn it from speaking engagements now under contract.

He decided to do this and also reduce costs by turning the *Magazine* into a monthly.

After the Progressive candidate lost the Wisconsin election on November 5, Belle wrote Bobbie his father had "stood the strain almost better than we could expect" but that "his heart is sad and heavy. Of course nothing could ever make your papa believe that Wisconsin or the country is going to be always reactionary. He says one better die than lose faith. But the time ahead at best looks short to people of our age. It is a great comfort to feel that you children will be ready to do your part."

Belle assumed her children, immersed in Progressive politics from an early age, would carry on the battle for the ideals of American democracy. Fola, the superb student and professional actress who used her talents to speak out for women's right to vote, had not disappointed her. Bobbie was next in line.

Belle wrote Elizabeth Evans telling her the *Magazine* would be changed to a monthly beginning with the next issue: "When I suggested to Bob this morning that we quit it altogether, he said, 'Well, if I do I will announce that I am going to quit politics altogether.' "

In her column on October 17, 1914, as war was waged in Europe, Belle wrote of what the Germans meant in her life. She explained that Sauk County, where she grew up, "was strongly German," and she had developed "a faith in the German character and regard for German people which has never been shaken."

She spoke further of what was on her mind: "What thoughtful person does not shudder at the idea of one nation conquering another? This idea that war is the only way of settling differences among nations is a survival of the dark ages. . . . It is folly to try to place the blame for the war. In the last analysis Society is to blame for *tolerating* war."

She added that she confessed "to the belief that women should have a direct vote in the control of affairs. Women produce human life and war destroys it. If women had a larger voice in the counsels of nations, there would be no war slogans, no dreams of empire which could lead to the great sacrifices of life, of which woman alone knows the real value."

In this column Belle reported on a group of Boston women who made rubber stamps that proclaimed "Make war on war. Advocate worldwide disarmament and an international court, properly policed." This same group also produced a printed postcard to be sent to President Wilson, stating: "I hereby register my protest against war and call on my government to work with all governments toward world-wide disarmament and an international court of justice, properly policed, because I believe that this alone can secure that absolute necessity of civilization . . . Worldwide Peace."

Bob's "rest cure" worked once again and he was now back on the lecture circuit and earning money to meet the pressing debts of the *Magazine*. He traveled in Texas, Iowa, Michigan, and Illinois as Belle remained in Washington with Mary, who was attending school there. Bobbie, to his parents' dismay, was continuing to have difficulties with his studies. On November 7 Bob sent his son a series of postcards with the request for brief daily reports that would put it "up to you each day *to look yourself in the face* and take stock of what you have *done that day*."

Bob wrote Bobbie again on November 18 describing how hard *he* once had to work to earn money to go to the same university. He told how he hauled a load of wood twenty-two miles instead of buying it, sawed wood, drove the farm horse team hitched to a lumber wagon, milked the cow—"four years of the hardest kind of work. . . . It seemed tough when I looked about and saw other boys having it easy, nothing to do but get their lessons." He pointed out that his son did not have to do "outside things" to attend the university.

He pleaded with Bobbie "to make yourself do your *job*, and do it better than any man in your class. Do it so that the faculty, your classmates, your fraternity will all have to say, 'Bob La Follette is the ablest man in his year. He proves that the second generation can be better than the first'. . . . I love you, Bobbie, and I'm bound you shall be a *winner* on your *own* mettle. You are just getting into form. Keep it up. Yours always and always, Dad."

But, despite their pleas, Bobbie was unwilling or unable to meet his parents' great expectations for him in the classroom. Belle was so concerned she took the unprecedented step of going to Madison to spend a few days sitting in on Bobbie's classes and talking to his professors. All agreed Bobbie was capable of doing the work. But he seemed disinterested in the subject matter and worse, his professors told Belle, he was not applying himself to his studies. For Belle, this was no excuse. She insisted Bobbie buckle down and send the daily postcard report of his progress. By late November, the postcards contained Bobbie's complaint he was feeling ill and "rotten."

While Bob was away, Belle heard the President's message on

December 8, 1914, delivered to a joint session of the Sixty-third Congress. In it he declared the United States was a champion of "peace and concord" and "we never shall have a large standing army." She reported in her column, "His peace utterances met with a great wave of approval which found expression in tears as well as applause. However divergent the views may be of its policies, few will question that the Administration's ideals of peace have kept us out of war."

She attended a mass meeting of 3,000 women on January 10, 1915, at the New Willard Hotel in Washington, where the Women's Peace Party was formed. Jane Addams was chosen chairman. Belle wrote in her column: "The purpose of the organization is to secure the united influences of the millions of women eager to join forces against the destruction of war. . . . If we cannot stop war, we can voice our protest and arouse the people to demand that civilized nations, like individuals, instead of deciding their differences by mutual slaughter, shall submit their disputes to an international tribunal."

She quoted the resolution that formed the organization: "We women of the United States, assembled in behalf of world peace, do hereby demand that war should be abolished. We understand that the planned-for, legalized, wholesale human slaughter is the sum of all villainies.

"As women we are especially the custodians of the life of all ages. We will no longer consent to its reckless destruction.

"As women we are called upon to start each generation onward toward a better humanity. We will no longer tolerate that denial of reason and justice by which war renders impotent the idealism of the human race.

"Therefore we demand that women be given a share in deciding between war and peace in all the courts of high debate.

"So protesting and so demanding, we hereby form ourselves into a national organization to be called the Women's Peace Party."

The program included 1) the immediate calling of a convention of neutral nations in the interest of early peace; 2) limitation of armaments and the nationalization of their manufacture; 3) organized opposition to militarism in the United States; 4) education of youth in the ideals of peace; 5) democratic control of foreign policies; 6) the further humanizing of governments by the extension of the franchise to women.

Belle commented in her column that only one newspaper, the *New York Independent*, gave any coverage to the founding of this organization. She also said, "We rejoice that the voice of women is to be heard against the 'greatest scourge of mankind,' for all wars are primarily waged on women and children."

Bob offered a resolution on February 8, which he and Belle hoped would help the President maintain neutrality and achieve an early peace. The La Follette Peace Resolution, as it became known, called for a conference of neutral nations to seek "an early cessation of hostilities" in Europe by issuing a joint offer of mediation to the warring nations. Bob thought this would hasten the return of peace and also believed it would lead to a more permanent international cooperation.

His resolution suggested the conference consider rules for limiting armaments and nationalizing the manufacture of military and naval equipment, as well as the regulation of exports of war supplies from one country to another. The resolution also called for the establishment of an international tribunal to pass upon international disputes and proposed that the conference consider plans for a federation of neutral nations to safeguard the peace of the world.

The resolution was forerunner of the legislation that created the League of Nations. The resolution received newspaper attention as editorials contained comments on its wisdom. The *New York Evening Post* described it as "a move in the right direction that would show what power we still believe to reside in moral forces." The *Baltimore Sun* said the resolution would meet an "immediate need." Many believed the plan would appeal to President Wilson, since it was in accord with his plea for neutrality, but he took a stand against it. The resolution was referred to the Foreign Relations Committee but there was no hope of action without the President's approval.

From the university in Madison Bobbie wrote that he was on academic probation but determined to do better. Belle responded the same day, February 5, 1915: "Dear Laddie, It is too bad you should suffer so from the inhibition of fear. I think it is the result of habit—because of lack of thorough preparation. You are passing through the nightmare stage. It will take time to outgrow the ugly dream and it will be an enormous relief when you are no longer haunted by fear. We all know you will win and we are proud of your pluck and spirit and I am not worrying about the outcome, only my heart aches for my bonny boy and I wish I could do something for his hurts and bruises. But I know he will get over them and perhaps be the stronger for the tribulation he has experienced.

"I know it sounds a bit like baby talk, but although you will be twenty tomorrow, there trudges beside you, in mother's memory, a beautiful sturdy little boy with golden curls and big blue eyes with long curling lashes. He wears a red sweater and red stocking cap and corduroy pants with leather leggings. He is, oh, so wise and understanding and full of energy and determination, such a gentleman! I have never doubted what kind of a man he would make.

"Good night my boy. Our arms are around you and our hearts beat with yours. Love ever, Mother."

Two weeks after the adjournment of the Sixty-Third Congress, Bob left Washington for a speaking trip that took him as far west as Iowa and North and South Dakota. On his way back in April, he stopped off in Madison and was alarmed to discover Bobbie ill with a streptococcal infection that had developed after an attack of tonsillitis. The physicians there decided he should return with his father to Washington and son and father arrived there April 12. Though Bobbie's health improved at first, the infection soon flared up again.

On April 16, former President Roosevelt in an interview in the *Chicago Herald* called the Women's Peace Party "silly and base" and said it was influenced by "physical cowardice" and "an ignoble abandonment of national duty." Belle responded in her column, saying the former President "can't see beyond the settling of international differences by war. The Women's Peace Party asks for settlement by mediation, conciliation and arbitration. And we answer Mr. Roosevelt that the rights and wrongs of the great war now raging are but incidents of the great evil of war itself."

The British ship *Lusitania* sailed from the port of New York on May 1. That same day an American tanker, the *Gullflight*, was torpedoed by a German submarine. An advertisement had appeared in many American newspapers in which the German embassy warned of the risk of traveling on the ships of Great Britain and her allies through waters Germany had declared a war zone.

On May 7, without receiving any warning it was under attack, the *Lusitania* was sunk off the coast of Ireland by a German submarine. The ship went down eighteen minutes after being torpedoed and 1,198 of the passengers and crew, including 128 Americans, lost their lives. The American public was profoundly shocked.

Feeling was divided as to how the United States should respond to the loss of American lives. Some pointed out the *Lusitania* was a British ship traveling through a war zone and that those who sailed on her knew they assumed a risk. Former President Taft counseled patience and reminded Americans war was not the only way to hold a nation accountable. But ex-President Roosevelt and others, critics of President Wilson's policy in Europe, clamored for immediate action.

Colonel Edward M. House, adviser and personal representative of the President, who had been in London on a confidential mission for Wilson when the *Lusitania* was torpedoed, was quoted as saying, "We shall be at war with Germany within a month." On May 7 he cabled the President, "We can no longer remain neutral spectators."

Bob left Washington to deliver fifty more lectures and Belle wired him a daily medical report on Bobbie. She telegraphed on May 5 in Nashville that Bobbie's temperature was 100 and a half, the same as the day before, but the doctor considered him better and there was no "return of depression." She also wrote, "Family lonesome without Dad."

On May 31 she telegraphed him in Hopkinsville, Kentucky, that the doctors planned to remove Bobbie's tonsils. On June 17, she wrote him in Providence that Bobbie did not seem well, "his leg appeared to hurt worse and I noticed three or four new red spots on his arms," when she gave him a bath. She added the doctor did not seem alarmed as long as Bobbie's temperature stayed normal. She also mentioned another matter that caused anxiety, saying she had found an envelope as big as a book containing unpaid bills and "nearly had heart failure." She ended the letter, "I am sending you a memorandum of them. In spite of your wonderful courage, which I never cease to admire and wonder at, I know it must take the gimp out of you to be always under such a load. Must go now. Yours, Belle."

The medical reporting on Bobbie continued on and off for the next four years as, at times, he fought for his life against a virulent streptococcus infection that would not abate.

Bob was speaking in the small town of Humboldt, Tennessee, on June 18 when he received news from a local reporter that William Jennings Bryan, dedicated to maintaining peace, had resigned as secretary of state in a dispute with the President over the contents of a note Wilson intended to send Germany. Bryan believed the note would lead to war.

That same day Belle wrote Bob she had "never known such political excitement as that stirred up by Bryan's resignation." She said that though she thought "the Washington folks" all seemed anti-

Bryan, she could not believe the President expected the country to go to war.

Later that month in her column Belle reported on the International Conference of Women held in the zoological garden of The Hague in Holland, "a unique event." For the first time in history, and "while a colossal war was raging, women from belligerent and neutral countries assembled to voice their protest against war and all that makes for war." Jane Addams was elected president of the conference. Resolutions were passed similar to those of the Women's Peace Party and the Women's International League for Peace and Freedom was formed, with Belle as a charter member. The League still exists today.

Bobbie did not return to Madison to finish his sophomore year, so severe was his streptococcus infection. It affected his muscles and lymph glands, causing swelling and constant pain. Though there were intervals of improvement, he went for months with a temperature as high as 105 and spent most of the summer in bed in Washington or at Maple Bluff Farm. At the time there were no antibiotics and this infection often proved fatal.

Bob wrote home almost every day. Having suffered from so much illness himself, Bob probably identified closely with his elder son. He wrote on June 29, "Bobbie, this has been a year of great disappointment to you. A bitter, trying, gruelling year. But laddie, it has been the year of your greatest growth, your greatest development of character and strength, and power and patience. . . . A fellow takes stock of himself—in a long stretch of sickness—as he never has before. He is tied up with himself. He cannot get away. He has to talk it out face to face with all his foibles, his mistakes. I think it is the one time when a fellow obeys the mandate, 'Know Thyself.' You have been doing the biggest and bravest and hardest things of your whole life since you were sick. It will all count in your larger growth."

From Arkansas Bob wrote Belle he found the women were "alive for suffrage" and "making the men pay attention." He said he was surprised to find nearly all the Southern Republicans were Progressive and that people were aware he had supported a number of Democratic measures. People wanted to "adopt" him, he told her.

Belle replied the family was glad "to feel your message is getting across and that you are awakening another section of our country to civil consciousness. . . . As I see it, you and Bryan have a distinct place in history because of your power to arouse the plain folks—who are the basis of democracy—to a sense of patriotic responsibility to the work of our time. In addition, you have your constructive legislative record, which will stand out more and more clearly as years go by. How much greater than merely being President. . . ."

Bob returned home by December 7 to attend the joint session of Congress and hear the President deliver his annual message. Wilson now reversed the policy he had advocated the previous year. He supported legislation providing for a strong preparedness program, which Roosevelt and other critics of Wilson's foreign policy had been demanding since the early months of war in Europe. The President also asked for immediate enactment of an espionage law. Bob was against all this, believing there were other ways to settle international troubles. But more American lives had been lost on ships, and sentiment in Congress had been steadily growing to take significant steps.

Bob announced his candidacy for the next presidential election on February 22, 1916, at a meeting of the Progressive Republicans in Madison. He explained he was a candidate for the same reasons he had been in 1908 and 1912. In presenting his program he advocated the nationalization of the manufacture of all munitions of war; an embargo on the export of arms and ammunition and a conference of neutral nations to cooperate for peace among nations and to consider the establishment of an international tribunal for the settlement of international disputes. All these issues were taken from the platform of the Women's Peace Party.

At first the returns from the Wisconsin primary indicated there might be a divided delegation. But in the final returns Bob received 110,064 votes while the next-closest rival, Governor Emanuel Lorenz Philipp got 70,813 as delegate at large. Bob returned to Washington to hear President Wilson announce that the torpedoing of the unarmed French channel ship Sussex, on which three Americans had been injured, might mean war.

Wilson sent an ultimatum to Germany on April 18 threatening to sever diplomatic relations unless Germany at once abandoned "its present methods of submarine warfare against passenger and freight-carrying vessels." It was generally understood this ultimatum meant war unless Germany complied. Germany agreed to limit submarine attacks.

In her May column, Belle discussed an attack made by former President Roosevelt on the Women's Peace Party. He had advised "every wise and upright man and woman" not to have anything to do with the movement until the people who advocated the platform "hold a meeting specifically to denounce the invasion of Belgium by Germany and to demand that in the interests of peace the United States do what it can to put a stop to these wrongs." Belle's answer was that mediation rather than invasion was the way to settle disputes.

Through the winter and spring of 1916 Belle and Bob followed with intense interest and increasing indignation the bitter controversy over the confirmation of their friend Brandeis as an associate justice of the Supreme Court. A vacancy occurred when Justice Joseph R. Lamar died on January 2. Bob was in Wisconsin but returned to Washington when Attorney General Thomas W. Gregory sent for him. Gregory believed Bob could help persuade Wilson to name Brandeis to the Court. Pointing out that both conservative Democrats and Republicans would oppose the liberal Brandeis, Gregory asked Bob if there were enough Progressive Republican votes to assure Brandeis's confirmation if he were appointed. Bob canvassed the senators, then reported to Gregory it would be safe to assure the President that though a strong fight would be made against Brandeis, enough votes could be mustered to confirm his appointment.

The President sent the Brandeis nomination to the Senate on January 28. Two days later Bob wrote Phil, "We are all very happy over the Brandeis appointment. I had something to do with it—(Sub rosa on this). Will tell you when we meet. There is going to be a big fight over the confirmation. *But he will be confirmed.*"

Hearings were held on the nomination, under consideration before the Senate Judiciary Committee for four months. Brandeis was the first Jew selected to the highest court of the land and much anti-Semitism was directed against him. Through editorials in the *Magazine* Bob reviewed Brandeis's long service in the cause of social justice and denounced attacks originating with the country's financial interests, "organized as never before to defeat a judicial appointment." Their campaign, Bob asserted, had "descended to the low level of widespread defamation and falsification of a long and honorable private legal career." He said the people of the United States owed "a great debt to President Wilson for this appointment, that in Brandeis he selected the ablest and truest and best-equipped servant of this day and generation for this high service."

Though several Progressive Republicans were absent at the final Senate vote, Brandeis was confirmed on June 1, 47 to 27. The night before the confirmation Belle wrote Alice Brandeis in Boston: "I am thrilled with the thought that Louis is to be confirmed tomorrow and Monday he will take his place on the bench. . . . As soon as Louis is a member of the Court his enemies will take to cover. I suppose some of them will be claiming they made him judge. The fight has been a bitter desperate one but it will end with the oath of office. There is that advantage over a political position."

She urged Alice to come to Washington for the ceremony on June 1, saying, "We will have a quiet dinner. Quiet to the outside world but we will draw the shades and dance on the table and do whatever we feel like doing in the way of jubilation."

To the end of her life Mrs. Brandeis remembered with pleasure this "quiet dinner" at the La Follette home on the evening her husband became a justice of the Supreme Court. In the years ahead he would gain fame for his decisions, which all had the aim and effect of extending democracy. They were also written in a language as eloquent as has ever appeared in judicial decisions.

Bob enjoyed a second victory that March, one that represented years of work—passage of the seamen's bill. His interest in this bill dated from the December day in 1909 when Andrew Furuseth had walked into Bob's office in the subbasement of the Capitol. In his autobiography Phil paints a vivid picture of Furuseth, president of the International Seamen's Union:

"Andy, as we always knew him was a tall, raw-boned Norwegian with a weather-beaten face, lined, Dad said, as if it had been 'clawed by an eagle.' He had a beaked nose and fearless eyes. Andy never married. He had gone to sea as a lad, and out of his meager pay he had bought books—history books—and absorbed them into the warp and woof of his being. 'Andy,' Dad used to say, 'knows more history—ancient, medieval and modern—and can apply it more pointedly to our times than any man I have known.' "

Furuseth had arrived in Washington years before Bob's first election to the Senate. He had lived on the same wage as that paid the janitor in the union headquarters in San Francisco. Furuseth walked the corridors of the Capitol, calling on any member of Congress who would listen to his plea. He was seeking to free seamen from what was, for all practical purposes, a form of slavery. Once signed on a ship, a seaman was chattel.

Phil once asked, "Andy, what is courage?"

"Courage. Courage." Andy hesitated for a moment, then said thoughtfully, "If a man understood how short human life is and what little progress we have made in bringing out the good in human beings and how eagerly the evil in us breaks forth; if he understood that the earth is a tiny speck in a limitless universe and that the earth in due time will die like unnumbered planets before us have died; knowing all this, if he has real courage, he'll spit in the face of destiny and go on fighting on the side of the angels."

Bob presented his seaman's bill in 1914, a bill that directly challenged the worldwide system of seamen's virtual servitude. It provided greater safety for both crew and passengers. After much debate, late in the afternoon of October 23, the La Follette seaman's bill was passed without a roll-call vote.

At that point the opposition shifted from Congress to the state department and White House. President Wilson had supported the bill verbally and in writing but the pressure on him not to sign, emanating especially from foreign shipping interests, was fierce. The short session of Congress was to end at noon on March 4, 1915, and if the bill was not signed, Bob would have to start all over again the next session. He asked for an appointment with the President, which was set for March 2. Furuseth had not been included in the invitation to the White House but Bob took him along. He asked President Wilson to listen to Furuseth for ten minutes.

Phil wrote, "Dad told us later that Andy made one of the most eloquent pleas he had ever heard. He got down on his knees and clasped Wilson's knees as, with tears in his eyes, he pleaded for freedom for the men who went down to the sea in ships. Dad said that as Andy talked, both Wilson and he had tears rolling down their cheeks. The next morning Wilson's secretary, Joseph Tumulty, phoned Dad and told him the President had phoned him and said, 'Tumulty, I have just experienced a great half-hour, the tensest since I came to the White House. That man La Follette pushed me over tonight on the seamen's bill.' "

The March issue of the *Magazine* carried a long cover article, the happy end of Furuseth's twenty-one year struggle to pass a seamen's bill. The article was headlined, *The American Sailor a Free Man*. It described the new legislation, which standardized the sailor's skill levels, limited the number of hours of uninterrupted work and provided for better living conditions on shipboard—more food, more water, more light and air, larger and more sanitary sleeping and living quarters. Also important for crew and passengers, the act required every vessel leaving an American port bound for a foreign country to carry lifeboats sufficient to accommodate at least seventy-five percent of those on board, and life rafts for the remaining twenty-five percent. These were the gains for which Bob had fought.

The year 1916 was a presidential election year and Belle, Bob, Bobbie, Mary and Justice Brandeis and his wife, listened to reports of the sessions of the Republican National Convention in Chicago, which nominated Charles Evans Hughes. In those days, before radio, the news was telegraphed and then telephoned across the country. As had been anticipated Wilson was renominated by acclamation on June 15 at the Democratic convention in St. Louis.

Bob was running again for the Senate this year and since it was a presidential election year, the campaign centered on national policies. The issue of war or peace became the main theme. The Democrats emphasized Wilson's reelection would keep the United States out of the European war.

The night of the election, November 7, as they had so often done, Belle, Bob, Bobbie, Phil, Mary, Alf Rogers and a few other intimate friends spent the evening before the wood fire in the dining room at Maple Bluff Farm. Bob's return to the Senate was assured. Wilson's election was in doubt for several days but he eventually won.

Bob considered his own reelection by an overwhelming plurality, the largest ever received by a Wisconsin candidate, to be a mandate to hold steadfastly to his course against war. He carried 69 of the 71 counties in what was a great personal victory. Throughout the country there was a Democratic landslide.

A week later Bob made a speech protesting a cut of $109,000 the Senate Appropriations Committee had made in funds for the Children's Bureau. He reviewed the work the Bureau had achieved under Julia Lathrop and pointed out the monies were earmarked to continue and extend an important study of the causes for the high death rate—one baby out of eight—among children in the first year of life. It had been shown, he said, this death rate bore a relation to the wages of fathers and the conditions under which babies were born.

In the midst of Bob's speech, President Wilson was escorted to the chair to address the Senate. From his seat in the front row of the center aisle, Bob heard the President's historic address in which he advocated "peace without victory." He stated the general conditions he thought would justify asking the American people to help "guarantee peace and justice throughout the world," a peace in which the rights of small nations were recognized as equal to those of the large ones. He asked for a world court to arbitrate future conflicts between nations.

When the President left the chamber Bob resumed his speech on the Children's Bureau. The roll was called and the appropriation saved by a vote of 31 to 17. That evening Julia Lathrop telephoned Bob and Belle to express her appreciation.

The morning papers on February 1, 1917, reported the receiving of a note from the German government announcing unrestricted submarine warfare would be resumed in the war zone except in certain lanes for a limited number of passenger vessels. No one knew what action President Wilson would take.

The following night, February 2, Bob wrote the family: "One cannot shake off the feeling that an awful crisis is impending. I have felt impelled to try and break through and see Wilson. But it is given out that he is locked up alone and seeing no one. . . . The headlines are blatant for war to begin. You can only stand and grimly wait for a chance to fight the devils off."

The next morning word was received at the Capitol that the President would hand the German ambassador his passport and would address a joint session of Congress at two o'clock. At that hour Bob sat directly in front of the President, who arrived promptly at two. Bob listened with anxiety and growing disagreement as he heard Wilson announce Germany's declaration had left him "no alternative consistent with the dignity and honor of the United States" but to break off diplomatic relations.

After he did this, the President invited neutral countries to take similar action but none did. All confined action to diplomatic protests against unrestricted German submarine activity in the war zone. This is what Bob and Belle thought the United States should have done.

When the Chicago branch of the Women's Peace Party passed resolutions asking for a conference of neutral nations, a referendum on war and the keeping of Americans out of the war zone, Belle wrote Bob calling his attention to the group's support of measures he was also advocating. Belle continued her work in Wisconsin with the Women's Peace Party by speaking at various meetings. After she addressed a gathering at the city library in Madison, her speech was reported critically in an editorial in the *Wisconsin State Journal*. Bob, who read it, wrote her on February 18, "Nothing matters so long as we are doing what is right. That's the only thing that lasts." A few days later he wrote saying he hoped the editorial would not make her so uncomfortable she would "pass up any invitations to speak. Let's have peace if we have to fight all Hell to preserve it."

Bob broke away for a while from a night session at the Senate on February 19 to go to the station to meet Bobbie, who was following Dr. Fox's advice to leave the severe Wisconsin climate for the winter. Each morning Bobbie and Bob went to work together. Bobbie had decided, now that he had recovered, not to return to the university for his junior year but work as his father's clerk. He would have access to the Senate floor and his assumption of office responsibilities would lighten his father's burden. The daily companionship of his twenty-two year old son proved a great comfort to Bob during this anxious period. It also helped compensate for the disappointment he felt at Bobbie's poor academic record. To an unusual degree, Belle said, Bob came to rely on Bobbie's clear thought, objective judgment and executive ability.

At a joint session of Congress on February 26, Wilson now asked for the power to arm United States merchant ships. Sitting as usual near the front of the chamber, Bob listened with arms folded across his chest. A friend noted Bob was so shocked at Wilson's demand that he "threw up both hands instinctively as though hope were gone."

The following day the armed ship bill, which would give the President the powers he wanted, was introduced in the Senate. Study of the bill convinced Bob it meant war. He thought it violated the letter and spirit of a fundamental provision of the Constitution, "which expressly vests the war power in Congress." It seemed to Bob the loss of life and tonnage on armed Allied merchant ships that had already occurred, showed that placing guns on merchantmen did not give adequate protection against submarines. Just two days before, the armed British merchant ship *Laconia* had been torpedoed twice and had gone down without firing a shot.

The bill had been drawn up by Wilson and presented six days before the session of Congress would automatically end at noon on March 4. Bob was convinced that in trying to force the bill through so late in the session, the President's aim was to be in a position to exercise sole power during the nine months before the new Congress met.

To Bob and Belle, Senator George W. Norris of Nebraska and other senators, the issue was fundamental to the preservation of democracy. When the Senate met on March 2 to debate the bill, Bob had a list of those ready to help defeat it. The time each would take to speak had been carefully calculated. Bob's was the last of eleven names on the list. All except Senator Harry Lane from Oregon were Progressive Republicans.

Only forty-nine hours remained until the automatic adjournment of the Senate at noon Sunday to consider the important legislation still pending. Bills carrying appropriations totalling $1,500,000,000, including the largest Army appropriation bill ever presented, with a provision for universal military training, had not yet passed the Senate. The Administration insisted the Senate pass the armed ship bill before adjournment.

Bob's strategy was to try to block the bill and force it over to the new Congress, which would gain time for antiwar sentiment to register on Congress. But this plan became more difficult than he foresaw. The publication in an exclusive Associated Press dispatch of the "Zimmerman telegram" on March 1, the day the armed ship bill first came up in the Senate, shifted the emphasis of debate. Bob was convinced the release of the telegram had been carefully timed and published to inflame public opinion and influence Congress. The telegram was signed by Arthur Zimmerman, the German foreign secretary, and carried instructions to von Eckhardt, the German ambassador in Mexico City. It announced the German government's intention of simultaneously returning to unrestricted submarine warfare on February 1 and of trying to keep the United States neutral. If neutrality could not be maintained and war resulted, Germany offered to make an alliance with Mexico—Germany would give financial support and help Mexico reconquer her lost territory in New Mexico, Texas and Arizona.

The telegram made Bob's fight against the bill far more difficult. Newspapers that had stood by him over the years condemned his current stand. The *Milwaukee Journal* accused him and his colleagues of misrepresenting Wisconsin.

The debate began on March 2, after a motion to take up the bill was agreed to by a vote of 64 to 15. Bob voted nay, as he continued to do until adjournment. According to customary procedure Senator William Joel Stone for Missouri, chairman of the Foreign Relations Committee, would have been in charge of passage of the bill but he broke with the President and joined Bob's small group opposing it. Stone had consistently fought American entrance into the war.

A filibuster started as the Senate met for its final twenty-four hour session. Belle sent a telegram to Bob: "My faith in the clearness of your vision, in the rightness of your action, was never stronger than in this hour of national peril. Strength be with you."

The session continued all night. Bob stayed at the Capitol, where he had two offices. The one in the subbasement looking out on a small grass plot was usually occupied by his secretary and close friend, John J. Hannan, and his clerk Grace Lynch. The other office, directly above, was his private office, where he slept that night as best he could. He expected to speak Sunday morning. Bobbie, as his father's assistant clerk, and Hannan stayed awake all night, kept watch of what took place and then informed Bob.

One by one the Progressive senators took the floor to speak against the bill, to warn of the certain involvement in war that would follow its passage. Senator Norris preceded Bob, the final speaker. While Norris addressed the Senate, Bobbie brought his father volumes of material he intended to use, plus stacks of telegrams supporting his position. Tempers were frayed, tension ran high in the Senate. About five a.m. Sunday morning, March 4, Bob received a note warning him the presiding officer would refuse to recognize him when he rose to speak.

Bob asked Bobbie to bring him his traveling bag. Bobbie knew it contained a small revolver Bob carried when on the road. Bobbie removed the revolver before he brought his father the bag. Norris finished at 9:30 a.m. and Bob rose to speak. He was not recognized, as he had been warned. He strode to the center of the floor, shouted, "I will continue on this floor until I complete my statement unless someone carries me off, and I should like to see the man who will try it!"

There was a rush from the Democratic senators and shouts for order. Senator Oliver James, a Democrat, was known to be armed. Republican Senator Harry Lane of Oregon, a doctor and a friend of Bob's, had equipped himself with a rattail file. He stood guard near James to protect Bob. Later he showed Bob the file, saying, "If you slip this file down inside a man's collar bone on the left side, you can reach his heart with one thrust and he will never move again. Ollie James, who was carrying a gun, started toward you with his hand under his coattails, but he never would have drawn that gun. I would have stopped him with this file. I was right within reach of him all the time."

The Democratic rush stopped before Bob could be harmed and the battle remained verbal. But the situation became even more tense as Bob refused to yield the floor. Bobbie, alarmed at the possibility of physical violence, sent his father a Belle-like note: "Daddy, I expect you to make your protest but there must be a limit to the lengths to which you go. You cannot afford to get into a physical argument or you'll be arrested by the sergeant at arms. You are noticeably and extremely excited. For God's sake make your protest and prevent passage of the bill if you like, but if previous question is made and sustained, do not try to fight the Senate physically." Unable to protect his father, he added, "I am almost crazy with strain."

Bob never did receive his chance to speak but by constantly bringing up "parliamentary inquiries" concerning his right to speak, and starting another debate about the fact one senator had spoken twice on the same subject on the same legislative day, a breach of rules, Bob managed to avoid a vote until the clock struck noon. The Senate had to adjourn immediately. At this time President Wilson entered the chamber to take the oath of office for his second term. He was furious.

After the presidential ceremony Bob went directly to his office in the Capitol with Bobbie and Hannan. There Bob found Gilbert and Netha Roe, Fola and Andy Furuseth. Bob said to Furuseth, "That bill meant war. I had only two choices. To resign or defeat it."

Furuseth put his arm around Bob, said, "Bob, they'll crucify you. But God bless you."

That evening Bob sent a night letter to Belle in Madison: "Fought it through to the finish. Feeling here intense. I must take the gaff for a time. But believe it will postpone aggressive action which would have resulted in our getting into war immediately until as I hope the crisis passes and we may in the providence of God be spared the awful catastrophe of entering this world war."

At the same time Belle was writing him from Maple Bluff Farm: "It is my heartfelt conviction that you have rendered the world the greatest service it has ever come to you to render and that you have used the power and opportunity that was yours for humanity and democracy. I could not and I cannot see how you could take any other course and I am filled with a deep sense of thanksgiving beyond all words to express."

She wrote Netha and Gil Roe on March 6, of Bob's victory: "Beloved friends, I am satisfied with one great big fact. Immediate war has been averted. There will be time now for second thought.

It may be that the world has gone mad and that the people of the United States are as eager to invest the President with autocratic powers as Congress seems to have been. But it is a great thing to have this respite, to be able to believe that we have not been dragged, or rushed, or befooled into war."

Belle may have felt relieved over Bob's defeat of the armed ship bill but she did not rest in her campaign for peace. In her column she urged men and women to send postcards to the President saying, "As a patriotic citizen of the United States, I am trusting you to settle the present crisis without war."

She also informed her readers, "The Senate military committee has reported favorably on the Chamberlain bill, which requires six months of compulsory military training for all young men from the ages of nineteen to twenty-six. In forty-one state legislatures, at this moment, there have been introduced bills of compulsory military training of boys in the public schools. Think of it! It is agreed among educators that military training is among the poorest methods for the development of youth. The action is automatic, stiff and repressive, totally opposed to the ideals of bodily exercise for freedom, control and expression."

She summed up: "Universal compulsory military training announces to the world that we have abandoned our ideals and that we are preparing to get into the war. Are the American people asleep, or dumb with fear, that they are not moving on their national and state capitals in protest against the compulsory military training of our youth!"

After adjournment of Congress at noon on March 4, Wilson returned to the White House in an angry mood at Bob's successful thwarting of the passage of the armed ship bill. He wrote a statement released to the press that night. It read: "A little group of willful men, representing no opinion but their own, have rendered the great government of the United States helpless and contemptible."

Bob fought the bill primarily because he and Belle believed representative government depended on the direct responsibility of the representatives, not to the President but to the people. Bob and Belle were convinced the majority of the American people did not want war. Any surrender of the legislative to the executive would in the long run result in the loss of fundamental democracy.

A resolution criticizing Bob and demanding he support the President was introduced in the Wisconsin state senate. The *New York*

Times published thirty-three editorials from different newspapers, three-fourths of which supported the President in condemning the "willful men." Other newspapers and magazines accused Bob and his adherents of "flirting with treason," of being "Benedict Arnolds," "unsocialized creatures," even "a little group of perverts." In a cartoon the *Cincinnati Post* pictured Bob as conversing with the Kaiser under the caption "His Master's Voice."

At a mass meeting attended by 3,000 in Carnegie Hall, New York, on March 5 under the auspices of the American Rights League, each mention of the senators who opposed the armed ship bill brought cries of "Traitor!" and "Hang Them!" Four days later the Emergency Peace Federation held a large meeting at Carnegie Hall that received far less publicity. A man present on both occasions, Ralph Pearson, wrote Bob, "I heard the war mass meeting at Carnegie Hall pillory you and the rest of the twelve as 'traitors,' but I also heard the peace mass meeting of last night in the same place give you one of the two greatest ovations of the evening."

Bob wrote Belle on March 8: "My letters came in yesterday and today at the rate of about five hundred a day. At least four to one are strong and beautiful in their support. They come from all over the country." Bobbie wrote Phil and Mary on March 14: "Gee there are sure a lot of people among 'the silent masses' that know how to talk when they want to. It would do your heart good just to read the letters."

Yet Bob met plenty of anger too. In a streetcar, a man spit on him as he returned to the Senate shortly before noon on March 5 to take the oath of office for his third term. As he rode to the Capitol the street scene was ominous. Regular Army troops, detectives, Secret Service men and policemen guarded the route from the White House to the Capitol, where the President was to deliver his inaugural address.

When Bob entered the Senate chamber and walked down the center aisle toward his seat in the first row, he found it occupied. He stood for a moment, looked around, then walked slowly back until he saw an empty seat. As he started to sit down, the *New York Times* reported, Senator Benjamin Tillman came up and "with a stony face put his own hand on the chair saying 'Pardon me,' and sat down." Bob then "walked around the hall until he found a chair between two desks, and sat there with no companion on either side of him."

The afternoon of the day Bob took the oath of office, the *Mil-*

waukee Journal published an editorial declaring he stood "repudiated by the whole press of America" and that the voice of the nation held him "unfaithful to his trust." That night he was hung in effigy by students at the University of Illinois.

As the newspaper attacks on her husband grew more violent, Belle wrote him on March 6 suggesting he might get his point of view over to more people by devoting the entire March issue of the *Magazine* to the armed ship bill and the near certainty that if the President ordered merchant ships to be armed, acts of war would follow. She also stressed that Wilson was asking for just the kind of "unlimited autocratic power that the Kaiser and Czar and all the other crowned heads of Europe and Lord Grey asked for. 'Believe in me. Go it blind. I have the divine insight, and am going to do everything for your good.' The people who say stand by the President, right or wrong, are doing exactly what the people of Germany and England and all the European nations did." Bob agreed, and he and Belle worked on the special issue.

He wrote her in Madison on March 8, "I have been on the verge of sending for you a dozen times. I have needed your counsel and help these days. It has been an awful trial." When Wilson issued a proclamation on March 10 declaring an extraordinary occasion required Congress to convene on April 16, Bobbie wrote his mother it was very important she be in Washington for the session.

Two days later Belle took the train for Washington, leaving Phil and Mary at the farm. She wrote them on March 12 from Chicago, waiting for the connecting train, "My heart aches more and more at the thought of leaving you. But I hope it is not for long. What joy it has been to be together in the quiet and protection of the farm."

The March issue of the *Magazine* was headlined "The Armed Ship Bill Meant War" and carried an editorial explaining Bob's position, which was excerpted by some newspapers. The *Congressional Record* reprinted the article in full. Bob also sent the editorial out in the form of a letter to the thousands who had written to support him.

Meanwhile came reports that a revolution had overthrown the imperial government in Russia. Bob hoped this meant the end of autocratic rule and hoped also it would contribute to the democratization of Europe. With Wilson's approval, the American ambassador to Russia, David R. Francis, was instructed to recognize the new provisional government and did so on March 22. The next day Great Britain, France and Italy took similar action. On the Sunday after the Czar's abdication, Belle and Bob walked to the nearest newsstand to get the New York papers. Belle wrote that day to a friend: "The Russian revolution is a world event of such tremendous meaning and possibilities that I can hardly think of anything else. Of course, there will be reaction and a long struggle, but what has happened must stir the world to new ideals and give the oppressed new courage and the believers in ultimate democracy a new faith."

Bob thought the President would not dare arm merchant ships without authority from Congress. But on March 12, a week after the defeat of his bill, Wilson notified foreign governments that American ships clearing for European ports through the German zone would sail with guns and gunners furnished by the Navy. He had used an executive order to bypass Congress.

Wilson summoned Congress to meet April 2, two weeks earlier than the date previously set. From the Senate Office building where she was working that day, Belle wrote Phil there was "tension and strain in the very air you breathe in Washington." The members of the cabinet were unanimous in their wish for a declaration of war. J. P. Morgan and Company announced a bond issue of $1,000,000,000 for a war loan to France. The clamor in the press for a declaration of war grew louder each day.

Belle wrote Phil and Mary on April 1 that the telegrams their father was receiving from all over the country seemed to indicate a growth of sentiment to resist war, though she feared it might be too late because Congress had been "too thoroughly and completely intimidated." On the streets of Madison, Mary was jeered and pointed out by her schoolmates as "the traitor's daughter." As loyal and as proud of her father as the rest of the family was, she calmly wrote him asking for the facts about the armed ship bill filibuster so she could defend his actions.

Phil, then nineteen and a student at the university, wrote his father March 10: "Oh dear Daddy, I love you so much for your courage, but most for the fortitude which gives you the courage and strength to do as you see without making you bitter. Oh I pray God that I may in some small way be worthy of you. I do so want to make my life worthwhile but you have set an almost unattainable ideal for us. *But I'll do the best I can.*"

On April 2, the day President Wilson was to give a special message to Congress, trains brought thousands of citizens to Washington, some to hear the President, others to appeal to him and Congress to keep the country out of war. All parades were prohibited and the authorities forbade the use of any government building for a peace rally. Bob and Belle believed one reason for prohibiting the two planned parades was fear the peace demonstrators might outnumber the war advocates.

Shortly after 8:15 that evening Bob went with other senators to hear the President's message at the House chamber. Directly in front of the Speaker of the House sat the Supreme Court justices but not in their official robes. For the first time anyone could remember, the diplomatic representatives of foreign countries sat together officially on the floor of the House, behind them the American cabinet officials.

The President, escorted by a troop of cavalry, arrived at the Capitol at 8:30. As he entered the House chamber, everyone rose. Cheers swept the vast room. Bob stood with arms crossed and head bowed, refusing to join in the applause. Throughout the message and the cheering that greeted it, he listened silently. In a thirty-six minute speech Wilson asked for a declaration of war against Germany.

Bob and Belle were convinced the people had reelected Wilson in the belief he would keep the country at peace and now they felt deep resentment and sorrow as they heard Wilson demand a declaration of war within one month of his second inauguration. The President ended his message with the famous phrase, "The world must be made safe for democracy," and the crowd applauded wildly. Throughout this demonstration, the *North American Newspaper Alliance* reported, two senators, Stone and La Follette, less than fifty feet from Wilson sat silent. Bob later said he thought an outburst of cheering was "a strange response" to a request for a declaration of war.

The President also asked for compulsory military service, which Bob resolutely opposed. To the end of his life he believed the draft a violation of the constitutional rights of American citizens.

When the Senate met at noon the next day, Bob was already in his seat. Senator Gilbert Hitchcock of Nebraska introduced the war resolution, asking for unanimous consent for immediate consideration of the bill. Under a rule designed to permit study of proposed legislation, objections by a single senator could compel the resolution to be held over for a day.

Bob now objected. Mistakenly assuming Bob's objection was due to the fact the resolution had not yet been printed, Hitchcock assured him a printed copy would be on every senator's desk in five minutes.

Bob, making no explanation, quietly insisted the rule requiring the resolution go over for a day be adhered to. The vice-president ruled in favor of Bob's request.

Returning to his office Bob found cards with encouraging messages from many who had called while he was on the Senate floor. One read, "God bless you. The people do."

Following the adjournment, Bob, Belle, Bobbie, John Hannan and Gil Roe stayed at the Capitol until after midnight, working into final form the material Bob would use the next day. He had asked the office force to stay all night if necessary. Ever since the debate on the armed ship bill, Roe had been spending as much time in Washington as his New York law practice permitted, working with Bob and Belle on questions of international law.

The next day Bob began speaking shortly before four o'clock in the afternoon. Senators who had been in the smoking room hurried to their seats. The crowds in the galleries leaned forward in expectation. Bob spoke for three hours. He had "the solemn attention of almost every senator," as the *Christian Science Monitor* reported. He said he did not believe in the doctrine of "standing back of the President" without inquiring whether the President was right or wrong. His comment on Wilson's denunciation of the "willful" senators who opposed the armed ship bill was that these men represented the voters who elected them.

He read the results of a referendum held in Monroe, Wisconsin, showing 954 for peace, 95 for war. He also read a few of the 15,000 letters and telegrams he had received, of which ninety percent approved his stand against entering the war. He challenged Wilson to submit the issue to the direct vote of the people.

Step by step he traced what he considered diplomatic blunders committed by the President and State Department. The European war, he maintained, "had originated from causes beyond the sphere of our influence and outside the realm of our responsibility. . . . The government of each country engaged in it is at fault for it." He predicted history would find the real cause in the fact "England would tolerate no commercial rivalry. Germany would not submit to isolation."

Belle, listening in the gallery, knew Bob expressed the deep conviction behind his opposition to war when he said, "The sovereign power of the people never dies. It may be suppressed for a time, it may be misled, be fooled, silenced. I think, Mr. President, that it is being denied expression now."

Bob went on in this vein: "The poor, sir, who are the ones called upon to rot in the trenches, have no organized power, have no press to voice their will upon this question of peace or war. . . . They will have their day and they will be heard. It will be as certain and as inevitable as the return of the tides, and as resistless, too."

When he finished speaking, he gathered up his manuscript and walked to the rear of the chamber. Several senators then spoke in support of declaring war.

As the resolution finally came to a vote, the silence was tense as the clerk called the roll. Many senators replied in voices that quivered with emotion. Bob said his "No" in a clear, firm voice, heard distinctly in the hushed chamber. Gronna, Lane, Norris, Stone and Senator James Kimble Vardaman of Mississippi voted with Bob against declaration of war.

As the senators left the chamber, Bob's colleagues avoided him. With Bobbie and Hannan at his side he walked to his office through corridors filled with hostile crowds from the gallery. A stranger came forward, handed him a rope. The next night the *Boston Evening Transcript* predicted his speech would "naturally be the end of him. . . . Standing against his own country and for his country's enemies, he is gone and fallen. Henceforth he is the man without a country."

The House voted to declare war on the morning of Good Friday, April 6: the count was 373 to 50. Nine of the eleven Wisconsin congressmen voted against the nation's entry into war, which Bob thought a courageous page in the state's history.

The night the House debated the bill, a "patriotic" demonstration at Cleburn, Texas, burned Bob in effigy on the public square as the crowds hurled derisive cries at the blazing figure. Toward morning in the nation's capital a policeman, responding to a call from the center of the business district at 14th and H streets, found hanging in front of a shop a makeshift figure of a man.

Down the back hung a broad streak of yellow and dangling from the feet a streamer bearing the word "Traitors." On one side of the figure was the name "Stone." On the other side, the name La Follette.

CHAPTER
12
....

The Partnership
Under Fire

[1917–1919]

It was not until late October 1917 that the first American shot was fired in the trenches of Europe but the Sixty-fifth Congress remained in session from April 2 until October 6. During this period the Administration's war program was formulated in legislation and approved by Congress.

Bob was a member of the State Finance Committee, which had direct responsibility for methods to finance the war. He remained true to his convictions while serving on this committee. He voted against conscription, believing a democracy should not enter a war it could not fight with volunteers. His proposal for a volunteer army was rejected by the Senate. He then proposed an advisory referendum to allow the people to decide whether the country should have a conscript or a volunteer army. This too was rejected.

Bob also drafted an amendment to increase by $50 a month the pay of all American soldiers sent to foreign countries, the money to be raised by increasing the tax rates on incomes over $25,000. He predicted to Bobbie that when his amendment was introduced, "Those gentlemen in their plug hats will vote against it." As they did.

Bob spoke out against war bonds as a means of financing the war, for this would saddle future generations with the war debt. He was in favor of taxing war profits—which Belle called "the conscription of wealth"—to pay for the war. This bill also was defeated.

Belle, who had gone to the farm for a few days, read of these defeats in the Madison newspaper. She wrote Bob on September 5 she thought the fight he had been putting up for the conscription of wealth was splendid: "They may vote you down but, like so many propositions which you have advocated that are essentially right and simple and plain for the folks to see and understand, it makes a record and creates opinion that cannot be resisted."

Bob spoke against the espionage bill, which he thought the "worst legislative crime" of the war because it threatened freedom of the press, freedom of speech, freedom of assembly, freedom from unwarranted search and seizure and other rights won by generations of struggle and sacrifice. It gave the President "extraordinary powers" and raised the question whether the government's war powers included empowering the executive to disregard the Constitution. Bob commented that in all his years in Washington he had never "heard so much democracy preached and so little practiced."

He also believed that the country, having entered the war, had an obligation to plan for "a just and enduring peace." He asked for an early declaration of war aims, fearing the United States might be dragged through years of war only to establish imperialism abroad and exploit weaker nations. Bob introduced a resolution referring to the secret treaties among the imperialistic countries of Europe that affirmed the constitutional rights of Congress "to determine and to declare definitely" the war aims of the United States. The resolution also disavowed any intention by Congress to continue the war "for purposes of territorial annexations or indemnities." It favored the creation of a common fund by all belligerents for the restoration of devastated regions. It also called for a public restatement of the Allied peace terms.

Belle first read Bob's resolution when it was published in the *Wisconsin State Journal*. She telegraphed him it "seemed to strike the keynote of an aggressive and determined effort to secure a rational basis for settlement of the awful conflict. I am sure it expresses the desire and judgment of a suffering war-exhausted world. No word can express my gratitude and satisfaction."

In other readers his resolution elicited outrage. The assertion of the rights of Congress was undesirable to the Administration. The proposal that all belligerents contribute to the restoration of war-damaged areas shocked the press. The *New York World* denounced it as "pro-German." The *Wisconsin State Journal*, edited by Richard Lloyd Jones, Bob's former admirer and friend, declared in an editorial that Bob's resolution was designed to "defend, comfort and help the greatest criminal the world has ever known."

Bob was invited to speak in St. Paul, Minnesota, on September 20, 1917, by the Nonpartisan League. This was composed chiefly of midwestern farmers, pioneer men and women who had known freezing winters without fuel, crop failures from drought and low prices in good years because they were helpless against the unfair practices of the grain combines, milling interests and railroads. Bob knew these people well. He had grown up as one of them and had been interested in the Nonpartisan League since its founding. He asked Belle to accompany him on this trip.

After they arrived in St. Paul, he shut himself in his room at the Hotel Frederic for thirty-four hours to shape the speech he had drafted, one he also intended to deliver before the Senate in connection with his war-aims resolution. It was based on careful research as to historical and legal precedents upholding the constitutional right of free speech and the right and duty of Congress to declare the aims of war.

Two Nonpartisan League leaders who usually agreed with Bob were afraid to let him deliver the war-aims speech in St. Paul. The conference had been misrepresented in the press and harassed by Secret Service men. The two leaders feared a speech on the subject Bob chose might bring further attacks on the League. Belle was indignant at such lack of courage. She urged Bob to refuse to address the conference unless he gave the speech he had prepared.

He offered to withdraw from the program but the two leaders objected, for he was to give the important closing address. Finally he was persuaded to go to the auditorium and speak extemporaneously for a few minutes.

As Belle and Bob approached the auditorium, hundreds of men and women in the street waited for them and applauded vigorously. Ten thousand inside occupied seats on the main floor and in a series of galleries that rose almost to the roof. Bob slowly made his way through the crowded aisles to the platform as the audience rose to give him one of the largest ovations he had ever received. The demonstration continued for five minutes after he stood on the platform. For six months the press had denounced him as he fought losing battles in the hostile atmosphere of the Senate chamber. But in the large St. Paul auditorium where the listeners were farmers and wage earners, there was faith in him, love for him.

Bob had no written manuscript with which to refute possible misquotations by the newspapers. But three stenographic reporters took down every word of his talk. One was the official reporter of the conference, another represented the Minnesota Conference of Public Safety and the third, the United States Department of Justice.

Belle and he heard not a single unfavorable comment after he finished speaking to enthusiastic applause. As they drove to the station he asked, "Now, Belle, aren't you glad we stayed?" They both felt the trip was worthwhile in spite of the strain. The next morning they arrived in Madison, went to the farm and spent a restful day. Bob inspected the fields, the barn, the dairy herd, the horses and the ponies. He was delighted to find the barn and barnyard "clean enough to eat in." He praised Belle for her careful supervision of the milk, now of such a high standard it was recommended by local doctors.

For both Belle and Bob the farm was their sanctuary. Belle said in one of her columns she would not trade Maple Bluff Farm "for Harriman's railroads or Rockefeller's millions." She wrote: "How much less comfort in stocks and bonds than in a farm with fields of hay and corn and oats and barley and potatoes; with a garden which grows asparagus and lettuce and radishes and onions and peas and beans and tomatoes and cabbages and cucumbers and melons and strawberries and raspberries and currants and gooseberries and black-berries and a few grape vines with the prospect of a few bunches of grapes; with an orchard that has cherries and plums and apples and pears; a farm with cows and horses and ponies that have little colts, and with chickens and ducks! (There should be sheep and hogs, but we have none.) Oh, the comfort of the farm in the spring and in the summer and in the autumn and in the winter.

"Comfort when we are here, comfort when we are away; for there is great comfort and peace in just thinking about the farm. And when the stress and strain are hardest, though a thousand miles lie between, it is easy to stand on the porch and feel the influence of the great old grapevine that covers it, and of the nearby basswood and the noble maple just far enough away, and the little grove on the other side, and of the distant view between. The tension is loosened, body and spirit relax, we know the comfort of a farm."

After only one day at Maple Bluff Farm a storm of abuse descended upon Bob. A late Associated Press dispatch had gone out after his speech in St. Paul to more than 1,000 newspapers. Under large headlines Bob was quoted as saying, "We had no grievances against Germany."

What he had actually said was, "We had grievances against Germany."

The Associated Press also quoted him as saying the sinking of the *Lusitania* was justified because the ship was carrying ammunition. Bob had said Secretary of State Bryan knew the ship carried munitions but the passengers were not warned.

Bob and Belle left Madison by train for Toledo, Ohio, where he was to speak on September 23 at a meeting arranged by the Reverend H. J. Hahn. He had been driven from his church because of his antiwar stand. When Belle and Bob arrived, Bob was handed a batch of letters containing threats of violence if he spoke. But he gave the speech despite the climate of fear, explaining why he introduced his resolution calling on Congress for a declaration of war aims.

This was the last public address Bob made outside the Senate during the war. He returned to Washington as Belle went back to the farm. She wrote Netha Roe on September 24: "The St. Paul and Toledo meetings were wonderful beyond imagination and description. They satisfied me as nothing other than the experience of being there could—how the American people, the working people and the farmers, are thinking and feeling."

While Belle was pleased with the support of the ordinary people, the false quotations sent out by the press, together with deliberately misleading interpretations and misrepresentations in many newspapers, began to snowball into an organized campaign for Bob's expulsion from the Senate. The Minnesota Public Safety Commission charged him with making a speech of a "disloyal and seditious nature" and petitioned the Senate to expel him, as did other groups.

Among those who took the lead in hurling epithets was former President Roosevelt. He called Bob the worst enemy democracy had, "at the moment loyally serving one country—Germany." He added, "If I were this minute a member of the Senate I would be ashamed to sit in that body until I found some way of depriving Senator La Follette of his seat in that chamber. . . . La Follette's proper place is in the German Reichstag, not in the Senate."

In the next issue of *La Follette's Magazine* Bob used his only available medium for refuting the false statements attributed to him. He quoted what the newspapers alleged, juxtaposed with the accurate quotation from the certified transcript made by the official stenographer.

The resolution of the Minnesota Public Safety Commission, in the form of a petition asking for Bob's expulsion, was presented to the Senate by Senator Frank Billings Kellogg of Minnesota on September 29, 1917. When reporters asked Bob for a statement, he declined to comment. That night he telegraphed Belle saying the petition for his expulsion had been introduced and referred to committee but no resolution had been introduced by any senator and he did not expect one would be offered. He wrote, "The war traders are making a campaign of it and the old tory crowd think it a good opportunity. Your counsel would be of great help but want you to be wherever it will be easiest for you."

As he expected, petitions for his expulsion and impeachment continued to flow in. The Executives Club of Toledo telegraphed a resolution to President Wilson asking that Bob be deported. Public-safety commissions, chambers of commerce, merchants' and manu-facturers' associations, Rotary and Kiwanis clubs, the National Se-curity League and Grand Army veterans demanded his expulsion. Even in Wisconsin, the reactionary elements asked that he be thrown out of the Senate.

Though Belle found it difficult to leave Mary and Phil alone in the hostile atmosphere that had taken hold of Madison, she felt Bob needed her even more. She left at once for Washington. On arrival, she found that though newspaper headlines reported demands for Bob's expulsion, small stories appearing on the inside pages and a stream of letters supporting Bob's position proved that many people had not been taken in by the distorted reports of Bob's speech. The delegates to the California State Federation of Labor unanimously adopted a resolution expressing confidence "in his integrity and loy-alty."

Alice Brandeis wrote Belle on October 4: "I can't tell you how shocked we are and outraged too, by these recent attacks on the senator. It is almost incredible that such things should come to pass—his long, long years of utmost service, his loyalty, his devotion all forgotten. It makes my blood boil, Belle."

That day Belle wrote Phil and Mary in Madison: "It has been a rather anxious day. The Senate Committee on Privileges and Elec-tions, which was considering whether to expel Bob from the Senate, did not take any action on the petitions that were before them. But we understand there was some heated discussion as to what they have a right to do." She added that the truth of the statements their father had made at St. Paul might be denied but his authority stood back of it and she hoped this might end the controversy. She concluded, "Otherwise it will be another sensation. Be careful what you say to others."

Bob was condemned in the assembly chamber of the Wisconsin state capitol by the annual Conference of the City Superintendents of Wisconsin Schools. They petitioned the Senate to expel Bob promptly and "give the people of Wisconsin the right to hold up their heads without shame." That evening a figure of Bob was hung in effigy in Sheboygan, Wisconsin.

The Senate committee met and nominated a subcommittee of five, directed to limit the inquiry solely to the accuracy of the facts in the St. Paul speech. Late in the afternoon a messenger delivered to Bob's office in the Capitol a letter addressed to him by the chairman of the committee, Senator Atlee Pomerene of Ohio, and a copy of the St. Paul speech sent to Senator Kellogg by the Minnesota Commission of Public Safety, whose stenographic reporter was one of three who had taken down Bob's words. Pomerene's letter to Bob asked if this were a correct copy of the speech and, if not, to state the errors and provide a correct version.

Bob read the copy and immediately wrote Pomerene that it was not correct. He promised to furnish a correct copy as soon as he could obtain an accurate transcript from one of the other two stenographic reporters.

The next day newspapers revealed that former Secretary of State Bryan had publicly declared he had not known until after the sinking of the *Lusitania* that it carried ammunition in the cargo. Bob had declared in his speech that Bryan had known and had notified the President prior to the ship's sailing that ammunition was aboard.

Senator Kellogg now attacked Bob on the floor of the Senate. Citing Bryan's denial, Kellogg said Bob's statements were not "a question of free speech" but "of an erroneous statement of facts" that tended "to aid and encourage the enemy and to cast dishonor and discredit upon this nation."

During Bob's extemporaneous speech at St. Paul a listener had interrupted him with the question, "*What about the Lusitania?*" Bob had answered that before the ship sailed, Secretary of State Bryan had warned President Wilson that this passenger vessel carried explosives and a large amount of ammunition in violation of a United States statute. This information had been given Bob by Julius Truesdell, a member of the Washington bureau of the *New York Times* since 1910 and a reliable man of integrity.

One of the reasons for Bryan's resignation in June 1915 was generally understood to be his disagreement with the President about allowing passengers to travel on munitions-laden ships. In a Senate speech on April 4, 1917, opposing United States entry into the European war, Bob had referred to the *Lusitania*'s cargo of six million rounds of ammunition destined for the British Army. The accuracy of this statement had not been challenged at the time. Five months later in St. Paul he had answered the question from the floor in the same vein.

Bob sent Pomerene on October 1 a printed copy of the transcript of his speech, certified by the official reporter of the St. Paul conference. He pointed out the important particulars in which it differed from the version the committee had received from the Minnesota Public Safety Commission.

Belle and Gilbert Roe looked up legal precedents and gathered material pertinent to the committee's investigation, regarding, in particular, Bob's request to the Treasury Department for the official manifest of the *Lusitania*'s cargo when it left New York on its final voyage. The Treasury Department had refused to furnish the manifest on the grounds it was a classified document.

Gilbert knew Dudley Field Malone, the collector of the Port of New York, and arranged for Belle and Bob to meet Malone informally while they were in New York visiting Fola and Mid. Malone told them he thought it outrageous for the Treasury Department to refuse to give a senator an official document needed for his defense, particularly when the senator was right. Malone sent Bob a copy of the ship's manifest, showing the *Lusitania* carried 4,200 cases of cartridges and 1,250 cases of shrapnel. Bob also obtained a statement from the Cunard Line to the effect they had been sending small-arms cartridges aboard the *Lusitania* for years.

Times reporter Truesdell came to see Bob and told him he would testify under oath in Bob's defense. Bryan telephoned on October 3 to inform Bob he intended to continue to deny Bob's statement. Consequently, over the next few weeks, as part of the preparation for the committee hearings, Gil Roe took testimony from Truesdell regarding a conversation he had with Bryan. This testimony was a direct challenge to Bryan's subsequent statements.

Bob's hearing was scheduled for November 26, then postponed until December 3, then further postponed because, it was alleged, it had been impossible to secure a quorum. Belle wrote Phil and Mary on December 2 that it was "hard to endure such flippant treatment, but what can one do?" Possibly the committee did not want to deal with the problem. It was more damaging to Bob to let the accusations hang unresolved.

On the evening of December 12 a thousand students and members of the faculty at the University of Wisconsin met to form a Loyalty League and sign loyalty resolutions. After the meeting fifteen university students paraded through a biting snowstorm to the lower campus in front of the library. There they hoisted a dummy labeled *Senator La Follette and The Capital Times*, a new Madison newspaper that defended Bob. The students touched a match to the figure and, joined by other students, did an Indian dance as it burned.

For months Bobbie had been carrying a heavy load on many fronts, including writing a newsletter that went to forty-five newspapers under the title *The Week in Washington*. On Sunday morning January 28, 1918, Bobbie came down to breakfast complaining the house seemed chilly and he thought he had taken cold during the night because he had been too sleepy to close the window when a strong wind started to blow.

Though he protested he was not ill, Belle did not like the look on his face and sent for a thermometer. His temperature was over 103. She called Dr. B. M. Randolph, and asked him to come to the house and examine her older son. Dr. Charles Mayo, a friend of Belle and Bob, happened to be in Washington, and he accompanied Dr. Randolph. Both doctors diagnosed streptococcal pneumonia.

By the end of January Bobbie was so seriously ill that in addition to Belle's constant care he needed two nurses, one during the day, the other at night. During the months he lay ill, brief intervals of improvement alternated with acute crises accompanied by intense pain. Bob could not sleep, so anxious was he for his beloved "laddie." At night he would slip into Bobbie's room to examine the nurse's chart. Throughout the day he stayed in the house. Hannan came every evening to report on the day's events and get Bob's advice on pending legislation.

The Senate committee considering Bob's case finally announced it would meet February 8. The day before, Bobbie's temperature again rose to 103 and Dr. Randolph advised operating immediately because of pus in the pleural cavity, which contains the lungs. In less than an hour Bob, Belle, and their son were at the hospital. Bob went into the operating room with Bobbie at eleven p.m. and was present while the doctor operated. Belle waited in Bobbie's hospital room until Bob returned at 12:15 a.m. She wrote Fola in New York before she went to bed that Bobbie had withstood the operation well and she thought Bob more composed than he had "been at any time since Bobbie was taken ill. Perhaps we all feel steadied by the hope that this may mean a clearing up of the poison in his system and yet we can not be sure. This experience brings us all close together. I seem to think of you all and long to be helpful to my nestlings in their distress. And I think with horror of all the needless agony of war. How can it go on?"

Five weeks after his operation Bobbie was allowed to leave the hospital. Plans were made for him to go away to convalesce. But once at home his temperature again rose and another crisis developed, this one lasting several weeks. The streptococcal infection attacked his throat and face. His eyes were swollen shut and for five days his throat and tongue were so swollen he was unable to swallow liquid nourishment. Bob sent for his "beloved" Dr. Fox and he came from Madison to spend several days with the family.

Belle wrote Phil on April 3 that Dr. Fox's visit "was a great blessing as always," but that Bobbie found "it hard to look forward to another day because he was so weary of illness." However, he seemed better two weeks later when she wrote, "Papa has had almost as hard a time as Bobbie. He has been so wrought up over him. He will not go to bed nights and hovers about his room. But he will be all right if Bobbie keeps going ahead."

The Senate committee knew of Bobbie's illness and postponed its inquiry. But on May 13 Gil Roe learned, through the newspapers, that a meeting of the Senate committee had been called for May 15 "to dispose of the charges against Senator La Follette." It had been eight months since the St. Paul speech.

The Senate committee met on May 21, with ten senators present. Bob was at home with his son, who had suffered another acute attack the previous night. But Gil was present to speak for Bob. For three hours he discussed the St. Paul speech, presented Bob's case and cited precedents. Gil steadily maintained there was nothing in the petition of the Minnesota Commission of Public Safety that called for any action by the Senate except to drop the charges. The next morning the *New York Times* and other newspapers carried reports of the hearing and quoted Gil's arguments.

Every day until the committee hearings were adjourned, Gil skillfully and calmly answered an unrelenting stream of questions, many an attack on Bob's loyalty. In a letter to Netha on May 23 Belle wrote: "I wish you could be here to get the impression of what has been achieved by Gilbert in the past two days—the result of his thorough understanding and able argument and perfect control. It was a most difficult situation and he so completely mastered it that it seemed a special opportunity created for the purpose of enlightening the committee and leading them out of the maze. Bob is deeply satisfied and restored in spirit. No words can express my gratitude and Mary and Bobbie and Fola are rejoiced." She added that the reaction to Gil's arguments had been "favorable far beyond anything we could expect."

The hearings were widely reported, many papers carrying excerpts from Gil's argument and brief. He had called attention to the numerous misrepresentations of the St. Paul speech by the press, pointing out the stenographic record proved Bob had said just the opposite. On May 24 the Associated Press apologized for misquoting Bob. A check of the stenographic record proved Bob said, "We *had* grievances against Germany," not "We had no grievances against Germany."

During the months the disloyalty charges against Bob had been before the Privileges and Elections Committee, he was beset by many financial burdens. Before Bobbie fell ill, Bob had received a letter indicating an extension of the $14,000 mortgage on his farm might be refused (he was eventually allowed a $6,000 increase). The bills from doctors, nurses and hospitals for Bobbie's care ate up Bob's salary month after month—by the middle of June the illness had cost over $3,500 and Bob had to borrow money to pay the bills. He wrote Alf Rogers on his (Bob's) sixty-third birthday, "If I live until the war is over I will yet go to the lecture platform and earn enough to pay my debts. If I don't, the life insurance will just about clean it up."

Late in May 1918 Phil wrote his father he wanted to enter the R.O.T.C. training camp at Fort Sheridan, Illinois. After the Army accepted him, he visited the family in Washington. As he was leaving on July 13 he handed Mary a letter for his brother. It said: "I have just told you good-bye but could not express to you dear old pal what my old heart felt. . . . You can never know how deeply my love for you permeates every fibre of my body. . . . Thine to the end of Time's journey."

Fola wrote Phil on July 31 that Bobbie had been "quite broken up when he read your letter. He said that he had longed to talk to you the night before but that he was afraid of breaking down and couldn't do it. He said again and again: 'I love Phil so—no one knows what he means to me. All the quarrels we used to have have gone into love.' . . . You are bound up in the inmost of his heart, Phil."

Though Bobbie was still so ill he had to have a day and night nurse, his condition improved during June. He had not walked in nine months but the doctors decided it was so hot in Washington he should be taken to the mountains. Fola made reservations at the Homestead Hotel in Hot Springs, Virginia, and on the night of July 20 Bobbie was carried on a stretcher to an ambulance. His father and a nurse rode with him to the train where Belle, Fola and the other nurse joined them. As Bob walked from the train to the hotel beside his son's stretcher, tears came to his eyes when he heard Bobbie say, "It's good to see the sky. I'm hungry. I'd like a lamb chop for breakfast."

That afternoon Belle wrote Mary they "were all surprised—Bobbie most of all—at the way he stood the trip. He enjoyed the view from the window, his appetite improved and he gained strength." Belle was troubled by the cost of the hotel and when a chance cancellation made available a large house near the hotel for a month, she took it. Bob sent word to Mary and Mid to join the family and instructed Mary to bring Bud, the English bulldog. Belle wrote Phil on August 12, "With all the beloved family under one roof, the thought of you away is always present. When I look around the table or when we are gathered together for any purpose, we say, '*If* only Phil were here.' "

After returning to Washington Bobbie improved enough so no night nurse was needed. Bob slept in his son's room and cared for him, waking the day nurse only when an injection was needed to relieve the excruciating pain. Dr. Randolph insisted on at least a year's convalescence in a place where Bobbie could take sunbaths and be outdoors most of the day. It was decided that early in September Bob, Belle, Mary and Bobbie, still unable to walk, would leave for La Jolla, California, where years before, on the advice of Dr. Fox, Bob had gone with Belle to regain his health. The family group had to change trains in Chicago and Phil, who managed a leave from Fort Sheridan, met them at the station and carried his brother from one train to the other.

In La Jolla they found a place on the ocean that cost fifty dollars for the first month and forty-five a month thereafter, "rent of new hair mattress bed two dollars extra." The following week they took possession of the house which the owners called Wayside but which the La Follettes christened the Kewpie Kot.

Bob had counted on another week with the family to make sure they were well settled but his holiday was cut short on September 23 by a telegram from Hannan urging him to return immediately. Debate in the Senate on the Susan B. Anthony amendment was coming close to a vote. The woman suffrage amendment had passed in the House and was now before the more hostile Senate. Hannan closed the telegram, "Your vote essential." Belle, who had worked years for this moment, urged Bob to return in time to vote. Reluctant though he was to leave, he took her advice.

He left La Jolla that night, Belle accompanying him to the bus that would take him to the train at San Diego. They talked of the work ahead and as they said good-bye she advised him "to pursue a calm and poise that will lift you above personal things." On the train he read in a newspaper the Senate committee had decided to postpone further consideration of the charges against him until after the November election. It was now more than a year since he had given the controversial St. Paul speech.

He arrived in Washington late Saturday afternoon, September 28, to find a filibuster had held up the vote on the suffrage amendment. At noon on Monday he entered the Senate chamber after an absence of eight months spent at his son's bedside. The *New York World* described him the next day: "His hair had materially whitened, but he seemed fit for the conflict." Many senators greeted him cordially. Senator Boies Penrose of Pennsylvania called out, "Glad to see you, Senator. How's the boy?"

That morning President Wilson had unexpectedly telephoned Majority Leader Thomas Staples Martin from Virginia to say he would appear before the Senate at one p.m. to urge passage of the suffrage resolution. The President had opposed the amendment granting the vote to women since 1912. But in June he reversed his position. Now, before the Senate, Wilson read from small sheets of paper for thirteen minutes, urging passage of the suffrage amendment as "vital to the winning of the war."

But this patriotic appeal changed no votes. When Senator John Sharp Williams of Mississippi offered an amendment to limit the vote to white women, Bob voted to table the amendment and all other efforts to modify the suffrage resolution. His hurried return had not saved the joint resolution, for a roll-call showed the amendment's supporters were two votes short of the necessary two-thirds majority.

Though the Susan B. Anthony amendment resolution failed in Congress, some states had already enacted woman suffrage laws and the League of Women Voters had been founded. In her June 1918 column Belle reported on a resolution passed by the league that advocated "abolition of child labor and compulsory education of all children to the age of sixteen. An eight-hour day and weekly day of rest. Abolition of night work for women and minors. Equal pay for men and women doing equal work. Establishment of a minimum wage. Insurance against sickness, accident and unemployment, with provisions for old age, invalid and maternity benefits. Rights of workers to organize and bargain collectively through their chosen representatives. Adequate appropriations and inspectors in each state department of labor and a special bureau of women in industry in each. An international labor commission."

In La Jolla, Bobbie was now exercising and trying to learn how to walk again. Soon he no longer needed crutches or a wheelchair. But at times he was in such pain that Belle would massage him for hours at night so he could sleep. When Bob heard of this he wrote her, "Be careful, Dear Heart, there are limits—even for you."

Mary helped Belle with the housework and attended a school founded by Ellen Scripps, wife of the newspaper publisher. She and other neighbors provided company for the family. Mary also helped her mother take care of Bobbie. The infection had caused sores to erupt all over his body and these had to be lanced and drained. Mary was responsible for changing the bandages, making sure they were sanitary.

Not long after Bob returned to Washington he wrote Mary and enclosed pin money, along with the message, "You are not to measure my love for you by the size of this measly check." He reported the senators' deep interest in Bobbie's health: "They want the latest word. And everyone has a good thing to say and a hearty wish for his recovery and return."

Bob's case before the Committee on Privileges and Elections was still dragging on. Gil had moved for dismissal of the charges five months before but no action had been taken. The congressional elections were absorbing Washington. The Administration considered Democratic control of the Senate vital since it would have to ratify any peace treaty. The election returns showed sweeping Republican gains throughout the country but the question of who controlled the Senate remained unanswered for several days. Final count showed the Republicans had a majority of two.

Senator Thomas Pryor Gore telephoned Bob three days after the election to report the *New York World* carried an editorial headlined *Battling Bob Controls the Situation in the U.S. Senate*. The editorial said, "With but two majority for the Republicans, Senator La Follette alone can be an endless source of trouble and worry. Several of the old Progressive Republican clique that was active in the Senate six years ago are still members. . . . He will require the aid of but one or two to make his program effective."

The President appeared before a joint session of Congress on November 11 to read the terms of the armistice to enthusiastic representatives and senators. The *New York Times* reported, "La Follette of Wisconsin sat silent . . . drinking in every word that the President uttered. He joined in the handclapping—his first show of feeling—that began the demonstration over the President's declaration: 'The war thus comes to an end.' "

Bob wrote Belle on November 15 that he stood alone in his room that night thinking about what the peace that had finally come meant to him and others: "When I pulled my curtain down preparatory to settling myself at my desk, I looked up at the nearly full moon and felt as if I could almost make you hear and feel me through her. You will be out on the front porch a little later feeling her wonderful spell and thinking of the absent ones so widely separated. And yet how favored we have been and are. We have lived with an awful fear in our hearts for our beloved boys so long that as we begin to come back toward normal life and conditions with both of them still with us and the balance of the flock well—that I want to pray or cry or sing my thankfulness for all our blessings."

Gil came to Washington from New York, hoping that at long last the meeting of the Privileges and Elections Committee set for November 22 would see action on the pending motion to dismiss the disloyalty charges against Bob. It proved a quick, quiet meeting. The vote was 9 to 2 in favor of dismissing the charges. The Washington newspapers carried the headlines *La Follette Case Ends* and *Charges Against La Follette Dropped*.

Bob also received good news from Bobbie written December 1: "Dear Daddie, I get around the house quite a bit now with a cane. I take a bath in the tub all by myself and go to the bathroom to shave and wash 'n everything, with abandon. Almost like a regular person. I am adopting a regular routine for exercises starting tomorrow. Have a schedule all worked out in which Mother will play an important part of course. Good night dear dad, I love you with every fiber of my being."

Phil received his discharge from the Army on December 26 and planned to visit Bob in Washington, thinking he must be lonesome with the rest of the family in La Jolla. But Bob wired him to join his mother in La Jolla and Phil walked in, unannounced, on the family there. By this time Bobbie could even drive their second-hand car. He had written his father on December 5, "It seems almost like flying to get at the wheel after being dependent on the wheelchair." Bob answered: "Oh, my boy, God was good to you when he picked out the woman to be your mother. She knew what was best. When I look back over the terrible months and think of the even steady way, the control, the deep insight with which she has met it all, she grows more wonderful to me as time passes. She is the only one who never became in the least degree 'batty.' I should have worn a 'straight-jacket' part of the time. Let us think of her first in everything while we live. . . . Put your arms around Mamma and love her for me too. She knows *what's* best and just *when* it's best."

Then he added: "One of the hardest things about the last two years is the feeling of repression we have had to carry around with us. It is an awful strain on one's poise and control. I know it has made me a very different person to live with. Sometimes I wonder if I will ever be just the same again."

Bob was distressed to learn American troops were fighting in Russia. The Allies and the United States had agreed to send five divisions of troops into Russia "at the request of 'leading Russians' to 'crush the Reds.' " President Wilson had responded to Allied pressure and ordered United States troops to Archangel in northern Russia. Senator Hiram Johnson, a Republican from California, had criticized the Administration on December 12 for this intervention in Russia's internal affairs. Bob was glad Johnson had opened up the subject though he did not agree with some of the Senator's arguments.

Belle wrote Bob on February 6, 1919, regarding the Allied troops in Russia: "These jolts hurt worse than wordy tirades. But what shall we do? Shall we dissociate ourselves from everyone who disappoints us and with whom we disagree? This war has shaken the foundations and is changing the face of the earth. Tremendous and unexpected results are following. New issues are arising. If we would preserve our sanity, if we would not be overwhelmed with bitterness, if we are to have any chance for usefulness, must we not cooperate where we can, concentrate mind and heart on the best that can be done, and keep faith in the outcome of every rightly directed effort? I am repeating this doctrine for my own benefit rather than yours. I find it very hard to convince myself any effort of individuals will avail. The forces set loose seem so beyond control. All we can do or say seems like the chatter of birds against a hurricane."

The Peace Conference was to open January 18, 1919, and Wilson sailed for Europe on December 4, arriving December 14 in Paris where he was welcomed with acclaim. Bob was distrustful of the Allies' purposes at the peace table as represented by the Big Four—the United States, France, Great Britain and Italy. Most of the dispatches from Europe made him heartsick at the prospects for an enduring peace. The shadow of the Russian revolution distorted the viewpoint of the Allied representatives who were to sit at the peace table, for England, France and Italy were afraid of the Bolshevik revolution. Bob was convinced these three countries had settled the "peace" terms in advance according to the secret treaties made in the early months following the outbreak of war. He was certain they would pay no attention to Wilson's peace proposals, The Fourteen Points.

Bobbie's birthday was February 6 and Bob wrote Belle, wondering how they celebrated it: "I see him in your arms for the first time, mamma, our boy-baby. I see him in little leather breeches, with his sweater and cap and curls—and then a chubby sturdy boy with his thick tangle of dark hair—his mother's honest eyes. I have been hunting bears with him in the Rockies again today. And so he has been in my mind all day coming down through the years, always a good pal and now a good counselor. I have been contrasting him as he is today with myself at 24. He has better book training than I had at that time. And he has a knowledge of affairs—a grasp of national and world conditions and problems equal to that of the men who are called the mature and profound statesmen of our time—of *today*."

Writing to his son he said: "You will start life as a man, Bobbie, standing on my shoulders. You have your mother's brain, my boy—the best brain in the world. With established health, what a service you can be to your community, your country and humanity! I greet you. Take one on me! Here is my check for ten."

A letter Belle had written Bob crossed in the mail: "Daddy dear. In some ways Bobbie seems to me singularly susceptible to environment and suggestion. With all his force and individuality, his problem seems to be to take the initiative, to assume the big responsibility of shaping his own career, or deciding what he shall do and be. All through his long sickness this idea that he had not met his responsibility, had not made the most of his power and opportunity, had preyed on him. . . . I should like to see him doing outdoor *work*—a work of his *own choosing*. I think it would be of immense value to Bobbie to *earn a dollar* doing something he really *wanted to do*. Love ever, Mama."

Belle's and Bob's ideas of what would be best for Bobbie differed widely now. Not surprisingly after his long and debilitating illness, Bobbie himself seemed personally insecure and without strong ambition. In a letter to his father, thanking him for the ten dollars, Bobbie added, "No, Dad, I don't stand on your shoulders by a long shot. If I did I certainly would set the world on fire."

A letter Belle wrote Phil at this time contained the words on top of the page, "Destroy this letter after you have acted on it." It was in answer to a letter he had written asking for money to repay a small debt. Her letter read: "My beloved Phil, All my life I have been discovering that we owed more money than I had known about. Daddy had not told me because he thought it would worry me. To this day he does not understand how much more the *uncertainty* wears on me than the definite facts would. Just because you did not tell me about the note, I cannot but fear that perhaps there are other amounts, that you and I cannot rest until they are *all* paid. Love eternal, Mother."

Congress adjourned March 4, 1919, and that night Bob went with Fola and Mid to the Belasco Theater to see *Adam and Eva*, a comedy Mid had written with Guy Bolton. Bob was feeling the long separation from his family but refrained from suggesting Mary join him because she was planning to leave La Jolla for Madison to enter the University of Wisconsin at the start of the second semester. She had always planned to attend the college of her brothers, sister and parents. Phil had written to ask her to arrive in Madison in time to be his guest at the junior prom. She hesitated because she could not afford to buy new clothes. Phil reassured her if she had two party dresses she would not need new ones because no one in Madison had seen any of her dresses. They would look new. He added, "And you are so pretty anyhow that clothes don't make much difference."

It was the custom to invite Wisconsin's United States senators, the governor and other high officials to the prom. But this year Bob's name was omitted from the list. The obvious slight caused the family deep distress. Under these circumstances Mary declined the invitation to the prom so Phil arranged to meet her in Chicago and take her out there.

Bob wrote Belle March 16, "I am so sorry for both of the kids. To have such a nasty feeling thrust into their university life will make a lasting impression, I fear. Now with me, it don't count. It is like the buzzing of a gnat after you have been having the time of your life in a den of rattlesnakes."

During the hours Phil and Mary were together in Chicago he persuaded her to give up her plan to enter the university. He thought she would be unhappy in a place that showed so much hostility toward her father. Mary decided to go to Washington to see her father and then to art school there, to pursue her first love.

Bob wrote Belle and Bobbie on March 25: "Well, what do you think happened to me this afternoon? I was moping away up here in my room, when there came a faint tap at the door. I opened the door and there *stood Mary—my Mary!!!* Do you know what I did? I just cried! That's what I did. I'm an old man all right. . . . Ye Gods but it was good to have my arms around her and hold her in my lap—my baby. . . . Mary and I haven't talked things over or made any plans—yet—and I don't know what she has in her head. But Washington is hers. She shall have anything she wants—and do everything she wants to do. Say, I *feel just as if I had been demobilized.*"

A few days later he wrote of Mary: "We have each of us worked all the evenings since she came . . . she in her room and I in mine—but we run back and forth as we think of things to say to each other. Yes indeed I like to talk over things with Mary—she sees everything with level eyes—and has clear strong thinking back of it all." Bob had a small fund available for clerical help and Mary took a job in his office while attending evening classes at the Corcoran School of Art.

In response to one of Bob's letters deploring the terms of the Peace Treaty, Belle wrote on April 16, 1919: "Whatever one's attitude toward the war and our part in it, is it not the part of true statesmanship to deal with the problems as they exist? Just as I do not believe we can ever return to the old kind of personal competition in the business world, so I think we must accept some changed conditions in the political world."

She went on: "It seems to me nations cannot stand *isolated* if they would or even if it is for their own particular good. Some kind of a federated world whose ideal *should be* the best good of all, is bound to come. Selfish interests are bound to do their best to dominate it. They had their part in framing our Constitution which we are disposed to believe was a great document for human welfare. And it was. But we know some of the framers were almost as fearful of any real rule of the masses as the governments of today are now scared at Bolshevism. The proposed League of Nations may be so bad you cannot support it. I am only suggesting the spirit in which I think it should be approached."

Bob fully agreed with Belle as to the need for some kind of international organization to promote cooperation among the nations of the world. Because of the war, membership in the Women's International League for Peace and Freedom had become practically nonexistent, except for Belle and a few other staunch survivors who kept the idea alive.

The reports Bob now received indicated there was nothing left in the treaty of Wilson's Fourteen Points "that couldn't be covered with a postage stamp." He wrote Belle on April 21, "There can be no permanent peace based on wrong and no League can be formed strong enough to maintain such a peace."

She wrote him in March that Bobbie had improved sufficiently so she thought it safe for her to return to Washington if Bob believed it necessary. He replied, "You know, Mamma, my arms will be open whenever you feel you can come. A lot of the biggest problems will be here, calling for the best that is in the family. I flounder along the best I can . . . there is no one I can counsel with—excepting as Gil gets over occasionally. Just as soon as Wilson returns the very atmosphere here will be surcharged with high-voltage currents of deadly power. I never needed you close to me more than I will when the battle opens—but you must be awfully worn and fagged."

Belle found a tiny cottage in La Jolla for Bobbie that rented for $16.50 a month. She made certain he was settled in, then on May 6 took the train to Washington via Chicago. As they parted Bobbie gave her a letter to read on the train. He had written: "You know Mother dearest just how hard it is for me to have you go. You are so fine and wonderful. . . . And yet I know how little of my love for you I seem to express from day to day when you are near. It's just something in my makeup that makes me so for I do love you Mamma, so awfully much. . . . I can never tell you just what your great fight with and for me means to me. I know something of what it has cost you, Mother dear. And if I too should ever amount to anything it will be due to your wonderful self."

She wrote him on May 8: "It filled my heart with joy and I have said to myself many times today that I have more than my share of happiness. You children all overappreciate me—not my love for you, but what I have been able to do for you. And Bobbie dear, you quite underestimate your power of expression. *I am always conscious of your love.* . . . Don't worry about the future. You have the power and you will succeed when you are ready to take hold again."

May 8 was Phil's birthday. At Belle's invitation they met in Chicago and "visited hard" for two days. In a note to Phil written as she rode to Washington, Belle confessed she only had $3.50 in her purse. She explained, "Really the only reason I mind being short of funds is that I wanted to make our day in Chicago more of a birthday celebration for you. But we could hardly have gotten more joy out of it if we had been millionaires, could we?"

While waiting for Belle to arrive, Bob wrote Bobbie: "I have the sense of *waiting, waiting,* that subconsciously drags at the wheels of time because I know our dear mama is to come." On May 14 he wrote Bobbie of Belle's arrival in Washington: "How was any poor mortal 'way down South' in this old benighted place ever to know when Lady Belle would make her appearance. Didn't she telegraph? Well not so as you could notice it any.

"So I notifies old man Hannan this morning to hand me a memorandum of every train from Chicago on both lines. And this afternoon Mary and I started in to do the list for a day and a half at least. We caught Belle trying to slip through the gate immediately following the arrival of the first afternoon train on the B & O. She surrendered with a fight—and one on each side Mary and I escorted her to 3320 16th and we now have her securely in hand."

Belle probably used the $3.50 for meals on the train and had no money left to telegraph her time of arrival. She had been away from Washington almost a year.

The Fight for Peace
and Teapot Dome

[1919–1923]

Belle fulfilled another of her goals in life three weeks after she returned to Washington. On June 4, 1919, she sat in the Senate family gallery, where she had spent so many of her days, and heard the Senate finally pass the Susan B. Anthony amendment.

Bob described the scene by letter to his sons that night: "Mamma sat in the gallery all day and was rewarded as were the other fighters for suffrage and equal rights by seeing the Susan B. Anthony amendment pass by 56 to 25—after a 70-year struggle. I started the applause *on the floor* and it swept the galleries again and again without any rebuke from the chair, President [Albert] Cummins [of Iowa] presiding. All felt that it was a great victory."

Belle did not stop in her work to advance not only the status of women but mankind as a whole. She became even more active in what she considered the current critical issue—world peace. The Peace Treaty was signed in Paris on June 28 and Wilson embarked on the *S. S. George Washington* the next day. Bob wrote his family on June 29: "Wilson has signed an agreement to bind us to fight in every future world war. He has entered into a treaty that is without parallel in all history as a spoils-grabbing compact of greed and hate."

Belle was again in the gallery on June 10 when Wilson placed the Treaty of Versailles before the Senate for ratification and reported on the work of the Peace Conference. The President received an enthusiastic welcome but, as the *New York Times* reported, his speech was "heard in silence" as he described the treaty in general terms.

Belle and Bob felt, as he wrote in the September 19 issue of their *Magazine*, "This League and Treaty is nothing but the old, old scheme, modified a little to fit the times—of an alliance among the

victorious governments, following a great war, by which their con-
quered enemies may be kept in subjugation and exploited to the
uttermost."

During July Belle became ill with an abcessed tooth, followed
by a systemic infection and high temperature. Her health had always
been exceptionally good. She had great physical energy—each time
the family moved from Madison to Washington and back (at least
twice a year) she packed sixteen or seventeen boxes of clothes, books,
papers. If she ever suffered aches or pains, she never spoke of them,
according to Mary. She recalled the only time she saw Belle take to
her bed, obviously suffering but not complaining, was one day when
she made doughnuts at the farm. Bob was particularly fond of her
light, crispy doughnuts and though she did not approve of fried food,
she made this concession for him. While pouring off the hot fat she
spilled some, burning her left arm badly. The doctor took hours to
arrive by horse and buggy. The burn left a mean scar.

Bob, who accepted his illnesses calmly, now worried about Belle
because it was so unusual to see her in pain. When the acute infection
cleared up, the doctor insisted she must get away from the midsummer
heat of Washington. Fola accompanied her mother to the West Virginia mountains. Mary had left for New York and Parsons School of
Art. Aware of Bob's anxiety about her, Belle wrote July 23: "It is
wonderful to have Fola to rely on. She does everything with the same
thoroughness you do . . . I feel it is hard for you to be there alone
but I know you will keep your strength for your work and trust you
to take care of yourself."

Bobbie had left La Jolla on July 3 and, at the suggestion of Dr.
Charles Mayo, stopped off at the Mayo Clinic for a complete checkup.
He reported to his father on July 29 that the doctors told him he
"could go home and work his head off."

After sixteen years of serving as his secretary, Hannan decided
the time had come to leave Bob. He wrote Bob on July 22 he would
"always cherish the memory of those years. . . . With each succeeding
day my personal attachment to, and affection for you have grown. . . .
Not only because of your kind personal treatment of me but because
with each day I have come to have a deeper appreciation of the high
ideals that govern your public service."

Bob now asked Bobbie if he wanted to take Hannan's place, a
way of entering the political scene. Bobbie was delighted at the offer.
It meant he would not have to return to the university. Before starting

on the job he visited his brother at Madison, where they had planned to meet before going together to Washington. Phil was out of the Army by Christmas 1918 and had returned to the university for his degree. He now decided to enter George Washington Law School in Washington. At long last Bob and Belle would have both sons with them in the same city.

Bobbie wrote his father from Madison that the memory of the "war hatred" there had changed his feeling about the city in which he was born and grew up. Bob replied: "Bobbie, don't let that feeling against our home place take hold of you for a moment. It is the same crowd that always fought me. What if I had grown to hate the place because they downed me half a dozen times and maligned and traduced and boycotted me as they did for years? I would not let a few cheapskates drive me away from the most beautiful place in the world—where I had made my home, reared my family, buried my dead. I whipped them. Eighty percent are our real friends. They have been bound hand and foot and gagged there as they have everywhere in this country and in the world. But *there is another day*. And where I have spent my life and done my greatest work, no set of living men shall tell me to 'move on.' "

Belle reported in the September issue of *La Follette's Magazine*: "The women of the United States may vote in 1920. On August 18 the state legislature of Tennessee ratified the constitutional amendment which declares that the rights of the citizens of the United States shall not be denied or abridged on account of sex. With Tennessee's ratification the suffrage amendment became a part of the Constitution. For the first time in American history women may vote in every state of the union for candidates of all offices—local, state and national—and women may hold any office now held by men, whether elective or appointive." Belle also pointed out, "The United States is almost the last of the great powers to grant the vote to women. England, Russia, Germany, Norway, Sweden and Denmark all preceded us."

Just before Election Day in 1920 Belle reported in her column a speech given before the College Woman's Club of Washington, D. C., by Mrs. Harriet Connor Brown. Mrs. Brown urged women to organize through their various existing organizations, whether college, professional, union or church, to make their votes felt in the coming election. Belle's column was headlined *Women to the Rescue*.

She wrote: "We have reached a crisis in the history of our nation and in the history of the world. All mankind wants peace and yet men prepare for war. One fact alone is hopeful: Women of the world, for the first time in history, have the power to compel an appeal to reason in disputes between nations. If our powers of organization and cooperation are equal to the task we may save mankind, otherwise the outlook for civilization is bleak. Two years hence every man in Congress who is in favor of large military expenditures and conscription of our sons can be retired to private life."

Bob now embarked on a running debate in the Senate in the fight surrounding the Treaty of Versailles. His personal contribution to the struggle against ratifying the treaty occupied hundreds of pages in the *Congressional Record*, including five carefully prepared speeches. The central theme of his argument expressed his conviction the President had exceeded his constitutional powers in negotiating the treaty. Bob maintained that under the Constitution the President should have consulted the Senate at the moment he started to use his power to negotiate because it was "too late for the advice to be effective after the treaty is made and signed and passes out of his hands and into the possession of the Senate."

His gravest objection was that members of the League of Nations acted on "secret treaties" made between the Allied powers for the distribution of the territory of Europe, Asia, and Africa, and the Senate was being asked to ratify the results. Bob claimed the Paris conference pursued not the terms of an armistice but followed, "line by line," national boundaries as they had been fixed in the secret treaties made in 1916 and 1917, including dismemberment of the Austro-Hungarian Empire.

He told the Senate: "The little group of men who sat in secret conclave for months at Versailles were not peacemakers. They were war makers. They cut and slashed the map of the Old World in violation of the terms of the armistice. They patched up a new map of the Old World in consummation of the terms of the secret treaties the existence of which they had denied because they feared to expose the sordid aims and purposes for which men were sent to death by the tens of thousands daily.

"They betrayed China. They locked the chains on the subject peoples of Ireland, Egypt and India. They partitioned territory and traded off peoples in mockery of that sanctified formula of Fourteen Points, and made it our nation's shame. Then, fearing the wrath of outraged peoples, knowing that their new map would be torn to rags and tatters by the conflicting warring elements which they had bound together in wanton disregard of racial animosities, they made a League of Nations to stand guard over the swag!

"Senators, if we go into this thing it means greater discontent, a deeper, more menacing unrest. Mr. President, whatever course other senators take, I shall never vote to bind my country to the monstrous undertaking which this covenant would impose."

Bob was not alone in his views. Many other senators expressed their disappointment with the covenant of the League of Nations. But he was undoubtedly one of the most articulate and eloquent.

Belle and Bob had been looking forward to seeing the family under one roof for the Christmas holidays. Belle wrote Mary in New York on December 5 that her father seemed to want "an old-fashioned party such as you had when you were all in high school." Belle said she had arranged a dance for the night after Christmas and assured Mary, "We shall have plenty of room for everybody." Belle had converted the attic into a temporary dormitory so the children could invite their friends as houseguests. Fola and Mid arrived a few days before Christmas. Bob enjoyed the party he yearned for, the happy reunion he had dreamed of during the year the family was separated while Bobbie convalesced in La Jolla.

A poignant moment occurred when Phil reminisced about his visit to them at their cottage by the beach: "The warm, balmy weather, the peaceful Pacific, and the awful load that was lifting from our lives gave us an inner peace at Christmas that seemed almost unbelievable. I don't think any of us had realized how horrible those two years had been. There were deep scars within each of us that we would carry as long as we lived. But the ceaseless strain and daily apprehension were gone."

Phil delighted both Bob and Belle by revealing his decision to study law and the extent to which the decision had been influenced by Belle. He wrote later: "She said that the study of law is invaluable even if one never practices it. It is not the learning of law that is so important as learning to think—especially in legal terms. The cornerstone of that thinking is that in issues between people, or peoples, there are at least two sides, so do not take sides until you understand and weigh the problem as a whole."

When Congress convened in January 1920, Bob did not feel well enough to attend the Senate sessions. He took no further part in the continued debate on the Peace Treaty. Instead, on January 26 he went to the Mayo Clinic with Bobbie to find out why he felt so ill.

By February 12 Dr. Will Mayo and Dr. Charles Mayo completed their examinations and agreed a return of gallstones was causing Bob's pain and other symptoms. The Mayo brothers advised removal of the gallbladder but did not want to operate during the prevailing flu epidemic. They suggested Bob return to Madison and undertake a limited schedule of work until the epidemic subsided, then he would undergo the operation.

Belle printed an analysis of the budget appropriation passed by Congress for that year in her May 1920 column: "Past Wars, 68%; Future Wars, 25%; Civil Departments, 3%; Public Works, 3%; Education, 1%." She commented: "Women are dead in earnest about using votes to turn this table, to reverse those figures, so that the resources of the world shall be made to flow into channels of production instead of destruction."

Bob left Madison for the Mayo Clinic on May 29 to prepare for the operation. The next day Belle, Phil and Mary arrived in Madison to organize the household at the farm so everything would be ready when Bob came home to recuperate.

On the morning of June 7 Dr. Will Mayo removed Bob's gallbladder and one gallstone. Bob recovered easily and Dr. Mayo predicted he soon would be fine. Phil stayed with his father until he could return to Madison while Bobbie traveled to Chicago to meet with the Wisconsin delegation and attend the Republican National Convention as an observer. Senator Warren G. Harding of Ohio was nominated for President on the tenth ballot and Massachusetts Governor Calvin Coolidge was nominated vice-president.

The Democratic convention in San Francisco nominated Ohio Governor James M. Cox for President and Franklin D. Roosevelt of New York for vice-president. The entrance of the United States into the League of Nations was the paramount campaign issue. Election Day brought a nationwide Republican landslide as Harding defeated Cox by 498,576 to 113,422.

Bob was present at the opening session of the Sixty-sixth Congress on December 6, 1920, when President-elect Harding was given an ovation as he took his senatorial seat. He returned to the floor after a ten-minute speech expressing regret at leaving his colleagues. As he passed Bob in the front row, he paused, patted Bob cordially on the shoulder, and said, "Now, Bob, be good."

Bob retorted, "I'll be busy making *you* be good!"

During the final congressional session of Wilson's administration,

Bob held a strong position because the Republican majority in the Senate was so small that by securing the cooperation of a few Progressive Republicans and Democrats, it was possible to block the old guard Republicans. Ten days after Congress convened Bob halted an attempt to ram through a bill introduced during the previous session that made it a crime for railroad employees to strike. The bill died at the end of the Sixty-sixth Congress.

The last days of 1920 saw a nostalgic, old-fashioned La Follette kind of Christmas. The family was together again, expressing love and care for each other and for the causes they mutually espoused. On Christmas Day Belle joined the "peace on earth" rally planned by the Women's Committee for World Disarmament, of which she was an executive. She was also the principal speaker at the rally.

It was a windy, freezing day as she spoke her mind and heart standing on a cold corner of Pennsylvania Avenue: "We women have the power to compel disarmament. We need not plead or beg. We have the ballot. On this issue of militarism we hold the balance of power. We propose to be practical. We propose to watch Congress. And here on this day precious to the Christian world, at the very door of the Capitol of our beloved nation, we vow to use our voices to *defeat* those senators and representatives in Congress who stand for militarism and war and to *elect* senators and representatives who stand for peace and disarmament. Real disarmament of nations will relieve the people of the world from the grievous burden of military taxation, thus paving the way to transfer to education and public welfare the aid so long denied."

Belle always believed once women got the vote they would use the power of the ballot to establish a purer form of government and a more peaceful world. This was the fight to which she dedicated her utmost convictions.

Bob was present on March 4, 1921, when Harding was sworn in as President and Coolidge, vice-president. Among Harding's appointments were Harry M. Daugherty as attorney general and Senator Albert B. Fall of New Mexico as secretary of the interior. Bob felt very apprehensive about these two nominations. Their confirmation had been rushed through by Harding so as to effectively block Bob's plan to oppose Fall's appointment.

Fall was a member of the Senate committee that investigated Bob's loyalty during the war. Fall had been voracious in his attacks on Bob and had, through parliamentary proceedings, effectively denied Bob his right to defend himself. Fall also had opposed all bills designed to conserve natural resources. Bob had reason to distrust him.

At Bob's suggestion Belle and two other members of the Women's Committee for World Disarmament called upon Progressive Republican Senator William Borah from Idaho early in the new session of Congress to urge him to introduce his resolution for a disarmament conference. Borah did so on May 4 in the form of an amendment to a Navy appropriation bill. Though the President opposed the amendment, the public demand for a conference had become so strong that on May 25 the Senate passed it unanimously.

The second marriage of a La Follette child took place on June 15, 1921, when Mary married Ralph Sucher, a law student and newspaper correspondent who was a classmate and friend of Phil's at the university. Their wedding was the last La Follette social event to take place at the house on Sixteenth Street. The rent had been raised and Belle and Bob could no longer afford the spacious house. Nor would they need it, with all the children gone except Bobbie.

After the wedding Belle and Bob went to Wisconsin. Bob began his reelection campaign and Belle worked with Mrs. John Blaine, wife of the governor, to further the disarmament and world peace movement. Bob had not spoken in Madison in four years because of the hostile feelings during the war. According to Phil, friends arranged for Bob to speak in the assembly chamber at the state capitol but cautioned, "Don't talk about the war. . . . The war hysteria is receding. Don't stir it up. Talk about domestic issues. Spread balm on the scars. Let your old friends who deserted us in the war days come back to our camp." Bob listened but made no comment, no commitment.

The day arrived and the assembly chamber was packed. Bob started his speech with formal graciousness by expressing his thanks to his friends and neighbors for cordially welcoming him back to the place where he was born and had made his home for a lifetime.

"Then," Phil recalled, "he changed. The muscles of his jaw tightened. His blue eyes shot fire. He raised his right arm, fingers together, hand upright and waving aloft like a banner. The words came out like salvos from a sixteen-inch battery: 'I am going to be a candidate for reelection to the United States Senate. I do not want the vote of a single citizen under any misapprehension of where I stand: *I would not change my record on the war for that of any man, living or dead.*'

"A few moments of deathly silence followed as the audience began to grasp what he was saying and what it meant. There he stood—sixty-five years old. After four years of as wicked a beating as ever came to a man in public life in American history: Defiant! No quarter asked or given! The fight was on!

"Pandemonium broke loose. He got the greatest ovation of his life. A member of the state senate who had fought Bob La Follette for nearly forty years—and would still fight him—sat in his seat, tears running down his cheeks as he shook his head, repeating to himself, 'I hate the son of a bitch, but, my God, what guts he's got!' "

After the Senate passed the Borah amendment, President Harding called a conference of the United States, Great Britain, France, Italy and Japan to meet in Washington. The purpose was to discuss ways and means to achieve substantial naval disarmament.

Belle used her column in the weeks before the conference to make an appeal that a woman be seated in the United States delegation: "Failure to utilize women's special fitness and power to serve efficiently in this great cause must be the occasion for keen criticism. It has been women's initiative, zeal and determination that have had such a large influence in calling for the conference. Public opinion causes the conference, but the public is not invited to participate."

The official name of the disarmament conference, as it was popularly called, was the Confederation on Limitations of Armaments. Senator Borah, whose legislation had created the conference, was deliberately passed over for a seat on the delegation. The American delegates were Secretary of State Charles Evans Hughes, Senators Henry Cabot Lodge and Oscar Wilder Underwood and former Senator Elihu Root. For twelve weeks the delegates met in secret sessions at the Pan-American building in Washington. The plenary, or open sessions, were held in the D.A.R. auditorium next door. Belle attended the opening sessions, reporting for the *Magazine*.

In the secret sessions Hughes proposed a limitation on naval construction for ten years; this was agreed to by the delegates. A ratio was also agreed upon under which Japan, France and Italy were each permitted three-fifths the tonnage allowed Great Britain and the United States. All the participating nations agreed to stop building battleships and to destroy some already built or under construction. But nothing was done to limit the number of submarines and naval aircraft or the size of land armies. Or, indeed, to end the institution of war.

As Senator Carter Glass expressed it, the agreement was "not a permanent scheme to prevent war but a temporary expedient to avert bankruptcy." The treaty won the necessary two-thirds vote by the margin of 67 to 27.

During the few sessions open to the press and public, four seats were reserved for women and Belle was able to attend these sessions. At the end of the conference she vented her frustration in her column of February 1922: "This conference was called in response to the demand of the great masses of people, especially women, for disarmament and the end of war. But the delegates selected to sit at the council table were all representatives of the conservative class and whatever progress was made was made from their point of view. These delegates sought to lessen the chance of war and to mitigate its horrors, but they continued to think in terms of war. There was no strong forward-looking spirit about that table demanding that the will of the great masses of plain people be made effective—that there be *no more war.*"

During the brief recess between the first and second Senate sessions, Bob went home to Madison to be with his sister Jo and brother-in-law Judge Robert Siebecker, now Chief Justice of the Wisconsin Supreme Court. Robert was critically ill and died shortly after Bob returned to Washington. Bob was heartsick at losing his old college friend and law partner. For nearly two decades he had been a leader in interpreting Progressive legislation in Wisconsin, making it work, and thus creating a model for the rest of the nation.

On May 31, 1921, less than three months after his inauguration, Harding issued an executive order transferring control of the naval oil reserves from the secretary of the navy to the secretary of the interior. This was done in spite of protests from a number of naval officers. Rear Admiral Robert S. Griffin told Secretary of the Navy Edwin Denby that if he turned the naval oil reserves over to the Department of the Interior, "We might just as well say good-bye to our oil."

There were three large Western oil reserves, two in California and one in Wyoming at Teapot Dome. These reserves were to be treated as storehouses, held in trust for future use by the Navy in event of scarcity, high prices or national emergency. Throughout the Wilson administration Secretary of the Navy Josephus Daniels had zealously protected them and Bob had repeatedly approved this policy on the Senate floor.

The President's executive order was reported on the inside pages of a few newspapers. A seven-line story in the lower corner of the second page of the *Washington Evening Star* on June 2, written by Jerre Mathews, a Washington correspondent, first drew Bob's attention to the report. Soon after the order was issued Harry Slattery, executive secretary of the National Conservation Association, who had worked with Bob in the 1919 fight to protect naval oil reserves, started an active inquiry into their status. Months of investigation revealed that claims on these reserves, which had been decided against the great oil company claimants under the Wilson administration, were being reopened by Interior Secretary Fall and, in hearings, were decided in favor of the oil companies.

Bob gathered the facts for a resolution. He asked to see President Harding's executive orders of May 31, 1921. The orders had never been published in full and were not on file at the State Department, where such orders were required to be filed.

Bob wrote Secretary of State Hughes on April 6, asking for a copy of the President's orders relating to naval oil and coal reserves. The same day, he wrote former Secretary of the Navy Daniels, revealing what he had learned "on reliable authority" and stating he intended to take the matter up in the Senate. He asked Daniels's opinion on recent developments. Bob also telegraphed officials in Wyoming asking for information about the leasing of the United States naval oil reserves at Teapot Dome.

Secretary Hughes did not reply directly but sent Bob's letter to Secretary Fall. He wrote Bob on April 12 enclosing copies of the Executive order. As Bob read the order transferring the naval reserves to the Department of the Interior, he was convinced this was a violation of the law—an order beyond the power of the President.

On April 14 the *Wall Street Journal* informed its readers that Teapot Dome oil reserves had been leased to the Sinclair Oil Company, of which Harry F. Sinclair of New Jersey was founder and president. The *Journal* remarked this was "one of the greatest petroleum undertakings of the age." Bob referred to this article two weeks later in a Senate speech. He also pointed out the article reported that during the interval between the signing of the lease and the official announcement by the Department of the Interior, when, as Bob put it, "mystery surrounded the public's business," speculation caused Sinclair Oil stocks to jump $30,000,000 on the New York Stock Exchange in three days' trading. Subsequent investigation showed that Attorney General Daugherty was among those dealing in Sinclair Oil stock at this time.

Bob introduced a resolution in the Senate on April 21 calling on Secretary Fall to furnish detailed information regarding leases on all naval oil reserves. His investigation had convinced him the President's transfer of the naval reserves to the Interior department was illegal and Fall's leases were obtained in a fraudulent manner. When Bob sought information from naval officers who, he knew, had been opposed to leasing the naval oil reserves, he discoered they had been ordered to sea or distant ports. He was certain he had enough evidence to demand a sweeping investigation.

When Bob rose in the Senate the afternoon of April 28 to introduce his revised resolution, he attacked the Department of the Interior. He called it "the sluiceway" for a large part of the corruption to which government was subjected. There was enough evidence available, he said, to prove the naval oil reserves were being "sacrificed to private exploitation at the hands of favored interests." He called the chicanery behind the leasing of the Teapot Dome oil fields "positively criminal."

Bob's resolution came to a vote early that afternoon. The Senate passed it unanimously and ordered an investigation of his charges. It uncovered shocking corruption in high places, as Bob had predicted. The Teapot Dome affair became one of the most famous scandals to rock the American government.

The next morning after his resolution had been passed, Bob arrived at his office to discover it had been broken into during the night. Though nothing had been stolen, it was apparent his desk had been thoroughly ransacked. Two years later Gaston B. Means, an "investigator" serving in the Bureau of Investigation of the Department of Justice, admitted he had searched Bob's office and desk to find "anything Bob had where he could be stopped in what he was doing." Means, who took his orders from Jess Smith, a close friend of Daugherty's, later became a private detective for President Harding.

The Senate investigation disclosed that Sinclair had made financial contributions to Secretary Fall. Five weeks after the Teapot Dome leases were signed, Sinclair had sent $233,000 in Liberty Bonds to Fall's son-in-law. They were subsequently deposited in various bank accounts belonging to Secretary Fall. The leases granted the Sinclair Oil Company the right to drill for oil, for profit, on the federally owned naval oil reserves.

Teapot Dome was not the only naval oil reserve involved in this scandal. The Senate investigation also disclosed the fact that Edward Doheny, a successful oil prospector, had obtained leases from Fall allowing him to drill in the Elk Hills reserve in California. The leases had been granted shortly after Doheny's son had carried $100,000 from New York to Washington in "a little black bag" and delivered it to Secretary Fall.

Fall's granting these oil leases, valued at about half a billion dollars, was denounced by the Senate as fraudulent. The contracts and leases made to Doheny were eventually voided by the courts because they had been "consummated by conspiracy, corruption, and fraud." The Sinclair lease of Teapot Dome was judged to have been made "by means of collusion and conspiracy." Secretary Fall was branded a "faithless public officer" by the United States Supreme Court and convicted of taking a bribe from Doheny but another jury acquitted Doheny of offering the bribe. Fall and Sinclair were both found guilty in what was known as the Fall-Sinclair conspiracy trial. Fall was sentenced to one year in jail and fined $100,000, becoming the first cabinet officer to serve a prison term. Sinclair served nine months in jail for contempt of the Senate and for attempting to intimidate the jury during the trial.

Bob's third Senatorial term was expiring and he knew the Harding administration was working for his defeat. On July 7, as she prepared to go on the road with her husband, Belle wrote to her children: "I could work over the lecture I once prepared for the Chautauqua on Daddy into a campaign speech. Likewise I figured that I could move my disarmament discussion into a 'No More War' speech. I will begin speaking on Tuesday the first of August. That makes just one month until the primary."

She used her July column to explain the "No More War" campaign and to urge her readers to participate: "Thirty-three states have scheduled No More War demonstrations for July 29 and 30 as part of an international celebration held on the anniversary of the outbreak of the great war. A quarter of a million No More War placards have been distributed. The simultaneous posting of these placards bearing these three words will appear everywhere on the morning of the 29. (If you can't obtain a printed placard, it is easy to make your own.) Demonstrations and parades are planned in many cities.

"No More War demonstrations began in three cities in Europe in 1920. They were carried out in 200 cities in France and Germany in 1921. This year ten nations are participating: England, France, Germany, Holland, Sweden, Austria, Czechoslovakia, Hungary, Portugal and Switzerland (as well as the United States)."

In a letter to a friend Belle wrote, "I love women and I am glad they have the vote. I wish men could realize that women are really a part of the body politic and not outsiders. . . . I can only repeat what I have so many times said: I believe there should be more women actively sharing the responsibilities of government."

In a six-week campaign Bob and Belle covered practically every county in Wisconsin, making two or three speeches a day in large cities and small towns. It was their first intensive campaign since 1916. Bobbie, who managed this campaign, wrote Ralph Sucher, his brother-in-law, on July 27, "Dad's meetings are one ovation after another. He has never had such meetings in his life." Phil gave speeches in his father's behalf in southern Wisconsin.

By midnight on primary day, September 5, it was evident Bob had been renominated by a landslide. He carried all but one of the 71 counties and that county, a traditionally Stalwart stronghold, he lost by only 481 out of 7,785 votes. The Associated Press reported he won by the greatest majority a candidate had ever polled in a Wisconsin primary. All the Progressive Republican candidates on the national ticket except one were nominated, as were those on the state ticket, headed by Governor John Blaine.

Throughout the nation the press pegged Bob as the strongest factor in the next Presidential election. An editorial in the *Raleigh News and Observer*, owned by former Navy Secretary Daniels, called Bob's success "under all circumstances the most remarkable exhibition of personal power in American politics in the present decade."

Belle wrote on October 2 to Fola and Mid, who had just returned to this country after two years in France: "Daddy is quite well and deep down happy. There is a general feeling that the primary settled everything and that there is no need of an election campaign."

Bob returned to Washington for the closing weeks of the session and was warmly greeted by colleagues as he entered the chamber. When Mid saw him, he reminded his father-in-law of the prediction he had made during the war. Bob had prophesied, "I may not live to see my own vindication but you will." Bob now said, "Yes, Mid. The circle is complete, all the rest is velvet."

Throughout the country the elections were against the Harding administration but in spite of the strong anti-Republican trend, Progressive Republicans had been elected in all states except Indiana in which they had won nominations. When the new congressmen took office the Republican majority had been reduced to eleven in the Senate and seventeen in the House—this meant the Progressive Republican group would hold the balance of power. The Progressives had not held such power since 1911 during the Taft administration. Summarizing the election result, the *New York Times* commented, "There is no overlooking the fact that Senator La Follette, standing alone, will be the most powerful legislative factor in the next Congress. . . . His influence, potent in the Senate, will be even greater in the House, for there he has eleven members from Wisconsin, who will follow him. Today La Follette is stronger than at any other time in his career."

Meanwhile, Belle had taken on the Navy. Posters and billboards throughout the country pictured sailors aboard United States warships enjoying visits to exotic places. The captions read, "Join the Navy and See the World." In her May 1923 column Belle wrote: "Many a lonely boy, in hard luck, out of a job, is induced to enlist by these alluring posters. When Uncle Sam advertises, he is in a very different position from a private business man." She pointed out that if a breakfast food or an item of clothing does not live up to the advertisement, people can register their displeasure by not buying the product again.

"But," she continued, "the United States government is *our* government and holds the position of trustee to every man who enlists. It is a violation of that trust to enlist men by advertising that creates hopes and expectations that cannot be fulfilled. A boy enlists in the Navy for *four years.* If life is not as represented, is he free to resign? If he yields to homesickness and tries to escape, he is a deserter and sent to the guard house. This deceptive feature of the posters reflects dishonor on the government."

In the June issue of the *Magazine* Belle compared the role of women in government in the United States with their role in other nations' governments: "It is strange how backward the U.S. has been compared to other nations in selecting women for high official places. In Turkey a woman is minister of education. We have no department of education. The U.S. has no woman in the cabinet. Denmark has eleven women legislators. Sweden has five. Germany has more women members of Parliament than any other country. The U.S. has only one woman in Congress."

Another marriage in the La Follette family took place on April 14, 1923, when Phil married Isabel Bacon, who went by the nickname of Isen, in Chicago. As Isen recalled in her unpublished autobiography, *If You Can Take It*: "My relations with Mrs. La Follette could have been difficult, as Phil adored his mother and thought that she could do no wrong. However, she was an ideal mother-in-law and never interfered with our affairs except to encourage us to enlarge upon our potentialities. Someone repeated a remark she had made about me at the time—that I 'had the capacity for growth', which puzzled me. But with the years I have come to appreciate what she meant and to think it a vital quality for one to wish for one's children and their mates."

Bob had not been feeling well in spite of his victory in the election. His close friend William T. Rawleigh, who had made contributions to some of Bob's projects and campaigns, finally succeeded in persuading him to undergo an intensive series of tests at the Battle Creek Sanitarium in Michigan. Knowing Bob had little money, Rawleigh generously insisted that he and Belle stay as his guests at the sanitarium for as long as the doctors advised. They arrived at Battle Creek on May 27.

Bob followed the prescribed regime faithfully, took all the tests. He wrote Rawleigh on June 5, "If there are any unexplored places in my interior geography they are not to be found on their anatomical charts. We are giving ourselves to this one thing for which we came and I am confident already, at the end of ten days—that it will add substantially to my working capacity. It is another of the many things for which I shall be everlastingly grateful to you, my dear friend."

This thorough medical examination showed nothing wrong with Bob's health. Hearing this, Rawleigh persuaded Belle and Bob to take a real vacation for the first time in their lives, a vacation in Europe, for which he would pay. Bob accepted Rawleigh's generous offer to pay for Belle, Bobbie and himself because, he said, he would make the trip to learn about conditions in the countries there. He wanted to form his own judgment "on a basis of personal knowledge," not rely entirely on picking his "way through the maze of inspired propaganda with which Congress is flooded."

The doctors consented in mid-July to Bob's going off on the trip, provided he avoided public receptions, banquets, speech making and anything else that could interfere with gaining his strength.

Belle and Bob looked forward to this trip. They planned it not as a vacation but the chance to study the effect of the war and the Treaty of Versailles on European nations, especially Germany. And they were eager to visit Russia, now under Communist leadership.

Postwar Germany, Communist Russia and Italy

[1923]

Belle, Bob and Bobbie took the train to New York on July 31, 1923, for a bon voyage dinner with Fola and Mid, who lived at 158 Waverly Place in Greenwich Village. The buzzer bore two names, Fola La Follette and George Middleton.

Fola and Mid had gone to Europe in 1920 for two months and stayed two years, mostly in London and Paris. Before leaving on their first European trip Belle and Bob wanted to have a pow-wow, to receive impressions of the European situation from two family members who had recently returned.

The following day the three La Follettes, along with their friends Basil Manly, the director of the People's Legislative Service, and his wife Mollie, boarded the *S. S. George Washington*, bound for Plymouth, England, excited at the idea of their first long sea voyage and exploring Europe.

The third day out, at six a.m. the room steward knocked on Bob's stateroom door to inform him of the sudden death of President Harding. As the highest-ranking United States official on board, Bob was asked to preside at the memorial service. Belle and Bobbie prepared a statement about the service, which the captain radioed Mrs. Harding, along with an expression of sympathy.

Their arrival in Plymouth on August 9 was reported in the London *Times*, which had recently carried a long article about Bob's growing national importance as the leader of a possible third party in the coming election. A telegram from Prime Minister Ramsay MacDonald expressed regret he could not be at Plymouth to welcome Bob and asked if there was any chance to see him in Scotland.

Many newspapers requested interviews. Bobbie was in charge of his father's program in London. Belle wrote Mary that Bobbie was "kept busy whenever we are in our rooms answering the telephone. The London papers seem quite as eager as our own correspondents. Bobbie is very courteous and patient—tells them all that his father has come to observe and learn . . . that he is here to acquire information that will be helpful in his work and must devote himself to seeing people who can best serve this purpose."

Mrs. H. G. Wells sent a cordial note in which she invited Bob and Belle to visit her. Harold Laski, whom Supreme Court Justice Felix Frankfurter especially wanted Bob to meet, sent a letter from Belgium that began, "I need not say that to any radical you are one of the few Americans for whom real veneration is possible."

Belle participated in many of Bob's interviews. They both went to Labour party headquarters to discuss the American political scene. Bob suggested the party establish some means of regular correspondence between groups in England and the United States. He discovered both liberals and conservatives hoped the United States and Great Britain would unite in dealing with European problems. Certain British leaders hoped the United States would assume the principal financial and military responsibility for enforcing the Versailles Treaty.

Belle enjoyed their brief visits to the historic spots of London. Among her cherished memories was the famous old grapevine at Hampton Court, which bore luscious purple fruit. It reminded her of the venerable grapevine over the porch of their Wisconsin home. They stopped at Windsor, Warwick and Kenilworth castles and, of course, Stratford-on-Avon. Belle wrote Mary on October 15, "Daddy regretted not having more time at Shakespeare's house, but he got a great deal out of it and it was a source of profound satisfaction to him to have visited this spot on which his imagination has dwelt since boyhood."

They arrived at the Hotel Continental in Berlin on August 19. Belle wrote Mary they dined with the American Ambassador, Alanson Bigelow Houghton, on August 21, who supplied consular reports of conditions in Germany. They met the new prime minister, Gustav Stresemann, various members of the Reichstag, heads of labor organizations, editors and businessmen. Belle confided to Mary that Bob was "getting pretty tired and today he started in with a cold which worried me, but he felt much better after taking a rest this afternoon."

They both collected data on the depleted food supply in Germany, seeing with their own eyes that, after years of undernourishment, the people's strength was sapped and they were falling prey to disease. Belle noted that in Berlin, "bread, butter, milk, potatoes and other necessities are rationed by the German government. It is a tragic sight to see hundreds of people, mostly women, waiting in line for these rations." Belle recounted to Mary a story told her of a mother who after dropping her daughter at school stood on the potato ration line. When school was over, the daughter took her mother's place on line. The mother carried out other chores, then replaced the daughter on line. When she finally reached the end of the line, all the potatoes were gone.

Belle also visited the home of a man whose wage was $1.50 a week. There were six children in the family and cabbage soup once a day was their only food. Belle commented: "The misery of these people is beyond the power to imagine. What was once a comfortable income now has the purchasing power of a few cents. These people must work long hours, or beg, or starve. They are actually disappearing. The increase in suicide is appalling." To pay the reparations demanded by the Versailles Treaty, the German government had resorted to printing paper money of little real value so that inflation was rampant. Belle bought a box of figs priced at 500,000 marks with a one-dollar bill and received change.

At a tuberculosis hospital Belle saw the victims of the alarming increase in childhood sickness. Babies six to eight months old weighed less than their birth weight. Over a million Germans were on the brink of starvation, totally dependent on charity. Belle wrote, "One concrete fact stands out as plain as a pikestaff: that to rescue Germany from the abyss, she must have a sufficient food supply for the approaching winter or Germany will be in a state of civil war." Bob warned that those "who believe in self-government and democracy should see that food is sent before starvation drives Germany's hard working, intelligent, disciplined citizens to extremes either of Communism or Fascism."

Belle wrote Rawleigh: "During our ten days in Berlin the senator saw all of the leading members of the ministry, including Stresemann. He saw many of the intellectuals of Germany and also many industrialists and financiers. It was all very interesting and depressing because one could see right before one's eyes the disintegration of a once great country. It is stamped on the faces of everyone that one talks to."

Belle and Bob had been assured by the representatives of the

Soviet government in London they would be free to study conditions in Russia. The group left Berlin for Petrograd on August 30. Their friend Lincoln Steffens, who had preceded them to Europe, and Jo Davidson, sculptor and friend of Steffens, who lived in Paris, had been invited to join them en route. The party of seven took a small boat at Stettin, expecting to sail directly to Petrograd. But when the ship put in at Revel to discharge cargo, they decided to go by train to save time. Manly described the conditions: "We were supposed to be in a sleeping car but there were no mattresses or sheets, just two shelves which let down and thus, with two seats, provided four bunks in each compartment on which anyone could lie down that wanted to and cover up with all the coats he could borrow from other members of the party."

Bob noted in his diary they were met at the station by "S. Asnis," from the United States Consulate, who lunched with them, then left them at the Europa Hotel, owned by the government, as were all the hotels. Asnis called for them at five p.m. and took Bob, Steffens and Davidson to meet Gregory Weinstein, head of the Petrograd branch of the Foreign Office of the Soviet government. Belle, Bobbie and the Manlys went out to explore the city.

Bob wrote in his journal: "I had a very interesting interview with Weinstein, who formerly edited a Socialist paper in the U.S. As I understood, he was deported during the war. I informed him I wanted to get the truth as to the Soviet government and the condition of the people socially, economically, and politically . . . that I wanted to see the seamy side as well as the outside of their government, the bad as well as the good."

Bob described Weinstein as "an earnest, intelligent man, courteous and direct," who answered all questions frankly, admitting the Soviet government did not tolerate criticism or opposition of any sort.

All of Bob's interview requests were granted and he talked with most of the Petrograd leaders. Through interpreters he was told that some leaders deplored the suppression of free speech and a free press and also deplored conditions that resulted. On his return Bob wrote in the *Magazine* that "in their eagerness to carry out the Marxian theory, the leaders of the Soviet government have sacrificed the cardinal principles of democracy."

He thought it significant, he said, there were 150,000,000 people in Russia, of whom between eighty and ninety percent were peasants, and that the elections were "completely controlled by the Communist party, numbering less than 400,000." He concluded: "If I were a citizen of Russia I should resist this communistic dictatorship as vigorously as I have endeavored to resist the encroachment upon our democratic institutions in America. I hold that government by one class, denying to other classes the right to participate, is tyranny."

While Bob interviewed Soviet officials, Bobbie and Belle walked the streets of Petrograd and visited a communal textile factory. Belle wrote: "The first impression of the people is that they are busy and hopeful. The streets are full of pedestrians. There are few automobiles." At the factory, Belle noted, "There is a sense of equality between the workers and their chosen superintendents. A large proportion of the workers are women. The women are paid a full wage (equal to a man's) but they are released from work two months before a birth is expected until two months after a birth. There is a complete nursery at the factory where children from two months to two years of age are cared for. The mothers take their children home each night." She was impressed with the health care and education available at these state-run nurseries.

She also visited the workers' quarters, located adjacent to the factory, noting, "Each floor has a community kitchen, laundry and bath. Each family has one good-sized room." Belle's English-speaking woman guide was quick to point out, "Of course our country is poor, very poor, and alone, which makes it very hard, but, oh, we have such faith in our future." When Belle asked about women's organizations the guide replied, "Men and women have exactly the same status—political, economic and legal. We need no separate organizations. We all get the same pay for the same work and all schools, occupations and professions are open alike to all of us."

They saw women traffic managers and streetcar conductors, as well as factory workers. The guide told her most dentists were women and that the Soviet Ambassador to Norway was a woman. This impressed both Belle and Bob, who believed Russia was destined to play a large part in international developments of the next decade. Before leaving he said, "World peace is impossible without Russian cooperation."

Steffens and Davidson remained in Russia while the rest of the party left for Warsaw, where they spent a day sightseeing. Belle wrote Mary on September 15 it was a relief to be in a place "in which we do not feel obliged to study the conditions." En route from Warsaw to Vienna on September 14, Bobbie wrote Rawleigh: "Every day this trip grows more interesting and profitable to each one of us. Dad is gathering information which will be of invaluable service to him in his work in the Senate and the campaign to come." It was assumed by family and close associates that Bob would run for the presidency in 1924.

In Vienna they visited the art museums and the Emperor's palace at Schönbrunn, and heard Maria Jeritza sing *Carmen*. Belle took advantage of these few days of comparative leisure to write her impressions of Russia for the *Magazine* before taking the train to Italy. Belle wrote Mary on September 19, "Our day in Venice was quite perfect. We rejoice that we came, wish we might stay."

Bob was awake at daylight when their train rolled into Rome. As always, he was interested in how men used the earth and noted at 6:30 in the morning that every inch of soil was being worked by laborers. He also wrote in his journal, "The soil looks old and tired. But the orchards and vines look good and vigorous." They spent four days sightseeing, drove along the Appian Way, visited the Coliseum in the moonlight, and went to Rivoli and all the places they had read about and had wished to see ever since their university days.

Belle wrote Mary on September 23, "It has been wonderful to be here even for this short time. Daddy has enjoyed it very much. We saw Mussolini. He has a strong personality." Bob and Belle especially wanted to meet the Italian dictator and had arranged for an appointment. He sat at a large desk at the rear of a very long room. He made no move to greet them halfway but waited for them to walk to him. Through an interpreter Bob asked about political freedoms, particularly of the press. Mussolini replied it was necessary to control the press until such time as democratic ideals could be realized. Mussolini did not want to discuss these questions. The interview became more of a monologue as Il Duce extolled the Fascist system, how efficient it was, how the factories were operating at capacity, how everybody worked, how the trains all ran on time. Bob and Belle left with no more sympathy for Italian Fascism than for Russian Communism.

They departed from Rome on September 23, passing through the Tyrolean Alps by daylight and arriving in Munich the next night. They rose early, went for a walk before breakfast and admired the bookstores and art shops. On the walls of the office of the Continental Hotel they also saw "some threatening cartoons on the Ruhr situation." Later they noticed "a regiment of soldiers drilling in the street."

Hitler had already become the popular leader of a movement to separate Bavaria from the Reich. He had organized his storm troops to stage a demonstration in which they called for revolution.

Belle and Bob spent a day in Nuremberg, where they visited the churches, the home of Albrecht Dürer and the house where Goethe lived when he wrote *Faust*. They traveled by train and then by boat down the Rhine to Cologne where Belle and Mrs. Manly stayed at a hotel while Bob, Bobbie and Mr. Manly visited Essen for three days. Bob wanted to see the actual conditions in the Ruhr under French occupation, to find out as much as he could about France's purpose "in seizing and holding this area in violation of the Versailles Treaty," as he wrote in the *Magazine*.

In almost the only letter Bob sent during the trip, to his sister Jo, he said: "In the Ruhr—in and about Essen—where we visited a number of towns, the suffering is unspeakable. France is as merciless and unfeeling as the rack and the thumbscrew." Belle had written Mary on October 2, "I don't see how Germany holds out. But there seems a sort of endurance and faith that if they keep on working, they will see better times after a while."

From the Ruhr the group returned to Berlin, where Bob caught another bad cold. In a letter to Fola, Belle wrote he suffered pain "such as he had before going to Battle Creek. . . . This pain has come on sometimes at night, waking him up out of his sleep. When it passes off, he feels quite all right again." In a separate letter that same day, Bobbie wrote Fola and Mid describing his father's pain as a heart that was "kicking up didos . . . It may only be a passing thing but you know *our* rule, to tell everything good or bad, so I am letting you know . . . What I would give to live here as you did for a year and let politics go its way without me."

The party left Berlin on October 5 and rode all day on the train to Copenhagen, where they stayed three days. Bobbie wrote Fola on October 7, "This lush little country seems like the anteroom to Paradise; after the want and fear in Germany one almost begrudges the people their too-red cheeks." They drove to Elsinore and stood on "the platform where Hamlet's ghost walked," Belle wrote the Roes. Bob studied the cooperatives and compared the situation of American and Danish farmers. The latter received eighty cents of every dollar the consumer spent on farm products, whereas the American farmer received only forty.

They then went to Paris, traveling via Holland, arriving the night of October 10. Jo Davidson, who had returned from Russia, met them at the train station and escorted them to their suite at the Hotel de Crillon. The next day, after making a duty call at the American Embassy, they visited Davidson's studio. He had sculptured a bust of General Pershing that had won him world renown. Bob and Belle were impressed not only with the work they saw in the studio but also by his request to do a bust of Bob. Davidson worked in clay and for the next few weeks Bob sat for him almost every day. Before they left Paris they thought the likeness was excellent. The bust was later cast in bronze and placed under the Capitol Dome in Madison.

Bob later told Mary, "It was wrong that Belle and I did not go to Europe thirty years earlier. Everyone should go to Europe and go in youth." Paris fascinated him and he regretted leaving it. One morning Davidson came upon Bob as he stood alone in front of the Hotel de Crillon looking out over the Place de la Concorde. His eyes were filled with tears. He said to Davidson, "It is a crime to have waited so many years to see all this beauty."

Bob and Belle had planned to return to London for a brief visit but Bob was feeling so poorly that, on the doctor's advice, they decided to book passage on the first ship home. In a few days they were in Cherbourg boarding the *S. S. George Washington* once again.

During the voyage home Bob wrote a brief summary of his view of the European situation: "Democracy is now being crucified in Europe. In Russia it has been crushed by the Communist oligarchy. In Italy it has been destroyed by Mussolini and his Fascist groups. In Austria it has been the pawn of the Allied money lenders. In Germany the democracy established with an enlightened constitution is being ground between the upper and nether mill stones of Communism and Fascism."

He concluded: "The greatest contribution that America can make to Europe and the world is to restore and perfect her democratic institutions and traditions, so that they will stand as a beacon lighting the way to all the peoples. . . . There are evils in our own democracy. No one knows it better than I do. But the cure lies in the application of genuine republican principles." Bob saw himself as the leader America needed.

When the *George Washington* arrived at Portland, Maine, on November 2, Bob gave a statement to reporters that included an appeal to send food to starving children in Germany. His warning that the hunger there constituted a menace to the world was quoted in the *New York Times* of November 3. In a series of articles in the *Washington Herald* and *La Follette's Magazine* published after his return, he predicted that what had happened in Italy and Russia might happen in Germany—a dictatorship "resting not on the will of the people but upon force of arms."

He also warned that until the "infamous" Treaty of Versailles and its sister treaties "have been completely wiped out and replaced by enlightened understanding among the European nations, there will be no peace upon the continent or in the world, and all the pettifogging conferences, councils and world courts will not prevent or seriously retard the new world war that is now rapidly developing from the seeds of malice, hatred and revenge that were sown at Versailles."

With these new convictions strong in his mind, Bob introduced a bill before Congress adjourned asking for $10,000,000 in relief aid for Germany to save the people from starvation and help preserve their infant democracy, stating the situation in Germany was critical. His bill was defeated 53 to 25.

Second Presidential Bid

[1924]

While Belle and Bob were abroad, Mary supervised the moving to their new house at 2112 Wyoming Avenue. After settling in, Bob wrote his former law partner, Alf Rogers, on November 9 that the trip to Europe "was the biggest experience of my life and I hope that I've done enough work on it to make the benefit lasting."

During the voyage home Belle, Bob and Bobbie each wrote reports of their impressions of the countries visited. This material formed the basis for six articles Bob had contracted to write for the Sunday edition of the Hearst newspapers for which he received $500 an article.

The family got together for Christmas to enjoy each other and talk politics, and to decide whether Bob should be a candidate on an independent ticket that might have more appeal to Progressive Republicans and Democrats than a third party ticket. Bob had refused the presidential nomination of the Labor party in 1920 chiefly because Communists and fellow travelers were supposed to be a large part of it. He warned Progressives to stay clear of any group that represented Communists and used its methods of infiltration. Now the Progressives decided to go the independent route.

Bob had a recurrence of the chest pain he suffered in Europe and his doctors insisted he must rest and cut down on his work. They told him if he carefully followed their instructions he would be able to resume his duties when the Senate convened. He was not present on December 3 when the session started but he went to the Senate on January 3, 1924, to take the oath of office.

Newspapers noted he was "warmly welcomed by senators on both sides of the aisle." A small leather booklet was given to him, signed by thirty-one members of Congress. The engraved dedication read, "With your many friends the nation over, we rejoice in your return to good health and active participation in the fight for Progressive legislation." The *New York Times* reported he at once "resumed active command" of the Progressive faction.

Early in January he and Phil, now twenty-seven and a junior partner in the law firm of La Follette and Rogers, opened headquarters for his presidential campaign in the old Auditorium Hotel on Michigan Avenue in Chicago. The La Follette for President Committee sought to secure as many signatures as possible on petitions asking Bob to become a candidate. In addition to circulating the petitions, Phil visited the Midwestern and Northwestern states to organize a state committee in each one. As he covered the Midwest and East he found "a groundswell of sentiment and, among many, a deep devotion for Dad. Though our lack of organization and money was appalling, somehow the enthusiasm we found kept us going just as if we had a chance to win." Bobbie, at twenty-nine, was elected chairman of the Wisconsin State Republican Central Committee in Washington, D. C.

Belle wrote her sons on February 5 about the searching for and selection of delegates for the forthcoming Progressive convention, which would choose a presidential candidate: "Dear Ones, The past week has seemed long and I expect this one will seem longer. I am disappointed that there are so few women delegates. I think this is a more serious political mistake than you realize. Mrs. Williams [wife of Jesse Williams, member of the Committee of One Hundred, prominent supporters of Bob] told me over the phone that since the Teapot Dome scandal they are all talking of La Follette for President and counted on him to have some *women* in his cabinet who could not be corrupted by big business. There is no doubt about a strong trend of sentiment in Daddy's direction these days. Mother."

After announcing his availability as a Progressive candidate, Bob again fell ill. Phil left Madison for Washington at once and "found Mother and Bobbie concerned by Dad's illness and disturbed even more about his presidential campaign."

Bob told Phil, "I know perfectly well what Doctor Kellogg told me last summer—all about my having to slow down—that if I kept up the same pace I'd be dead in a couple of years.

"Well, Phil, I have had a wonderful life. I'd like to live it all over again. But I don't want to—I just can't—live rolled up in a cotton blanket in a damned wheelchair. I want to die, as I have lived, with my boots on. . . . We are going right ahead with our plans, with a full head of steam in the boiler."

Phil pointed out to his father that he faced heavy odds. He was sixty-nine, his health was not good, and outside of Wisconsin and Minnesota he had no political organization or adequate financing. "None of us for a moment thought we had any chance to win," Phil later wrote. "But we hoped that we might get enough votes to deprive any candidate of a majority in the Electoral College and thus throw the election into the House of Representatives, where Progressives might hold the balance of power. At the very least, we might get a large enough popular vote to lay the foundation for what most of us wanted above all—a new political alignment in America that would unite the Progressive forces."

Belle wrote Phil on March 22: "Beloved Phil, Dr. Marbury said this morning that Daddy was improving, that the physical signs were favorable. I feel encouraged, even though I cannot see any marked change and the temperature remains the same. Mother."

And the next day: "Beloved son, Daddy's temperature is higher. It was 102 this morning, the highest it has been. There is nothing to indicate *why* it goes up because other signs are good. We have a nurse. Love, Mother."

Then the following day: "Dear one, Daddy's temperature was over 100 this morning at nine o'clock. Dr. Marbury was pleased and said he hoped the temp would go down and stay there. Dr. Marbury and Dr. Randolph can find no enlargement of the pneumonic area in the left lung and therefore are at a loss to find the cause of the temp. . . . Mother."

Bobbie wrote Phil and his wife Isen in Wisconsin on March 26: "The doctors say that it is largely a case of Dad wearing out the germs. They regard the case as serious but not dangerous. It will be at least six weeks before Dad could take up his work again. This is hard luck and it jolts Dad pretty hard. Worlds of love, Bob."

Because of the plans for an independent candidacy, Bob did not enter his name on the Republican presidential preference ballot in the April primary in Wisconsin. But the Progressives had a slate of delegates to the Republican National convention. They elected twenty-eight of the twenty-nine delegates on April 1. Bob received more presidential preference votes, all write-ins, than did President Coolidge, whose name was on the ballot. At the convention the Wisconsin delegation submitted a minority report on the platform, as had been done at each convention since 1908. Coolidge, who had served as President for one year following Harding's death, was nominated, with Charles Dawes as his running mate.

The Democrats, balloting 103 times for a candidate in New York City's Madison Square Garden, chose John W. Davis, a New York lawyer, for president and Charles Bryan of Nebraska for vice-president.

The Conference for Progressive Political Action met on July 4 at Cleveland and wired Bob the organization's request he become a presidential candidate for them. Their members included representatives of organized labor, the Socialist party, agricultural groups and a roster of distinguished names such as the poet Edwin Markham, Congressman Fiorello La Guardia of New York, and Senator Henrik Shipstead from Minnesota. The *New York Times* reported that "a more complete cross section of American life was never assembled in one hall."

That afternoon Bobbie read a statement from his father addressed to both the La Follette for President Committee and the conference group. Bob made it clear his was not a third party candidacy, believing this sponsorship would harm the Progressive movement. The umbrella organization for his candidacy was the La Follette for President Committee, and his running mate was Democratic Senator Burton K. Wheeler of Montana. Wheeler had been a member of the special committee in the Senate that investigated the Teapot Dome scandal.

The Conference for Progressive Political Action unanimously endorsed Bob as its presidential candidate. Then followed what Phil called "the gigantic task" of getting the names of La Follette and Wheeler on the ballots of the forty-eight states.

For an independent candidate, political machinery had to be created almost from scratch in every state. This meant establishing campaign headquarters, gathering petitions and recruiting volunteers. Despite all these problems, in less than two months the La Follette-Wheeler ticket was on the ballot in almost all states. Money, as always, was a problem. Rawleigh was by far the largest campaign contributor but his contributions could not compare with the large sums available to Democrats and Republicans, though they gave the La Follette Committee its modest start.

The final reported campaign expenditures were: Republicans, $4,360,000; Democrats, $820,000; La Follette, $222,000. Only two individuals contributed $5,000 or more to Bob's campaign and about one-third of the total came from ticket sales and collections at speaking engagements.

A national organization of more than seventy prominent women was formed to support Bob's campaign, including Jane Addams, Mabel Costigan, Freda Kirchwey, owner of *The Nation* magazine, Ellen Scripps and Zona Gale. To help with the increased work, Rachel Young, a high school classmate of Bobbie's, was added to Bob's office staff.

Belle wrote Elizabeth Evans on July 21: "This campaign is such a tremendous undertaking and all our resources appeared so puny relatively that I could not see how we could cope with it further than to get the name on the ballots in all the states and see what would happen."

To help make things "happen," Belle went out to stump for Bob. She was the first wife of a presidential candidate ever to do this. She spoke September 28 at Mountain Lake Park, Maryland, before starting an extensive tour Gil Roe had arranged for her through New York, Pennsylvania, New Jersey, and Connecticut. The *New York Times* reported her as saying at the Mountain Lake Park meeting, "I am not going to talk technical politics. I am going to talk to you as neighbor to neighbor, friend to friend. I want especially to speak to you women, to talk things over with you, get your views, answer your questions, and see if we can't mutually understand and agree."

The *Times* reported on October 1 that "the distaff side of the La Follette party" addressed a capacity meeting in Town Hall, New York City, where she received "an enthusiastic reception." Again speaking in an intimate manner Belle described the long fight she and Bob had shared. "He never advocates a reform that experience has not shown is needed," she said. "In all these years his opponents have tried to frighten the people with the bugaboo that he was too radical, that his platform was a menace, and that something terrible would happen if he was elected again. But the people kept right on electing him." She volunteered the belief she was more radical than he, that Bob was "almost old-fashioned in his worship of our institutions."

In an interview in the *New York American* on October 12, Belle said, "I have loved my life. I have been fortunate, marvelously lucky in having all these years a companion. True companionship is the greatest thing in the world. We have been through everything, my husband and I, bad times and good times, disappointments, illness, poverty, hard work, the struggle for principle, the climb to success.

But when you have a companion to count upon through thick and thin, it's all easy. We two have kept together because—well, because our minds and our hearts matched."

Zoe Beckley, in a special article in the *New York Times* of October 19, wrote of Belle: "On the platform she looks taller than she really is. Her quiet, cultured speaking voice takes on a ringing tone that carries to the backmost rows. She uses much gesture and a smile of winning sweetness . . . and carries herself with grace and sprightliness. Her hair is graying blond, parted, waved and done in a simple knot behind. Her eyes are blue and kind and understanding, her features small, her mouth particularly attractive, and there is a hint of dimple in her chin. . . . She and Senator La Follette look amazingly alike: people often speak of it. Mrs. La Follette laughs and says it is because they've lived so long together."

Later in the campaign Belle fell ill with a severe cold and was in bed for a week at the Brevoort Hotel in New York, which forced her to cancel a speech scheduled for October 27. Fola read her mother's words to an audience of 2,000 at Cooper Union, receiving an "ovation," according to the *Brooklyn Daily Eagle*.

While Belle convalesced at the Brevoort she followed newspaper reports of the campaign. Bob and Mid stopped to see her on their way to speak at Yankee Stadium. Mid wrote: "I was in Bob's car, escorted by a motorcycle squad with screeching horns. It whisked him at full speed through halted traffic, to the awaiting thousands. I walked with him from the entrance to the platform. Twelve thousand pairs of eyes fixed on the man beneath the snow-powdered pompadour, now nearing seventy, smiling, happy at the cheers. . . . How the old war horse tossed his head and, with all his eloquence, faced as tumultuous a reception as any candidate had ever received! My experience of the intense evangelical zeal he threw into that campaign was an unforgettable one."

Bob loved to campaign and now he enjoyed a new political procedure. Along with Coolidge and Davis he appeared in a brief sound motion picture. Produced by DeForest Phonofilm, this was the first time "talkies" were used in a presidential race. Bob tried out another technological "first" that cost $3,000. He opened his campaign with a Labor Day radio address. Radio had been used to broadcast political speeches delivered at open meetings but his was the first ever delivered exclusively over the radio and broadcast from a studio. Bobbie stood outside the glass booth giving his father signals as to how his voice was coming through. Bob's speech reached three million to four million people. He commented he never had a more respectful audience—or fewer interruptions.

During the campaign Bob, Bobbie and Phil traveled in a special Pullman car hitched to regular trains. Phil spoke first to warm up the audience. He had his father's gift of stage presence. As one reporter put it, "In his campus garb of blue coat and grey flannel trousers, this blue-eyed chap looks hardly old enough to vote. But how he can talk!" In Minnesota, after a particularly enthusiastic crowd cheered Phil, Bob walked over to him with tears in his eyes, hugged him and said, "You are my boy!" For Phil, who always felt somewhat in the shadow of his older brother, this was the ultimate accolade. Bob gave the main speech, they then passed the hat and collected enough money to get to the next stop.

After the first weeks of the campaign, the *Baltimore Sun* reported of Bob, "The effects of last week's appearance after appearance before great cheering crowds, far from wearing down the vitality of a man nearing seventy years, has been a tonic to him. After a week of sleeping cars, he is in better condition than many of the men half his age who are with him. This flaming old man and his two attractive sons present the one dramatic, colorful spectacle of the campaign."

But this was not enough. Shortly after the polls closed on November 5, 1924, it was obvious Coolidge had won by a landslide. As the family drove home that evening to Maple Bluff Farm from the capitol, where they heard the returns, Phil, as he later wrote, said that both he and Bobbie "spoke out in wrath at labor's betrayal of our cause, but Dad brought us up sharply. He said: 'You have never known real poverty. Oh, we have had hard times but never the haunting fear of losing your job, or losing those paychecks that are all that stand between starvation and their families. Don't blame the folks. They just got scared.'"

Phil went to bed that night "tired—and still bitter." In the excitement and strain of his father's campaign, he had forgotten he had been elected district attorney of Dane County, the job his father had won in 1880, forty-four years before, the job that had started his father on his political journey.

Coolidge received 15,718,783 votes, Davis, 8,378,962 and Bob, 4,822,319. Bob's showing was greater than any other third candidate had ever received. He went down in defeat planning future battles. Heartened by the support of so many voters, he started at once to organize Progressives for the next campaign. Throughout the rest of November he and Bobbie stayed at the farm with Phil and Isen. Belle remained in Washington to keep Mary company while she awaited the arrival of her baby. Six days after the election Belle wrote Bob, "It was good to hear from you last night and be assured you were all well." The following day, November 11, Bob received a telephone message that Mary's baby was born and had been named Robert La Follette Sucher.

Two days before Congress was to convene, Bob and Bobbie left for Washington. When Bob entered the Senate on December 1 he received a warm welcome, even from those who had once voted him out of the party. That night he wrote in his diary: "Was surprisingly well received. Everybody cordial, many coming to my desk to greet me." He wrote Jo on December 27: "It was not easy to face the old gang with the election just over and every state lost except Wisconsin. But I sailed in, my head up and all smiles. You may be sure I would not give any outward evidence of the taste in my mouth."

Bob had not seen his first grandchild because he had a severe cough but when it cleared up he went with Belle to visit Mary and her son. He wrote in his diary that day, "Mary looking well and very beautiful. Her face shows the change—indescribable but divine—that goes with motherhood. The boy, blessings on him! He fills the heart and hopes—a beautiful head and a certain look that speaks for the things to come. God give him a long and useful life."

Belle wrote Phil and Isen on December 21: "The house is something of a hospital although I trust no one is seriously sick. Daddy was able to attend the Senate the last three days of the session. . . . He is resting in bed this morning. He says he feels comfortable. There was a decided drop in the temperature and the house is still cold. I think he plans to get up for his midday meal."

She also reported that "Bobbie came home from the office a week ago yesterday feeling bum. He went to bed and has been there since. Dr. Marbury thinks it is intestinal grippe. He has a nurse from Providence Hospital whom he likes very much. I think on the whole he is getting a good rest."

She wrote of Mary's baby as having crying spells and not gaining weight but reported the doctor reassured her the baby would be all right within the next few weeks. Belle also told Phil and Isen she had not been well but was feeling better. In the last paragraph of her long letter, the only paragraph not mentioning someone's illness, she said:

"I wonder Isen if you could not put up to Zona Gale the basic importance of a university president who stands for constructive opposition to militarism. I fear the Kronshages [the university president and his wife] are under the Hearst influence. It is difficult to write a letter that might not be misinterpreted. But I think you and Phil might *talk* to Zona safely. Love ever, Mother." Zona Gale, an old friend, writer and supporter of Bob, was now on the board of the University of Wisconsin.

Bob's doctor had advised a vacation in Florida and on January 14, 1925, Belle and he left for Fort Lauderdale and days in the sun. They took walks along the beach and enjoyed a much-needed vacation after the hectic campaigning they both had endured.

Nurse
to a Dying Fighter

[1925]

While enjoying the Hotel Bramard in Fort Lauderdale, Bob and Belle kept in touch with the Washington and Wisconsin scenes through Bobbie and Phil. Belle brought her typewriter so she could continue her columns while Bob wrote letters in his clear script, often making carbon copies for his files.

In line with their plans for a quiet summer at Maple Bluff Farm—no campaigns, no Chautauqua circuits this year—they began to plan a few conferences with leaders from the Progressive states to discuss the formation of a new party. Out of this came the decision to hold a meeting in Chicago of the Committee for Progressive Political Action. They exchanged almost daily letters and telegrams with Bobbie regarding action to be taken before the meeting.

They all agreed the only effective way to organize a new Progressive party was on the basis of individual membership with the states as the units of organization. They hoped the Chicago conference would end with a decision to call state meetings during the summer for the purpose of selecting delegates to a convention to be held in the fall. They were aware Communists and other delegates were determined to turn the fall convention into an opportunity to form a new party based on group membership along Marxist class lines.

Bob wrote Jo on December 27 that he hoped the new party could be formed on principles that would appeal to every American citizen who believed "*in a government of the people, by and for the people.*" He added, "I cannot go into any new party movement upon any other basis."

Belle wrote Bobbie, Fola and Mid, Phil and Isen on January 18, 1925, from the Hotel Bramard that "Daddy has picked up wonderfully. His appetite has come back. We took quite a walk yesterday without his feeling serious fatigue. Bobbie, please send us one of the sacks of buckwheat. You will find it in the basement pantry. Be sure and have it well packed. Send it by *express* or parcel post. All love, Mother." As always, one of Belle's primary concerns was proper nutrition and a simple diet.

She wrote Bobbie on February 11 in reference to his taking responsibility for the forthcoming conferences, "You have been wonderfully patient, Bob, and I admire the way you hold to the proposition in spite of all the discouragement. It is the spirit of Daddy all over again."

Bob thought his older son had carried the heavy burden of decisions about the conferences like a veteran. He sent a telegram: "Absolute confidence in your judgment and ability to meet all requirements tactfully and wisely. All love."

They had expected to remain in Fort Lauderdale until April but their plans suddenly changed. Bob received messages from Senator Reed and Senator Norris urging him to return at once to help prevent the confirmation of Charles Beecher Warren as attorney general. When President Coolidge first nominated Warren, the People's Legislative Service investigated his record and uncovered a close connection with the Sugar Trust, notorious in its violation of the Sherman anti-trust law. To many senators Warren's record appeared to disqualify him for the post of attorney general, since he would decide whether corporations with which he had been actively associated for years should be prosecuted. On March 10 the Senate, by a roll-call vote of 41 to 39, for the first time in more than fifty years refused to confirm a presidential cabinet appointment.

Two days later Coolidge, in a petulant mood, again submitted Warren's nomination to the Senate. The margin against Warren had been so close that Reed, Norris and other Senators thought Bob's vote would be needed in the second Senate consideration.

So Belle and Bob left Fort Lauderdale as soon as they could get train reservations. Arriving in Washington March 15, Bob learned the Senate had agreed to vote on the Warren nomination not later than Monday at 2:30, with the understanding no senator should speak more than thirty minutes. On Sunday, newspapers reported anger had flared in the Senate late the day before. Two senators had obtained advance press dispatches stating the President had announced at the White House that if Warren was not confirmed, he would appoint him after the Senate adjourned, in a so-called recess appointment, used only in emergencies. Bob and Belle thought such a move would be unconstitutional and, furthermore, would set a dangerous precedent.

The galleries were packed before the Senate convened on Monday morning for this struggle between the White House and the Senate. When the Senate met at 10:30 Bob was still working in his office on a five-minute speech protesting both Warren's nomination and Coolidge's threat to override the Constitutional provision that presidential appointments be made "with the advice and consent of the Senate."

A ripple of applause was heard in the galleries when Bob took his seat in the first row directly in front of Vice-President Charles Gates Dawes. The roll call was taken and it was announced the Senate had "refused to consent" to Warren's nomination by 46 to 39. Bob was one of ten Republicans who had joined the Democrats in opposing Warren's appointment.

The special session adjourned on March 18. Congress would not convene until December and Bob looked forward to months free of the pressure of Senate sessions and committee work.

Bobbie, "tired to the bone," accepted an invitation to go abroad with a friend for a short vacation. Bob noted in his diary on March 30, "Cold and spitting snow. With Baby Bob [Mary's son] most of day. Growing and becoming playful. Fine little fellow. Will be a great joy to us all."

The following afternoon Bobbie left for New York to spend the day with Fola before sailing. That night Bob wrote in his diary: "It was a pull to see him go, though we were all for it. . . . I have to struggle to keep from being sentimental about it. I am awfully dependent on the lad—and feel guilty at taking so much out of his life to keep me company as the years come on me. It is the most pronounced symptom I note of their advance."

On Sunday afternoon, May 17, a clear day with bright sun, Bob drove with Belle, Mary, Ralph Sucher and the baby for several hours through Potomac and Rock Creek parks. "Life is good," he said to Mary as they watched children at play. At sunset they returned home and, as Bob closed the door of his car, he stopped for a moment, smiled at Mary and said, "We had a good time, didn't we?"

Later in the evening, as he and Belle sat on the lawn, he complained of feeling chilly and went to his room. He awakened at dawn with a severe chill and acute, shooting pains in his chest. Not wishing to disturb Belle, he wrapped himself in blankets and sat close to the radiator, trying to get warm.

After Dr. Marbury and a heart specialist had made a careful examination, Belle wrote Phil and Fola the specialist insisted Bob remain in bed a month, explaining he had had a heart attack. Belle said: "The specialist believes Daddy can rest this way and restore the heart tissue and build a reserve on which to take up work again—the extent of course to be determined by his condition. I have not talked to Daddy but he is always reasonable. The attack which was so loathe to yield to control was a shock and a warning he must heed. I am sure he will adjust himself to the doctor's decision. And we must all unite in making it easy for him."

Bob enjoyed Mary's visits and he asked to have the baby brought to his room, saying, as he watched his grandson play on his bed, "See how he reaches for things beyond his grasp. That will always be true—and it is right and good to have it so."

When Bob had been in bed a week, Dr. Marbury and Dr. Randolph said all the symptoms had disappeared and they were confident he would recover.

Bob had been looking foward to his son's return from Europe and on the day the ship was due in New York, woke feeling so well he insisted on shaving himself. That afternoon he had another attack of pain. Though it was less severe than the previous one, Dr. Marbury thought Bob should have a night nurse. The next day Belle wrote her "Loved ones" that Bobbie's "coming did us all a lot of good. It did not seem to tax Daddy's strength to visit with him." Bob wanted to hear his son's latest impressions of Europe.

Bobbie wrote Phil and Isen on June 3 that "Drs. Lee and Marbury both feel that our dear Daddy has lost ground in the last forty-eight hours." Bob's blood pressure on June 13 rose to 140, the highest since he had been ill. On his seventieth birthday, Sunday, June 14, he enjoyed the flowers and messages his friends sent.

That day Bobbie wrote his brother: "Mother bears up well under the strain, although I fear that she is much worn. I find it difficult to get her to leave the house at all, even though I am here."

Bob had a good night on June 15 and when Fola and Mid, Phil and Isen arrived the next day, his condition improved. The doctors were again hopeful of recovery. At noon that day Bobbie gave a statement to the press saying, "Though the condition of Senator La Follette is somewhat more serious than before, he is holding his own and the physicians hold every hope for his ultimate recovery."

Each day Bob seemed "to pick up in strength and be so like

himself for an hour or two with all his keen wit and quickness of mind," Belle wrote Elizabeth Evans. She added that neither she nor his physicians could believe he was not going to get well.

On June 18 at eight a.m. Bob suffered a severe heart attack. Dr. Marbury was summoned and came at once. He later called the family into the room, where they all remained until Bob died at 1:21 p.m.

In a letter to Elizabeth, "Boston mother" to the four La Follette children, Fola described the last moments of her father's life: "We were all in Daddy's room when the end came. Mother seated by his bed, holding his hand; speaking to him, pouring out the love and devotion of a lifetime in the last long farewell; all hesitation gone from her speech; her voice clear and sweet; telling him her vision of the nobility and beauty of his life and work. If he heard, it was with other senses than those that he had used through the years, for as far as nurses and doctors could tell he was 'unconscious' just at the end. But we heard—we who were gathered about—and we can never forget. And if he could have heard, there has not been and never can be any tribute which would so deeply have satisfied his mind and heart.

"His passing was mysteriously peaceful for one who had stood so long on the battle line. Never have I seen so slight a demarcation in the transition from life to death. And yet within an hour of the final silence he had spoken quite naturally and simply, had shortly before evoked a smile by one of his inimitable little jests."

She concluded: "But his heart was tired and refused to carry on. He went to sleep, and we shall not hear his voice again—strangely, that was the thought that came to each one of us when dear Dr. Marbury looked up and signed to us all that our yearning and love could do no more for him. . . . We kissed his brow in silence and turned to mother—and she gave us of her strength speaking of how Daddy had loved life and found it good. And from this thought it seemed as if everything flowed. Through all the hours and days that followed each one gathered strength and courage from the other. There was an almost mysterious accord as to how everything should be done. Each detail was met as if Mother's thought had shaped our minds before she spoke. We have done and do what we can for her, but it all seems so little and inadequate compared with what she gives us."

None of the family wore black on the afternoon of June 19 as they followed the gray casket out of the house. Bob had always disliked mourning garb. There was no ceremony in Washington though the thousands gathered at the Union Station stood silent as the casket was lifted into the same special car in which Bob had traveled during the 1924 presidential campaign. Trainmen in the yards dropped their tools and bowed their heads as the train bearing his body passed on the final trip home from the nation's capital, where he had lived and worked for twenty-two years.

Belle traveled in the special car with her four children, her sons-in-law, George Middleton and Ralph Sucher, and Gil Roe, Basil Manly and Grace Lynch. Senator Wheeler and Senator Lenroot and other members of the Wisconsin congressional delegation rode in another car. As the train passed through towns and villages on the way to Madison throughout that afternoon, night, and the next morning, crowds gathered to pay a last tribute. Farmers stopped working in the fields to bow their heads. At every railroad center or yard where stops were made, workers gathered with bare heads to pay homage to "their fallen leader," the words used by the *Washington Daily News* on June 20.

In Chicago the car bearing Bob's body homeward was hooked up to a special train for the journey to Madison. As the train rolled into the rich green land of Bob's home state, hundreds along the way sorrowfully watched the funeral car. Slowly the train rolled to the state capitol.

Between long lines of quiet men, women and children, the casket, draped in the United States flag, was placed in the East rotunda of the capitol. Flowers from organizations and individuals throughout the country, including President Coolidge, were banked behind the balustrades of the main balcony. All through the night state soldiers in civilian dress and several members of the legislature stood guard.

The *Chicago Tribune* on June 21 carried a story filed by a correspondent on the train. Its headline: "Fighting Bob, On His Shield, Home at Last."

CHAPTER
17
....

Last Labor of Love

[1925–1931]

The burning question after Bob's death was, who would take his place in the Senate? Who could possibly fill his shoes?

In his autobiography Phil wrote, "Politicians of all shades of allegiance had a unanimous choice—my mother, Belle Case La Follette. Select her, all said, to serve Dad's unexpired term of three years. Fitting recognition for a woman of rare ability and special qualifications. All politicians—but all—in Wisconsin were for her. Thousands of women, not only in Wisconsin but all over the country, wanted this honor for her and for their sex."

Belle would have been the first women senator in the United States but she refused, explaining why in a public statement. She said she wished to express her "heartfelt appreciation of the great honor and confidence implied" and she wished also "to acknowledge the generous endorsement of political leaders, of labor organizations, the courteous consideration of the press and the many kind messages received from all parts of the country."

She then addressed herself to her fellow women "because your petitions present to me the most compelling reason why I should entertain the suggestion to become a candidate. I realize that my election might pave the way for other women to be elected to the Senate, and I am deeply mindful of the importance of women sharing the responsibilities of high office and of having a direct voice in shaping a government of the people."

After giving careful thought "to the special obligations circumstances placed upon me," she said, "I cannot, however, bring myself to believe that it is my duty to enter the [political] field."

She explained: "For many years I have gladly shared with Mr. La Follette the rewards and hardships of public life. My faith in the righteousness of his chosen work has been, like his, unshakable, but I know from long experience the exacting demands, the ceaseless strain of public service. At no time in my life would I ever have chosen a public career for myself. It would be against nature for me to undertake the responsibilities of political leadership."

She declared this a critical time in the history of the Progressive movement. Progressives in the Senate were few but vested with great responsibility and power and, she added, "I need not suggest how vitally the choice of Mr. La Follette's successor may affect the cause."

She asked the Progressive voters of Wisconsin to choose a candidate "on the basis not only of the unswerving devotion to the cause, capacity and fitness, but also of the iron resolution, enthusiasm and faith necessary to carry on the work Bob has laid down."

She cited "one common, comforting and encouraging note of assurance" appearing in the messages and tributes to Bob that had come to her and her children from all over the world. The message: "That the spirit of Mr. La Follette's work shall go on. To this end I hope to contribute my share in the future as in the past."

Belle's overriding goal was to complete her husband's biography which, she believed, would be of great value to the Progressive cause. She estimated it would take three years for her to finish this work. She described the first part of her husband's story, which he had written and published, as having served as "an inspiration to thousands of men and women. The writing of the record of that period, including the World War, offers a great opportunity for service. I undertake the work humbly but gladly. In so far as is in my power, I shall make the record true and complete. To this undertaking and to the continuance of La Follette's Magazine I shall dedicate my time and strength, confident that it offers me the largest field of usefulness."

She explained she was making this public statement because she wanted the many who had urged her to become a candidate for her husband's unexpired Senate term to know the motives that influenced her decision. She concluded, "I am confident that when you understand the compelling reasons you will approve my decision."

Belle wanted Bob, Jr., to fill his father's unexpired term, then run for Senator on his own. (Phil, even as a child politically ambitious, would have given anything for the opportunity but, at 28, was too young to qualify.) Governor Blaine had the authority to call a special election, even briefly considered himself a candidate, but then decided to run for the governor again in 1926. This left the way open for a somewhat reluctant Bob, Jr., to toss his hat into the ring. As one reporter was later to write of the two brothers: "Bob was pushed. Phil jumped!" Bob had absorbed all the intricacies of parliamentary procedure and Senate operations. He also had what his brother called "an extraordinary gift" for working with other people. Phil said of him, "He was firm, had deep convictions, but could state his side without offending the opposition. He could find common ground among men of diverse views and he had a first-class mind, which, put to work on a given subject, could master it." Unlike his father and brother Bob did not, however, enjoy campaigning or speechmaking. And it showed. "You ain't as good as yer pa was, and ya never will be," Bob was informed by a grizzled old farmer after giving a carefully reasoned, but passionless speech.

"No one knows that better than I, my friend, no one knows that better than I," he replied.

Nonetheless, Bob, Jr., won the special election by a wide margin. Just meeting the minimum-age requirement of thirty, he became the youngest senator since Henry Clay. Rachel Young, his high school sweetheart, stayed on as his personal secretary.

Belle was with Isen and Phil at the hospital in Madison when Isen gave birth to a nine-pound, ten-ounce boy in 1926. Isen asked her mother-in-law what name to give to the baby. Belle replied, "Whatever you and Phil want, but it would be fine if you named him after Daddy." A few hours later, Bob, Jr., arrived at the hospital and Isen asked his advice on a name. "Whatever you and Phil want, but it would be nice to name him after Daddy."

Isen said, "But what if you have a boy of your own?"

"Better not count on that," he laughed. He told Phil he was still "playing the field."

After his father's death Phil handled Belle's legal affairs. They sold off enough of Maple Bluff Farm to pay the mortgage and, at long last, Belle, "with her modest needs, felt a financial freedom she had so often been without," Phil wrote.

When her father died and her brother bought out her share of the Case farm in Baraboo, Belle had used part of the money to buy a lot overlooking Rock Creek Park. She had hoped that someday she and Bob might build a house there, but Bob considered Washington only a temporary home and preferred to rent. The area had now become quite fashionable, so Belle sold the lot for $18,000 and bought a small house on Cathedral Street, where she and Bob, Jr., lived and where she began work on Bob's biography.

On December 8, 1927, Belle received a letter from Phil in which he said that Alf Rogers, Fred Holmes, the managing editor, and he had conferred at length about the finances of the *Magazine* which had been losing more money each year, with the current cash balance very low. The three men agreed the *Magazine* had reached a point where it could not continue operating without considerable loss and they were now confronted with a situation where money had to be borrowed to run it.

Phil was "strongly opposed" to Belle's putting any more money into the *Magazine*, pointing out she had already given $2,000 and that to continue was, in his judgment, wrong. The value of the *Magazine* to the Progressive movement meant those interested in the movement should support it, Phil believed.

He concluded his letter to Belle: "I know that a suspension of the *Magazine* will now, as it would have at any time, be a keen disappointment to you, especially, but I still cannot see any other conclusion than that so far as you are concerned, you have not only done all, but done more, than was necessary and proper to keep it alive. . . . After you and Bob have talked it over, I wish you would write me or Holmes as to your judgment in the matter."

Four days later she responded, explaining that though the *Magazine* suffered a heavy loss for one summer month and the monthly reports for 1927 "have not been good," she still thought finances would improve as the time for renewals came. She continued: "I have, however, given the matter a great deal of thought and am settled in my mind as to the policy to be pursued. It seems to me a very serious matter to stop the *Magazine now*. I think we should keep it going—and *going at its best*—for another year if we can without incurring a loss that is prohibitive and foolish."

She was convinced they would "need every agency possible to get to the people. While our subscribers are relatively few, the *Magazine* does carry weight with them and has indirect influence besides. It may be the money needed to keep it going another year would count more if put into the campaign literature. I think Bob's friends will subscribe to his campaign and I will make my contribution by keeping the *Magazine* going *if it can be done without too great a sacrifice*."

She warned, "The reactionary forces realize how much there is at stake. Daddy's long career is an object lesson of what can be done, at least to hold them in check. They will do their utmost to get the

La Follette brothers *now* before they are fairly started." Bobbie would be up for reelection in 1928.

She wrote Fred Holmes on January 16, praising the content of the January issue, though she was "disappointed in the press work of the letter on the back page." She asked, "Can you tell me the reason for this sort of blurring?" She also pointed out an error in the front-page editorial, "which I was sorry about." She suggested as a subject for the lead editorial in the February issue, "the Wisconsin platform." She added, "For articles, as I remember, you have the one on Felix Frankfurter by Mrs. Evans, the seaman's law by Andrew Furuseth, the United States of Europe by Mrs. Brandeis, Abraham Lincoln by Bridgman, and Navajo rug-weaving by Fanny Dennis. I think Fola will have an interesting review of Marie Howe's life of George Sand. . . . I should like to know if I am right in estimating that we have enough material for February. I will get it off my mind and concentrate on other work I have to do."

She was referring to her work—research and writing—on the biography of Bob, which would eventually run into two volumes of 1,305 printed pages and be published after her death when completed by Fola.

On January 25 she wrote Holmes she realized the magazine faced a financial crisis and that she thought "we should face the situation as we would a crisis in illness. We must find out what is the matter, determine the cause if possible, and act promptly in applying the remedy, if there is any." She asked Holmes for his diagnosis of the falling off in renewals: "Is the loss general or is it especially noticeable in Wisconsin or any other states?"

She added that if he thought $1,000 could be spent at once to hold subscribers, to better advantage than a month or two later, he should let her know and she would send a check. She ended the letter, "I may be mistaken—I hope I am—but it does seem there must be something wrong with the Wisconsin political situation when the Progressives cannot be aroused to rally to the support of Mr. La Follette's *Magazine*. Thanking you, as always."

About this time Belle published a letter with the salutation, "Dear Readers" in which she asked them to renew their subscriptions and get one other subscriber. She wrote: "Mr. La Follette's followers often tell me they would like to contribute to the building of a monument to him. Throughout his long public service he concentrated on doing the work right at hand. He founded his *Magazine* and kept it going in the belief that each number would be a living force that would help to win back for the people the control of their own government, lost to them by the encroachment of corrupt politics and all-powerful monopoly."

Belle assured the readers, "I speak whereof I know, when I tell you the highest tribute you can pay our great leader and editor, and the kind of tribute he would care most about, is to make his *Magazine* fulfill the purpose he visioned at the beginning, which stayed with him to the end of his life.

"At this time when so much is at stake in Wisconsin; when a presidential campaign is on; when many Progressive senators and representatives in Congress are up for election who exercise a balance of power in legislation; when questions that deeply concern every home are in the balance—the question of just taxation, the question of conservation, the question of electric light, heat and power, the question of great naval preparation and rivalry, of universal military training, of intervention, involving war or peace—is this not an opportune time to build up *La Follette's Magazine*, which is a clearing house of Progressive thought and action on these and other measures that vitally affect the common welfare?"

Belle's appeals were effective. The magazine, renamed by her *The Progressive*, survives to this day.

Phil wrote in his autobiography that he could not say when he actually decided to run for governor. He just "grew into it." It was clear that the Progressives had no other potential candidate. In April, 1930, he had a legal matter before a federal commission in Washington and arranged to meet Belle and Bob, Jr., in Atlantic City for "a quiet weekend to talk over the situation in Wisconsin." Out of this weekend meeting came Phil's decision to make the race for governor. As Belle once advised Bob, she was now advising their two sons.

Phil started to prepare the announcement of his candidacy for governor, to draft a platform and organize the reference material to take with him on the campaign, as he had seen his father do so many times. He sent the first draft of the formal announcement to Belle and Bob, Jr., for their comments.

After reading it, Belle called him. She said she and Bob, Jr., did not like it "at all." She added she was sending Mary's husband, Ralph Sucher, to Madison to lend a literary hand (he had been a newspaperman). Then Belle asked to speak to Isen. Isen had written a number of articles for the *Magazine* and Belle had been impressed with her writing. She asked Isen what she thought of her husband's draft. Isen replied she did not know anything about politics.

Belle said, "You are an intelligent woman. If what Phil writes doesn't appeal to you, rest assured it will not appeal to others."

Ralph, Isen and Phil went to work "on the dining room table at Maple Bluff Farm." The substance existed in the draft but Ralph was "of great help in smoothing and polishing the rough edges" and thereafter Isen became Phil's "best critic," he wrote.

Belle gave him $500, with which he bought a new Ford four-door sedan to campaign with. As election time neared, she wrote: "You were surely right in thinking your announcement should convey the impression of reserve and steadiness. And I think that is the spirit to preserve above all else throughout your campaign. You know Daddy grew calm and self-controlled in proportion to the strain and excitement he had to meet, and I know you also have that power. . . . I am convinced that you will gain strength in the long run if you plan your campaign so that it doesn't look like you are making a 'whirlwind' tour of the state. . . . Conduct your campaign so as to leave on all your audience the impression of poise and repose that is inherent in your nature."

Phil knew that before each campaign his father had drawn up and issued his personal platform, which, if he won, became the basis for proposed legislation. Now Phil did the same. He also sent Belle, Bob, Jr. and Ralph the draft of this platform for their comments. After they approved it he was ready to start his speaking tour of Wisconsin. Phil felt he had three headline speakers—his brother, Senator John J. Blaine of Wisconsin, and himself—and as the campaign developed, he found a fourth in Isen.

Despite her admitted "natural distaste for politics," she was continually pressed to work for "the cause." In her memoirs Isen recalled a talk she gave at a country school near Madison. "As the women filed by to shake my hand after the talk, one inquired, 'I bet you don't remember my name!' I tried to evade as best I could, but an older woman standing by my elbow remarked accusingly, 'Well, you certainly aren't like your mother-in-law! When she gave a reception for Teddy Roosevelt, 10,000 people came down the line, and she knew the names of every one of them!' "

In the next sixty days Phil covered all but one county, delivering 261 speeches. He reported to Belle that his right hand had swollen to nearly half again its normal size from "vigorous handshaking" and it subsequently remained larger than his left and he had to unbutton his right cuff to get his shirt on.

He never lost his temper and never mentioned his opponent, Governor Walter J. Kohler, by name, but Kohler did not do as well. In the closing weeks of his campaign he referred to Phil as an "upstart" and "a whippersnapper."

On primary day Belle wrote her younger son from Washington that she and Mary "have risked our reputation as prophets—at least I have—by predicting you were going to be the next governor of Wisconsin. . . . From this distance it looks as though the campaign had been the kind that satisfies our ideals of what a campaign should be. . . . After the count is made today, we will know where we are at and how much work there is ahead."

She warned him, "If you are elected, your personal responsibility will be very great. I know your endowment and how you have been seasoned, but I dread the long fight you will need to make before you get results. I am working on that period of Daddy's biography. What a struggle! You stand on his shoulders, but the task looks almost as tremendous as it did then. My constant thought is how he would glory in the way you and Bob are carrying on his work, each in your own way."

Election Day evening, Phil, Isen, Bob, Jr., Rachel Young and other close friends gathered at the farm to hear the results of the primary. The final count was La Follette 395,555, Kohler, 267,687. The next day Bob, Jr. and Rachel were married in a simple ceremony at the farm as Bob, Jr., ended "playing the field."

That Phil would carry on in his father's footsteps was clear from a paragraph he wrote at this time: "The stock market had crashed a year before my nomination. For months, in every waking hour, my mind had wrestled with one deep, haunting thought: What was the cause—what was the answer to the problem of hunger, want, suffering, for millions of human beings amid enormous plenty? Why, with unsalable farm surpluses, were people hungry? Why, with stupendous undone work, were people workless? Why?"

In the November election Phil easily defeated his Democratic opponent Charles Hammersley, 393,000 to 170,000. The Progressives had control of the state assembly but the state senate with its four-year term was controlled by Democrats and conservative Republicans. As had his father before him, Phil would face a fight to get through legislation that would help the growing number of families now dependent on others for economic survival.

With Mary and Fola leading full lives, with Bob, Jr., in the Senate, and Phil in the Wisconsin governor's office, Belle could now concentrate her energies on completing her husband's biography. It proved a demanding task. As she had so often done when the pressures of life seemed overwhelming, Belle would visit her favorite sanctuary in Rock Creek Park, the Marian Hooper Adams Memorial Statue by Saint-Gaudens.

Of this area, which she said reminded her of the Wisconsin woods outside the log cabin in which she was born, she wrote: "The big cone pine tree and the high encircling evergreens give the spot seclusion and no matter how many go and come, you seem to be alone with the wonderful, draped figure, trying to fathom its meaning. To me it brings repose like the thought of my mother; and I have observed that while those who see it first usually speak of its sorrow, as they contemplate it, they grow thoughtful and uplifted—not depressed. Saint-Gaudens was himself reluctant to interpret his masterpiece with a name, and once said that it was about 'all there is in life.'

"One day it came to me quite suddenly that after all there was no mystery in this great work of art, that like all fundamental truth it was simple. It is not grief, not resignation, nor peace, nor satisfaction. It is all of life, not a phase. It is—Experience—Life's Composite. One has lived all and felt all—has known happiness and has suffered so much that there is nothing more to fear; yet is not bowed down, but is strengthened—a soul—prepared to live, ready for eternity. It is the strengthened, glorified, chastened look of those who live with courage, conviction, faith, hope, readiness for all things; those who understand and accept life as a part of the infinite plan. There is no beauty in the world like it."

On August 16, 1931, Belle, then seventy-two, went for a routine medical checkup at the Georgetown University Hospital. The examination was supposed to take only an hour, after which she would return home. But during the examination the doctor inadvertently punctured her intestines. Peritonitis set in. There were no antibiotics in those days to combat such an infection.

Rachel called Phil in Madison to tell him Belle was in the hospital and in serious condition. She urged him and Bob, Jr., who happened also to be in Madison, to come at once to Washington. Bob, Jr., caught the morning train. Phil was delayed by the rebandaging of an infected foot but caught up with his brother by chartering a light plane.

At the hospital they found Belle still conscious but within a few hours she slipped into a coma. By late afternoon, August 18, she was dead.

Her sons arranged for the funeral to be held in Madison. On the afternoon of August 21, services were conducted at the state historical society. Floral tributes were heaped in the flag-draped rotunda, sent by officials, organizations, friends and admirers. At the foot of the casket lay a wreath of White House ivy from President and Mrs. Hoover and a large basket of lilies and iris from the United States Supreme Court justices.

None of Belle's children wore any signs of mourning, knowing this would have been their mother's wish, as it had been their father's. After the services the casket was taken to Forest Hill Cemetery, where hundreds of Belle's friends waited under an oak tree near Bob's grave covered with flowers. Standing in the bright afternoon sunshine, in a scene reminiscent of a day six years before when they stood at the very same spot, the family and friends heard the Reverend H. H. Lumpkin say of Belle:

"Her spirit rose always to challenge life and in these lines of an ancient poet of another race and time there is beaten out a fitting measure to the music of her life." He quoted from the poem she so loved, "The Salutation of the Dawn," saying it expressed her philosophy of life:

> For yesterday is but a dream
> And tomorrow is only a vision
> But today well lived, makes
> every yesterday a dream of happiness
> And every tomorrow a vision of hope,
> look well, therefore, to the Day.
> Such is the Salutation of the Dawn.

After her death Lincoln Steffens wrote of Belle in his inimitable style:

"Belle La Follette is, historically and romantically, the woman triumphant.

"From the time when, a pretty young girl with a gypsy spirit, she found her man—who was a man—and put her eager, warm, firm hand into the fist of Bob La Follette—to the day when she laid down the just pen which was retracing with love the story of their life—which was a life—to look for the last time around upon their children and their children's children—she was the mother marking a straight, sure, deep line which she could see run straight on—sure and deep into the future of the race on this earth, forever.

"She used to have, this gypsy woman, a funny little chuckling laugh which she half laughed when a word or an act fixed a fact. She must have chuckled it to herself, a little, as she relaxed her closed wings at the end of her long walk.

"For she walked, this winged thing. She wanted to fly; she inspired flight and she bore fliers, but she herself—Belle La Follette—walked all her life on the ground, to keep the course for her fliers."

Jane Addams also wrote of her longtime friend and co-worker, looking toward the future.

"Her children and grandchildren have the fragrant memory of a life which was an unending commerce of the fine deed and great thoughts, so that even in this hour of sorrow and loss we congratulate them upon this goodly possession.

"It is given to but few in any country to possess so fine a heritage from both a father and mother and to almost none to so adequately live up to that heritage.

"The dead are not dead if we have loved them truly, if in our own lives we give them immortality, take up the work they have left unfinished, preserve the treasure they have won, and round out the circuit of their being to the fullness of an ampler orbit."

Belle Case La Follette lived a life based on the ideal that a better, more just, more humane society was possible. She believed that future generations must realize equality throughout our nation and peace among nations in a world without war. She acted on her beliefs with dedication, spirit, and courage. She was unable to achieve her goals, but she chartered a course for future generations to follow.

EPILOGUE

....

No doctor, of the myriad of doctors my grandparents sought to determine the cause of Bob's illnesses, nailed it better than Belle. As she noted after Lincoln Steffens tried to persuade her not to let Grandfather take on the "terrible load" of *La Follette's Magazine:* "He knew Bob well enough not to expect me, or anyone else, to try to stop him when his mind was made up. Bob habitually overtaxed his strength, always keeping in harness until exhaustion or illness compelled him to stop." Although Belle did not know it—indeed, few doctors of that day understood the malady either—from my own medical history I believe Grandfather suffered from manic-depression.

Even as a child people remarked on my "energy." I used to take it as a compliment. Now I know it is a warning signal that I am "high," that I am exhibiting the "manic" symptoms of manic-depression.

As a teen-ager and as a young adult, I also suffered mysterious pains and depression. My parents sent me to countless doctors and psychiatrists who treated me with pills, therapy, or both. None of it worked. And so I bounced along, either very up and feeling great, or very down and hurting. Two things changed my attitude, if not my life.

Upon hearing producer and director Joshua Logan courageously describe his bouts with manic-depression on network television, I was clobbered with the realization, "That's me!" I further gleaned from Mr. Logan that the illness is basically biological, caused by a chemical imbalance that is usually inherited. I immediately thought of Grandfather. Even the name—La Follette—means "a little crazy." How far back, I wondered, has this been going on?!

This journey in search of my grandmother is the second thing that is changing my life. For in finding her, I discovered the "mental gymnastics" she prescribed for Bob. He was unwilling—or unable—to follow them. I determined to try. In so doing, I have found the "prescription" to cope with myself.

Knowledge, or even better, self-awareness is power. I now consciously control those exhilarating highs and pull myself down, however reluctantly, from that heady stratosphere before I hit the inevitable crash. Most of the time Belle's mental gymnastics work. I find I am able to manage my mood swings. And without medication. For as Belle warned Bob, unless he stopped relying on medicine, "You will never really and truly realize the strength and recuperative power that is in yourself."

In researching this book it soon became clear that Belle might come across as too perfect. We looked hard for chinks in her crystal-pure character. The one negative we could find was that both she and Bob demanded an unachievable standard of perfection for the next generation.

As a young woman I remarked to a cousin that our mutual grandparents could not be perfect, because nobody was. To which she responded, "Well, they were!"

Phil, my father, in writing home from the University of Wisconsin during the armed ship debate stated: "Oh, I pray God that I may in some small way be worthy of you! I do so want to make my life worthwhile, but you have set an almost unattainable ideal for us."

Both sons, but especially Bob, Jr., were haunted by the fear of failure. In addition to suffering from, as Belle put it, an "inhibition of fear," his intelligence never seemed to come through in a testing situation. Perhaps it was easier not to try in the belief that, if you don't try, you can't fail. Bob, Jr., also, as Belle noted, felt an added sense of failure during his years of illness. It continued to haunt him when he ran for his father's seat in the senate. This feeling of inadequacy was not helped by comments such as the one he received from a grizzled old man during the special election of 1925: "You ain't as good as yer pa was and ya never will be."

To which young Bob replied, "No one knows that better than I, my friend. No one knows that better than I."

Two generations later I look back at the lives of my grandparents with wonder, pride and appreciation. I also know they were one hell of an act to follow.

—Sherry La Follette

BIBLIOGRAPHY

....

Derleth, August. *The Wisconsin*. New York: Farrar and Rinehart, 1942.

La Follette, Belle Case, with Fola La Follette. *Robert M. La Follette: A Biography*. New York: The Macmillan Company, 1953.

La Follette, Isabel Bacon. *If You Can Take It*. Autobiographical manuscript in the personal collection of Sherry La Follette.

La Follette, Mary. Interviews and correspondence with Sherry La Follette and George Zabriskie. Washington, D.C. 1979–1985.

La Follette, Phillip. *Adventure in Politics: The Memoirs of Phillip La Follette*. Edited by Donald Young. New York: Holt, Rinehart and Winston, 1970.

La Follette, Robert M. *La Follette's Autobiography*. Madison: The University of Wisconsin Press, 1960.

Madison, Wis. Wisconsin State Historical Society. Ada L. James papers, 1911–1922.

Madison, Wis. Wisconsin State Historical Society. Series I Correspondence of Robert M. La Follette, 1900–1925.

Madison, Wis. Wisconsin State Historical Society. Gwyneth K. Roe papers, 1880–1968.

Merk, Frederick. *Economic History of Wisconsin: Civil War Decades*. Madison: Wisconsin State Historical Society, 1916.

Middleton, George. *These Things Are Mine*. New York: The Macmillan Company, 1947.

Muir, John. *The Story of My Youth*. Boston: Houghton Mifflin Company, 1913.

New York. The New York Public Library Microfilm Collection. *La Follette's Magazine*. Writings by Belle Case La Follette, 1910–1931.

Washington, D.C. The Library of Congress. The Congressional Record. Testimony before the Senate on Woman Suffrage: April 26, 1913.

Washington, D.C. The Library of Congress, Manuscript Division. The Robert M. La Follette Family Papers, 1855–1925.

WPA Writers' Project. *Wisconsin: A Guide to the Badger State*. New York: Duell, Sloan and Pierce, 1941.

INDEX

....